The

RESTITUTION

of ALL THINGS

The
RESTITUTION
of ALL THINGS

ISRAEL, CHRISTIANS, *and the*
END OF THE AGE

JOSEPH FARAH

 WND Books

THE RESTITUTION OF ALL THINGS

Published by WND Books, Washington, D.C. WND Books is a registered trademark of WorldNetDaily.com, Inc. ("WND")

Book designed by Mark Karis

WND Books are available at special discounts for bulk purchases. WND Books also publishes books in electronic formats. For more information call (541) 474-1776, e-mail orders@ wndbooks.com, or visit www.wndbooks.com.

Scripture quotations are taken from the Holy Bible, King James Version (public domain).

Hardcover ISBN: 978-1-944229-50-4
eBook ISBN: 978-1-944229-51-1

Library of Congress Cataloging-in-Publication Data
Names: Farah, Joseph, author.
Title: The restitution of all things : Israel, Christians, and the end of the
age / Joseph Farah.
Description: Washington, DC : WND Books, 2017. | Includes bibliographical
references and index.
Identifiers: LCCN 2016025209 (print) | LCCN 2016038204 (ebook) | ISBN
9781944229504 (hardcover) | ISBN 9781944229511 (e-book)
Subjects: LCSH: Church--History of doctrines. | Judaism (Christian theology)
| Israel (Christian theology) | Christianity and other religions--Judaism.
| Judaism--Relations--Christianity.
Classification: LCC BV598 .F37 2017 (print) | LCC BV598 (ebook) | DDC
230--dc23
LC record available at https://lccn.loc.gov/2016025209

Printed in the United States of America
16 17 18 19 20 21 LBM 9 8 7 6 5 4 3 2 1

CONTENTS

PREFACE

And he shall send Jesus Christ, which before was preached unto you: whom the heaven must receive until the times of restitution of all things, which God hath spoken by the mouth of all his holy prophets since the world began.
—ACTS 3:20–21

IT'S A FUNNY THING, the way the world tracks time.

Practically everyone knows what year it is right now.

Something very dramatic and life changing must have happened nearly 2020 years ago that made people take notice. It had to have been rather spectacular and amazing for all nations to adopt this new calendar.

Not surprisingly, there have been some feeble protests.

Notably, many in Israel keep track of what year it is in two ways—one "civic" date and another religious.

North Korea, an isolated, totalitarian country led by a series of madmen who rule as if they are gods, build weapons of mass destruction, and starve their people, has repeatedly tried to persuade the rest of the world that time really began when the first of its dynasty of rulers, Kim Il-Sung, was born, April 15, 1912.

When the bloodthirsty, communist, revolutionary Khmer Rouge took over Cambodia in 1975, murdering millions in the process, the leadership declared it was the year 0, just as the French revolutionary leaders, in opposition to all religious influences, had declared 1792 Year 1.

Let's just say such efforts have been . . . in vain.

Of course, most people know why the world marks time the way it does (though I note with horror that many Twitter users remarked on New Year's Day 2014 that they believed it marked America's 2,014th birthday!): Jesus, the Savior of the world, the Messiah, and the Son of God, came into the world—and life was never the same again.

He came as a baby born of a virgin, fulfilling hundreds of Hebrew prophecies about the coming Redeemer. He lived approximately thirty-three years in Israel and never traveled beyond Egypt and what we call Syria or Lebanon and Jordan today. He taught that the Hebrew Scriptures were God-breathed, true, and valid.

Jesus healed the sick, raised the dead, was crucified, rose after three days, ascended into heaven, and foretold that He would come again as a conquering King of kings, establishing an everlasting kingdom of pure justice, righteousness, and peace.

Since then, there have been efforts to portray Him as:

simply a great teacher who told magnificent parables

a lunatic who happened to be at the right place at the
right time to captivate billions of followers

the leader of a group of Bronze Age peasants
    in a backwater called Israel

a magician or sorcerer

a misunderstood socialist and advocate for
    the poor and downtrodden

a revolutionary zealot

merely another in a long line of Hebrew prophets

A few even insist, despite the overwhelming and well-documented historical record, that He never really existed. "They are without excuse," the Bible warns (Rom. 1:20).

Despite efforts to conceal the nature of His unique, calendar-changing life with the use of terms such as *CE* (Common Era) and *BCE* (Before the Common Era), everyone with any grasp of history knows it was Jesus who reset mankind's clock. The original terms used to divide time were *AD* (abbreviating the Latin *Anno Domini* or "in the year of our Lord") and *BC* ("Before Christ"—"Christ" being Greek for "the Messiah").

While most people know why we measure time the way we do, you will seldom hear it mentioned. When the lighted ball drops in Times Square at midnight each New Year, there's always a lot of chatter. Yet in all the years I have watched that phenomenon, I have yet to hear even one celebrity reference what happened two thousand years ago to change our concept of time. Not one participant braving the cold night air in Manhattan, not a single musical guest, not one news commentator, not one host.

In fact, in the sixty-two years I have been alive, I've never seen anyone in public life make the point I am attempting to drive home today—that Jesus, or Yeshua, as He was known to His Hebrew brethren, is the one and only life in the history of humanity that changed everything—even the way we count the years going by. (Not only that, we also use His earthly life to count the years before

He came. We simply do it backward.)

I don't believe followers of Jesus make this point effectively enough. I don't even think *we* appreciate it enough. We rarely use it to share the good news that Jesus came to share, let alone underline it every chance we get. Clearly, we don't recognize how important it is to stave off efforts to popularize terms such as *CE* and *BCE* rather than *BC* and *AD*.

In short, we are not doing enough to remind believers and nonbelievers alike just how much it's all about Jesus, the Alpha and the Omega, the Word, the Lamb of God, the Way, the Truth, and the Life. Neither do we talk much about the subject of this book: His second coming and what it portends.

Oh, I know, some of you don't believe in such things. You think it's just a bunch of silly superstition. Even some Christians don't believe in the Second Coming.

But as a journalist, I can't ignore hard evidence—no matter where it may lead me. And the more I study the prophetic scriptures of the Holy Bible and look at the condition of our world today, the more convinced I become that we are nearing that time. In fact, I think we are very close.

For just as Jesus' virgin birth in Bethlehem was foretold by the Hebrew prophets hundreds of years earlier, so too was His return to earth predicted. The only question is when.

The most dramatic evidence for His imminent return that our generation has witnessed was the rebirth of the nation of Israel in 1948. The Jews, God's chosen people, were, as prophesied, scattered over the whole earth for nearly two millennia beginning shortly after Jesus' death on the cross. Yet, the Scriptures leave no doubt that the Jewish state would exist, once again, before He returned. (See Ezekiel 22:14–15; Luke 21:24; cf. Ezekiel 34:13; 38:8.)

Interestingly, Orthodox Jews have long taught that the world would last for six thousand years before the Messiah would come and usher in a millennial period of restful human history. Since God created the world in six days (Gen. 1:31), and rested on the seventh day (Gen. 2:1), they reason that the world's history would climax the same way. Specifically, they cite Psalms, which says, "For a thousand years in thy sight are but as yesterday when it is past" (90:4).

Likewise, Christians have looked to 2 Peter: "Beloved, be not ignorant of this one thing, that one day is with the Lord as a thousand years, and a thousand years as one day" (3:8).

The early church understood this six-day theory of world history. It was widely accepted teaching for the first three centuries of the church. From the time of Adam, genealogical records show that four thousand years passed until the time of Christ. From Jesus' time until the present age represents another two thousand years, for a total of six thousand years, or six days.

I can't help but notice that six thousand years are almost up. You can make of it what you will.

There's also a three-day theory: Jesus rose on the third day (1 Cor. 15:4). Would the beginning of the third millennium—or thousand-year period—not be the likely time for His return to earth? There is even strong scriptural evidence for such a theory in Hosea: "After two days will he revive us: in the third day he will raise us up, and we shall live in his sight" (6:2). Note that this prophecy is not about the resurrection of Jesus; it's either about the resurrection of Israel after two thousand years of dispersal or the physical return of the Lord.

In 1776, Edward Gibbon published *The History of the Decline and Fall of the Roman Empire*. In it he cited early documents suggesting that the Christian disciples of the first century were taught that Jesus would return after two thousand years. We'll soon find out if they were right.

For many reasons, I believe Jesus is returning soon. But I'm especially drawn to 2 Timothy, which describes the state of the world in the "last days":

> This know also, that in the last days perilous times shall come. For men shall be lovers of their own selves, covetous, boasters, proud, blasphemers, disobedient to parents, unthankful, unholy, without

natural affection, trucebreakers, false accusers, incontinent, fierce, despisers of those that are good. Traitors, heady, high-minded, lovers of pleasures more than lovers of God; having a form of godliness, but denying the power thereof. (2 Tim. 3:1–5)

To me, that sounds exactly like our world today.

But the critical question addressed in this book is not, when will Jesus return? It's, what will it be like when He does return?

Even among self-professed followers of Jesus, there is so little expectancy, so little talk about this age that all the prophets yearned to see.

Who wouldn't want to see a one-thousand-year period of peace, justice, and righteousness?

We *all* want peace on earth and goodwill toward men. And almost everyone desires justice, mercy, and truth.

In one way or another, people everywhere dream of a return to the garden of Eden. You can see the theme running universally through art, music, and film.

Interestingly, the same Bible that tells us of that all too brief, paradise-like existence on earth also foreshadows a return to a glorious period of one thousand years in which justice, mercy, truth, peace, love, and goodwill among people dominate the earth.

It will be a return to the way God intended men, women, and all creation to live in the world. It will be what the apostle Peter called "the times of restitution of all things" (Acts 3:21).

The Bible gives us many hints of what this period will be like, from many different angles and perspectives. In fact, it is, as Peter suggested, the good news that all of the prophets spoke about since the world began.

Think about that. There's a common denominator in what *all* the prophets spoke about. Obviously they all foreshadow a Savior, a Redeemer, a Messiah. But they also point to a period of time, a kingdom to come, in which truth, light, justice, and peace prevail. That's pretty exciting stuff.

Many other authors and teachers have asserted that we might be very close to that time and that place. The Bible is replete with glimpses of that kingdom.

That begs a question: Why don't we hear much about it in churches? Furthermore, why aren't more books written about it? Why don't we see movies about that period instead of the brief, most violent and catastrophic times to come on earth that precede it?

Why do even prophecy students and teachers focus so much attention on the death, destruction, and the cataclysm of what the Bible promises to be a very short period of future history, and so little on what is called the *millennial kingdom*, when earth will experience the restoration of all things?

Good questions, all.

Shouldn't mankind be looking toward the coming kingdom of God as our great hope for the future? If so, then why are we so preoccupied with such a short period of tribulation?

Peter added that "the prophets from Samuel and those that follow after, as many as have spoken, have likewise foretold of these days. Ye are the children of the prophets, and of the covenant which God made with our fathers, saying unto Abraham, and in thy seed shall all the kindreds of the earth be blessed" (Acts 3:23–24).

Even the most famous prayer of the Bible, the one Jesus recited when He instructed His brethren on how to communicate with the heavenly Father, spoke of a better time and place:

> Our Father which art in heaven, hallowed be thy name. Thy kingdom come, thy will be done in earth, as it is in heaven. Give us this day our daily bread. And forgive us our debts, as we forgive our debtors. And lead us not into temptation, but deliver us from evil: for thine is the kingdom, and the power, and the glory, for ever. Amen. (Matt. 6:9–13)

Twice in that short prayer Jesus referred to the coming kingdom, in which God's will for mankind will be done.

This book seeks to shed light on what few sermons teach about, few authors expand upon, and few Bible studies explore. It's also about the standards for entering the kingdom and appreciating it to the fullest extent.

But the question remains: why don't we hear, read, and see more about this coming kingdom of God here on earth today?

Why don't people think much about it, let alone talk about it?

The answer, I suspect, is fear of accountability for our actions.

Warning! I'm going to suggest that you may be *blown away*, *disturbed*, and possibly even *offended* by some of what you read in this book. It is not my intention to offend, but it is my desire to get you thinking in a new way and studying the Bible as it is written rather than as others tell you it is written. That is why I provide so many scriptural references.

One admission: I am a most unlikely person to be tackling such an endeavor.

What qualifies me to write about spiritual matters?

Do I have a seminary degree? No.

Have I pastored a church? No.

Do I have any formal training in religion? No.

But while I am best known for a career in journalism, writing books, making movies, and launching the first independent online news source in the world, I have always had a passion for knowing God and His ways more deeply.

I was raised as a nominal Roman Catholic. As long as I can remember, I always loved Jesus—at least what I knew about Him, which, honestly, wasn't much as a child.

Coming of age in the 1960s, I got caught up in the radical politics of the day, first in anti–Vietnam War activism, then in the counterculture movement, and finally, in a kind of nihilistic, revolution-for-the-hell-of-it activity, which brought me into contact with some of the most notorious characters of the '60s and '70s—from Abbie Hoffman and Jerry Rubin to Bill Ayers and Bernardine Dohrn.

With the help of the American Civil Liberties Union, I successfully fought suspension from high school for refusing to recite the Pledge of Allegiance to the flag.

I wrote for left-wing underground papers and even started some.

In high school, with hair down to my waist, I was arrested and jailed for attempting to shut down Washington, DC, with thousands of protestors in 1971. Again with the help of the ACLU, all charges were dropped. Many, though not I, were actually *paid* hundreds or thousands of dollars by the federal government for false arrest.

As a teenager I helped foment campus rebellions, uprisings, and building takeovers.

I was even recruited to perform acts of terrorism by adult radicals who liked the idea of exploiting juveniles in their schemes because they were unlikely to be severely prosecuted if caught. At one point in my young life as an Arab American, I dreamed of joining Yasser Arafat's Palestinian Liberation Organization to conduct terrorist attacks on Israel.

None of this activity was costly to me. In fact, it set me apart in a strange and worldly way. I was elected vice president of my class— probably could have won as president, but I wasn't interested in the work it would entail. As a senior in high school, I found myself being wooed with offers of full-ride scholarships to prestigious universities, not because of my academic achievements, but because of my reputation as a hard-core radical in the making.

I turned the offers down because I sensed these institutions and offers represented, in French Revolution parlance, "bourgeois" efforts to buy me off. Instead, I accepted admission to a state university just outside of Manhattan, where I expected to organize the working-class students into revolutionary soldiers.

It was there, in that university, that I discovered two passions that would change my life: Jesus Christ and journalism. How did all this come about? First, I met someone who would become my best friend for life—the son of a Spanish-speaking Baptist minister from Venezuela. For the first time in my life, he evangelized me, gave me a copy of Hal Lindsey's *The Late Great Planet Earth*, and I accepted Jesus as my Lord and Savior. (Jesse: You have my eternal gratitude! Love you!) Second, when it came time to decide a major, journalism would be my career.

The common denominator between these two paths? In my mind, they both presented the opportunity to seek the truth. And that's what I had been doing all along—even while looking in all the wrong places.

I became editor of the college newspaper and took every communications and writing course offered. In a series of stories that ranged from over-enrollment of the university to unreported moonlighting, my reports resulted in a top-down shakeup of the institution. At night I was a part-time correspondent for a daily newspaper, covering government meetings.

So my formal training and my experiential education are in journalism. I've been doing it now professionally for four decades.

Shortly after graduating college, I got my first job reporting full-time for my hometown daily, the *Paterson News* in New Jersey. I went home to tell my father, who, with tears in his eyes, confided in me for the first time that I got the job he had wanted when he was my age. World War II had interrupted his college studies, and he had been forced to get his degree over many years of night school while he worked as an upholsterer to provide for his family. He went into teaching instead. I had tears in my eyes, too. It made me appreciate the opportunity more than ever.

I worked hard at the paper and advanced quickly—getting better beats, more money, and some experience as an editor. In 1979, I applied for a job at the Los Angeles *Herald-Examiner*, then one of the biggest dailies in the second-biggest city in the country, and got it. I spent the next nine years there, the last six running the newsroom.

But there was more going on in my life than long hours at the paper.

One day, I was watching television, and a commercial came on. Hal Lindsey was promoting his new book, *The 1980s: Countdown to Armageddon.* I decided to interview him for the paper.

We hit it off. I wrote a story telling readers that through the decade of the 1970s, Lindsey's books had sold more copies than any other author's. Thus we began a decade-long collaboration on his books, his newsletter, and his TV show, which still airs today. From that point on I got immersed in prophecy and worked in similar ways with other famous teachers.

It was Hal Lindsey who first taught me about the centrality of Israel in the Bible, and during that period I began visiting Israel as a Middle East correspondent. I've had many other teachers along the way, including Chuck Missler, Chuck Smith, Jack Van Impe, Greg Laurie, Mark Biltz, Joel Richardson, and Jonathan Cahn, who helped deepen my walk with Jesus and gave me many insights into the coming kingdom.

I've belonged to many different kinds of churches and Bible study groups over the years—Catholic, Presbyterian, Baptist, Calvary Chapel, some charismatic, others not, denominational and nondenominational.

Meanwhile, and simultaneously, I got the opportunity to serve as editor-in-chief of two major-market dailies, in Los Angeles and Sacramento. I also started a nonprofit foundation committed to sponsoring investigative journalism—all the while collaborating on books with other authors, including Rush Limbaugh's number one *New York Times* best seller, *See, I Told You So.*

In 1997, I founded the first independent online news service, WorldNetDaily—now known as WND.com. The focus, then and now, was the kind of reporting the press was supposed to do—exposing fraud, waste, abuse, and corruption in government and other powerful institutions. But it also became a haven for Christian journalists and brought a distinctive Christian worldview to the media marketplace.

Today, it is one of the largest news sites in the world, the largest Christian content website in the world, and one of the largest websites of any kind in the United States. The business has expanded into book publishing, boasting the highest percentage of *New York Times* best sellers of any publisher in the world, along with producing movies. *The Isaiah 9:10 Judgment*, based on Jonathan Cahn's *The Harbinger*, became the best-selling faith movie of 2012 and 2013.

But there's someone in my life who has been as inspirational as all of these gifted and learned teachers and wonderful experiences. It's my wife, Elizabeth. When it comes to the Word of God, her curiosity knows no end. And her passion for truth and understanding God's way remains boundless.

And that's why, I believe, God has put it on my heart to write this book.

I waited for a long time for someone else to do it. I even tried to recruit others to do it. Though I have written thirteen books over the years, it's harder and harder for me to find the time as the business of WND has grown.

But I, like my wife, still have a passion for the truth in a world full of lies—and that's why I have written *The Restitution of All Things*. It's the result of my lifelong pursuit of truth—even if some of that life turned out to be terribly misguided and misdirected.

What did my wife have to do with this book? My interaction with her and our studies of the Bible together, along with our children, have led to many profound questions and discoveries over the years. The one that led to this book came with one of those loaded questions: Why don't we observe the fourth commandment?

It was a question I couldn't answer—not with a clear conscience. I just didn't know. I'd never come across anything in the Bible that explained it clearly. So we studied—and studied some more. Those studies deepened our faith, opened our eyes, made the Bible come alive in ways I could never imagine.

We searched for the truth. We didn't just ask our pastors. We went deep into the Bible and into history for clues.

It's a study that continues today and will probably continue into the kingdom to come. That's when we will all learn more about our faith and the truth than we can possibly learn in this lifetime.

Speaking of truth, did you know that the word *truth* is found 224 times in the Bible? Truth is even one of the names for our God. Here is just a small sampling of verses about truth:

- "The LORD, the LORD God, merciful and gracious, longsuffering, and abundant in goodness and truth . . ." (Ex. 34:6)

- "He is the Rock, his work is perfect: for all his ways are judgment: a God of truth and without iniquity, just and right is he." (Deut. 32:4)

- "Into thine hand I commit my spirit: thou hast redeemed me, O LORD God of truth." (Ps. 31:5)

- "He who blesseth himself in the earth shall bless himself in the God of truth; and he that sweareth in the earth shall swear by the God of truth; because the former troubles are forgotten, and because they are hid from mine eyes." (Isa. 65:16)

- "When he, the Spirit of truth, is come, he will guide you into all truth." (John 16:13)

Meanwhile, there are still many people walking around the world today, asking the same question Pilate asked of Jesus: "What is truth?" (John 18:38). They wonder if there is any truth—because they wonder if God is real.

We want to be like Jesus, who said, "And ye shall know the truth, and the truth shall make you free" (John 8:32).

Knowing Jesus is, of course, knowing the truth with a capital *T*.

I didn't write *The Restitution of All Things* because it was time to write another book.

I didn't write it because I needed something else to do.

I didn't write it because of pride.

I certainly didn't write it for the money.

I wrote it because I felt God calling me to do it.

I no more wanted to take on this project than Jonah wanted to evangelize Nineveh. But I did it because I had a hunger to know more about what Peter and all those prophets were talking about when they described the way God, in the person of Jesus, would restore all things, make them new, and remake the world the way it was intended to be before the Fall.

After all, if all the prophets were looking toward this glorious, victorious time of peace and harmony, shouldn't we be considering it too? Shouldn't we understand our destiny and that "blessed hope"? And shouldn't we be preparing ourselves for this amazing new life?

But in my mind, this is more than another prophecy book—much more.

I had a desire to learn and convey why the church of the first century was so effective in such a brief period of time and, sadly, why the institutional church over the last nineteen centuries has been at times so ineffective and even counterproductive—often not part of the solution but part of the problem. I wanted to share what I have learned about the spiritual traditions of men sometimes overshadowing the commandments of God. And I wanted to expose the vicious lie that has become known as "replacement theology." In short, I wanted to awaken the world to the truth of the Bible, of the reality of Jesus the Messiah, the King, the High Priest, the Redeemer and Son of God.

In Matthew 16:19, Jesus promised to give His disciples "the keys of the kingdom." This book explores the nature of those keys and that kingdom, which, I believe, can be found only in the Scriptures, under the leading of the Holy Spirit. What I found in my study of this time, this period, this kingdom, affirms what Peter said—every prophet provided glimpses of this great hope.

Would you like to learn more about those keys—and get your hands on them?

Would you like to unfold the mysteries of that kingdom that could be your destiny, and understand your true inheritance as a believer and follower of Jesus?

That's what this book is all about—along with the responsibilities that citizenship in that kingdom requires.

It is my hope that it challenges you to dig deeper into the Scriptures.

There's little doubt in my mind that you are going to be confronted with some controversial ideas in this book. You may even react with *horror* to some of those ideas. Certainly, many of them will *not* be popular among believers.

All I ask is that you put these ideas to the ultimate test of truth. Don't take my word for it. If anything I write here is not supported by Scripture, don't believe it. Be like a Berean: receive the word with all readiness of mind, and search the Scriptures daily, to ascertain whether what you read here is so (see Acts 17:10–11).

Now, here we go, on a journey to discover the truth about Jesus' one-thousand-year reign as King and High Priest on planet earth, and many other matters that relate directly to that glorious new world awaiting us—a world in which truth, justice, and peace will finally prevail during God's "restitution of all things."

ACKNOWLEDGMENTS

I WANT TO THANK JESUS-YESHUA, my Lord and Savior, for everything He has done for me and for all He is doing to restore the world and humanity to a state of justice, love, peace, and harmony, however difficult it might be for us to imagine and believe.

Deep thanks also to my blessed wife, Elizabeth, for her love, comfort, forgiveness, and understanding of me. Though we are two entirely different personalities, we agree on so much and were clearly made for each other. This book would not be possible without her passion for the Bible and the deep studies we engage in together.

My love and thanks to my children for the blessing they have been in my life. Here's to you Ashley, Alana, Alyssa, Kathleen, Grace; my sons-in-law Mark and Benjamin; and my precious grandchildren—Ryder, Hunter, Maxwell, and Charlie.

A special thanks to Geoffrey Stone and his team for the editing, and Mark Karis for the cover design.

Last but not least, thanks to Hal Lindsey, Chuck Missler, Joel Richardson, Mark Biltz, Jonathan Cahn, and other great teachers for inspiring me through their own glimpses into the kingdom of God. None of them, however, should bear any responsibility for viewpoints expressed in this book with which they may disagree.

1

DID JESUS COME TO START
A NEW RELIGION?

Beware of the leaven of the Pharisees and of the Sadducees. —MATTHEW 16:6

I'M CONFIDENT MOST EVERYONE READING this book has
read the four Gospels. You may have read them many times, studied
them systematically, even walked through every verse in Bible study
groups.

But now I'd like to challenge you to do it again with a certain
perspective in mind that will, with the Holy Spirit's leading, give

you fresh insight into what Jesus taught that was so radical, who He talked to during His short ministry, and what practices He tried to correct before going to the cross as the ultimate atoning sacrifice for the sins of the world.

The key question I want you to ask yourself in this fresh look at the Gospels is this: *Did Jesus come to start a new religion called Christianity?* The answer may surprise you:

Jesus came to do many things, to fulfill many roles. But none involved starting a new religion.

- He came to save the world from its sin.

- He came to bear witness to the truth about God and the fallen world.

- He came to fulfill what was prophesied about His coming kingdom.

- He came to be a light to the Gentiles.

But He did not come to change or do away with His Father's commandments. I don't believe that for a minute. I don't see it in Scripture. In fact, the evidence is overwhelmingly just the opposite. Somehow, though, most people who claim to follow Him have missed that.

I'm not suggesting that the Creator Himself didn't know what would happen after His death. On the contrary, He knew—He most definitely knew. That's why He warned us ahead of time. What did He say?

Matthew 7 gives us His warning:

Wide is the gate, and broad is the way, that leadeth to destruction, and many there be which go in thereat: Because strait is the gate, and narrow is the way, which leadeth unto life, and few there be that find it.

> Beware of false prophets. . . . Not every one that saith unto
> me, Lord, Lord, shall enter into the kingdom of heaven; but he
> that doeth the will of my Father which is in heaven. Many will
> say to me in that day, Lord, Lord, have we not prophesied in thy
> name? and in thy name have cast out devils? and in thy name
> done many wonderful works? And then will I profess unto them,
> I never knew you: depart from me, ye that work iniquity. (Matt.
> 7:13–14, 21–23)

Have you ever read those words with bewilderment, or even
with fear and trembling? Who are these people who call Jesus "Lord,"
prophesy, cast out demons, and do wonderful works—all in His
name—but are turned away on Judgment Day? Have you thought
about that? Have you wrestled with that question?

More than a billion people alive today call themselves "Christians."[1] Will they all enter the kingdom of heaven? Will most? How
many of us have ever prophesied or cast out demons in Jesus' name?
Very few, I suspect. I sure haven't.

Yet even some who have done or will do these "wonderful works"
will be turned away by Jesus when He returns. That should give
every self-proclaimed follower of Jesus pause to consider: *Am I on
the broad, destructive path, or the narrow one that leads to life?* "Few
there be that find" that one, Jesus emphasized.

If all we are expected to do, as many television preachers suggest, is "give our hearts to Jesus" in one momentary, "born-again"
confession of faith, why will so many be lost? Don't many teachers
today say that Jesus came to give us an easier path to salvation—to
unburden us from the law, which was such a stumbling block under
the old covenant? How do we reconcile this teaching with what
Jesus said in Matthew 7?

These are the questions that should be on your mind as you
take another walk through the Gospels. Ask the Holy Spirit to
reveal to you what may have been previously obscured from your
understanding.

Here's another provocative question: Why did Jesus use parables in His teachings? Do you think He used them to make His message easier to understand, so that more listeners would discover the truth and find the narrow path?

That's what I once believed. But the Scriptures tell us a different story.

In two of the gospels, the disciples asked Jesus why He spoke to the people in parables. His very direct answer, recorded in Luke 8, was, "Unto you it is given to know the mysteries of the kingdom of God: but to others in parables; that seeing they might *not* see, and hearing they might *not* understand" (v. 10, emphasis added).

Matthew provides more detail:

> He answered and said unto them, Because it is given unto you to know the mysteries of the kingdom of heaven, *but to them it is not given.* For whosoever hath, to him shall be given, and he shall have more abundance: but whosoever hath not, from him shall be taken away even that he hath. Therefore speak I to them in parables: because they seeing see not; and hearing they hear not, neither do they understand. And in them is fulfilled the prophecy of Esaias, which saith, By hearing ye shall hear, and shall not understand; and seeing ye shall see, and shall not perceive: For this people's heart is waxed gross, and their ears are dull of hearing, and their eyes they have closed; lest at any time they should see with their eyes and hear with their ears, and should understand with their heart, and should be converted, and I should heal them. But blessed are your eyes, for they see: and your ears, for they hear. (13:11–16, emphasis added)

In other words, Jesus did not speak in parables so the masses would see and hear more clearly. Instead, He did so to fulfill a prophecy: "And he said, Go, and tell this people, Hear ye indeed, but understand not; and see ye indeed, but perceive not. *Make the heart of this people fat, and make their ears heavy, and shut their eyes; lest they see with their eyes, and hear with their ears, and understand with their heart, and convert, and be healed"* (Isa. 6:9–10, emphasis added). Obviously, He did *not* intend that all should understand His parables. He used them for the opposite purpose.

When Isaiah—called Esaias in the Greek Scriptures—asked God how long the people would have to wait to receive understanding, He said: "Until the cities be wasted without inhabitant, and the houses without man, and the land be utterly desolate, and the Lord have removed men far away, and there be a great forsaking in the midst of the land. But yet in it shall be a tenth, and it shall return, and shall be eaten: as a teil tree, and as an oak, whose substance is in them, when they cast their leaves: so the holy seed shall be the substance thereof" (Isa. 6:11–13).

The time would come when the children of Israel would understand with their hearts, be healed, and be saved, but it was not in Isaiah's time—and it was not in Jesus' time. Those were times of pending judgment. The die had been cast.

Only a few were chosen. This is the way of the narrow path. Broad is the way of destruction.

In the Gospels, we see that Jesus dealt sternly with the religious leaders of Israel. Why? What was the great offense of the Pharisees and the Sadducees of His time? I've asked many Christians this question, and their answer is always the same: "They were hypocrites."

Well, yes, Jesus did sometimes refer to them as "hypocrites,"[2] but we're all hypocrites, aren't we? So what were they doing *specifically* that outraged the Messiah, and John the Baptist, too?

For the sake of expediency, let's walk through just the first gospel. In Matthew 3 we read:

> In those days came John the Baptist, preaching in the wilderness of Judaea, and saying, Repent ye: for the kingdom of heaven is at hand. For this is he that was spoken of by the prophet Esaias, saying, The voice of one crying in the wilderness, Prepare ye the way of the Lord, make his paths straight. And the same John had his raiment of camel's hair, and a leathern girdle about his

loins; and his meat was locusts and wild honey. Then went out to him Jerusalem, and all Judaea, and all the region round about Jordan, and were baptized of him in Jordan, confessing their sins. (vv. 1–6)

John was preaching the urgent message of repentance—a familiar report from all the prophets of the Tanakh (Old Testament) before him. As he was baptizing in the Jordan those who came to accept his cries in the wilderness, along came some of those religious leaders—the Pharisees and Sadducees.

How did he greet them? Was he happy to see them? Did he nicely invite them to be immersed in the cleansing rite of baptism, coaxing them to repent of their sins? Did he say to them, "Hey, guys, just accept the Messiah into your heart and you will be saved"? No. Not at all:

But when he saw many of the Pharisees and Sadducees come to his baptism, he said unto them, O generation of vipers, who hath warned you to flee from the wrath to come? Bring forth therefore fruits meet for repentance: and think not to say within yourselves, We have Abraham to our father: for I say unto you, that God is able of these stones to raise up children unto Abraham. And now also the axe is laid unto the root of the trees: therefore every tree which bringeth not forth good fruit is hewn down, and cast into the fire. I indeed baptize you with water unto repentance. but he that cometh after me is mightier than I, whose shoes I am not worthy to bear: he shall baptize you with the Holy Ghost, and with fire: whose fan is in his hand, and he will throughly purge his floor, and gather his wheat into the garner; but he will burn up the chaff with unquenchable fire. (vv. 7–12)

Did you catch that? He called them snakes! He taunted them with the question of who had warned them of God's coming judgment on Israel. And he cautioned them not to rely on the promises to their father Abraham for safe haven in the coming kingdom.

Why would John be so harsh in condemning the Pharisees and the Sadducees? What were they doing wrong? How did these deeply religious men get off the narrow path? A pattern that can be seen throughout the Gospels begins here.

In Matthew's next reference to the Pharisees, in the Sermon on the Mount, Jesus says, "For I say unto you, that except your righteousness shall exceed the righteousness of the scribes and Pharisees, ye shall in no case enter into the kingdom of heaven" (Matt. 5:20).

Apparently, the best example the people of Israel had for righteousness in those days was the Pharisees. Yet, they came up short. They missed the mark. Again, what was it that they were doing wrong? And why did John call them vipers?

We meet the Pharisees again in Matthew 9, shortly after Jesus' encounter with the tax collector whose book would bear his name:

And as Jesus passed forth from thence, he saw a man, named Matthew, sitting at the receipt of custom: and he saith unto him, Follow me. And he arose, and followed him.

And it came to pass, as Jesus sat at meat in the house, behold, many publicans and sinners came and sat down with him and his disciples.

And when the Pharisees saw it, they said unto his disciples, Why eateth your Master with publicans and sinners?

But when Jesus heard that, he said unto them, They that be whole need not a physician, but they that are sick.

But go ye and learn what that meaneth, I will have mercy, and not sacrifice: for I am not come to call the righteous, but sinners to repentance.

Then came to him the disciples of John, saying, Why do we and the Pharisees fast oft, but thy disciples fast not?

And Jesus said unto them, Can the children of the bride-chamber mourn, as long as the bridegroom is with them? but the days will come, when the bridegroom shall be taken from them, and then shall they fast. (vv. 9–15)

The Pharisees were very interested in Jesus. Sadly, they seemed particularly interested in catching Him in behaviors that were not part of their tradition and customs and were, therefore, sinful.

But *was* it a sin to eat with tax collectors and sinners? Where might we find such a law in Scripture? I invite you to search through the Torah, the five books of the law. You will not find such a prohibition. So we can surmise that the Pharisees had determined for themselves—by their own traditions and the teachings of men—that it was unacceptable.

And what about fasting, as the Pharisees did? Is it good to fast for spiritual strength? Yes, it can be a powerful weapon of spiritual warfare, as Jesus demonstrated during His forty days in the wilderness when He was tempted by Satan (see Matt. 4:1–11). Later, when the disciples were unable to cast out a demon, Jesus told them, "This kind goeth not out but by prayer and fasting" (Matt. 17:21).

So, fasting can be a good thing, but it is not a commandment, and is not found in the Torah as such. Even the Day of Atonement, which is to this day associated with fasting, is described simply as a day to "afflict your souls" (Lev. 23:27, 32). While fasting might be one way to do that, Scripture doesn't explicitly command it.

In other words, the Pharisees, in confronting Jesus, were taking on a holier-than-thou attitude. They were following man-made traditions as if they were commandments from God. In some cases, they even considered these traditions to be superior to the commandments found in the Torah.

Again, we see a pattern developing that will become overwhelmingly clear as we examine more exchanges between Jesus and the Pharisees throughout the Gospels.

Continuing in Matthew, we read this account: "As they went out, behold, they brought to him a dumb man possessed with a devil. And when the devil was cast out, the dumb spake: and the multitudes marvelled, saying, It was never so seen in Israel. But the Pharisees said, He casteth out devils through the prince of the devils" (9:32–34). The Pharisees were actually accusing Jesus of being in league with Satan—bearing false witness against Him for doing miraculous good works!

Shortly after, Jesus doubled down on His work, healing everyone who came to see Him of every imaginable malady. He empowered His disciples to do likewise, sending them out to do the same healing work. But first, He gave them fair warning of the opposition that would come from the Pharisees—specifically referencing their accusation against Him:

> But beware of men: for they will deliver you up to the councils, and they will scourge you in their synagogues; and ye shall be brought before governors and kings for my sake, for a testimony against them and the Gentiles. . . . And ye shall be hated of all men for my name's sake: but he that endureth to the end shall be saved. But when they persecute you in this city, flee ye into another: for verily I say unto you, Ye shall not have gone over the cities of Israel, till the Son of man be come. The disciple is not above his master, nor the servant above his lord. It is enough for the disciple that he be as his master, and the servant as his lord. *If they have called the master of the house Beelzebub, how much more shall they call them of his household?* (Matt. 10:17–25, emphasis added)

In the next chapter, Jesus again upbraided the Pharisees to His disciples, illustrating that their accusations against both Him and John were not only false, but contradictory: "For John came neither eating nor drinking, and they say, He hath a devil. The Son of man came eating and drinking, and they say, Behold a man gluttonous, and a winebibber, a friend of publicans and sinners. But wisdom is justified of her children" (Matt. 11:18–19).

Then there is the confrontation with the Pharisees after Jesus and His disciples picked some grain on the Sabbath and "when the Pharisees saw it, they said unto him, Behold, thy disciples do that which is not lawful to do upon the sabbath day" (Matt. 12:2).

Picture this scene: Jesus and His disciples are walking through a wheat field, perhaps going to a synagogue or returning from one. They are hungry, so they begin plucking off some of the wheat kernels and eating them. Is this a violation of the Sabbath law? No, it is not. Scripture tells us it's unlawful to *work* on the Sabbath, but it is not unlawful to eat. Nowhere in the Old Testament will you find any prohibition against plucking grain and eating it on the Sabbath. It would be a violation of the Sabbath to grind the wheat into flour and bake the bread, but not to munch on grain that is abundant around you, as you would in the garden of Eden. That is clearly not a sin.

Jesus never broke the law; of that you can be certain. His role as Messiah and Redeemer required that He live a sinless life so He could die as an unblemished sacrifice for all who fell short of the mark. As the Messiah of Israel, Jesus could not break any of God's commandments. We know He didn't. He died a sinless death so He could atone for the sins of the world.

Many well-meaning believers and teachers today cite Matthew 12:2 as evidence that Jesus was overturning the Sabbath. He was doing no such thing, as you will see in chapter 5.

Once again, it's a false allegation against Jesus and His disciples. But here's what you need to know about this pattern of confrontation that is emerging: the Pharisees were actually *adding* to the law, making up new rules, which Scripture soundly condemns: "What thing soever I command you, observe to do it: thou shalt not add thereto, nor diminish from it" (Deut. 12:32).

So, it was the Pharisees who were violating the commandments—not Jesus.

This is the big beef Jesus had with the Pharisees. They had placed their oral law and traditions ahead of the written Word of God—doing so in violation of the Torah. As you will continue to see in this study, that is the source of the major conflict between Jesus and the Pharisees, as recorded in all four gospels. It continued after Jesus' death and resurrection in the book of Acts. It is a central theme, and you simply cannot truly appreciate why Jesus came and what His ministry was about by not comprehending this important point, yet few do.

Why is it so important?

Because, as Jesus said, He did not come to destroy the law but to fulfill it (see Matt. 5:17). He was referring to the Torah, not the man-made laws of the Pharisees, which, at the time of His ministry, dominated Jewish spiritual life in Israel. It's an important distinction that has resulted in profound misunderstandings for the church for the last nineteen hundred years. More on that later, but for now, let's continue our study of Jesus' confrontation with the Pharisees to see what else we can learn from them.

To explain His disciples' Sabbath behavior, Jesus told the Pharisees:

> Have ye not read what David did, when he was an hungred, and they that were with him; how he entered into the house of God, and did eat the shewbread, which was not lawful for him to eat, neither for them which were with him, but only for the priests? Or have ye not read in the law, how that on the sabbath days the priests in the temple profane the sabbath, and are blameless? But I say unto you, that in this place is one greater than the temple. But if ye had known what this meaneth, I will have mercy, and not sacrifice, ye would not have condemned the guiltless. For the Son of man is Lord even of the sabbath day. (Matt. 12:3–8)

Again, Jesus was not advocating any breaking of the commandments of God here, though this can be a tricky passage unless you are steeped in the study of the Old Testament. Why was David permitted to eat the showbread, reserved for priests, when he was running and hiding from Saul? There are both practical and spiritual answers to this question.

In 1 Samuel, we see the practical answers: David had asked Ahimelech the priest for five loaves of bread.

And the priest answered David, and said, There is no common bread under mine hand, but there is hallowed bread; if the young men have kept themselves at least from women. And David answered the priest, and said unto him, Of a truth women have been kept from us about these three days, since I came out, and the vessels of the young men are holy, and the bread is in a manner common, yea, though it were sanctified this day in the vessel. So the priest gave him hallowed bread: for there was no bread there but the shewbread, that was taken from before the Lord, to put hot bread in the day when it was taken away. (1 Sam. 21:4–6)

So, there were extenuating circumstances that both the priest and David agreed permitted exceptions to the rule: (1) David and his men needed food and were in a relative state of purity; (2) the hallowed bread was now common, as it was being replaced as show-bread by freshly baked bread.

On the spiritual side of the equation, David was not breaking the law because even before he became king, he occasionally performed tasks otherwise assigned to kings and priests. In Psalm 110, the Lord Himself tells David: "Thou art a priest for ever after the order of Melchizedek" (v. 4)—meaning not a priest after the order of Aaron, since he was not of the Levite tribe, but after the order of Melchizedek, king of Salem and a contemporary of Abraham. In the same way, Jesus, in the genealogical line of David, not Aaron, is also a priest after the order of Melchizedek (see Heb. 7). One more spiritual clue is given in Leviticus: "There shall no stranger eat of the holy thing: a sojourner of the priest, or an hired servant, shall not eat of the holy thing. But if the priest buy any soul with his money, he shall eat of it, and he that is born in his house: they shall eat of his meat" (Lev. 22:10–11). David, a man after God's own heart, was, in a sense, a soul purchased by the ultimate High Priest, like all of Jesus' followers. But David holds a special position in the Lord's economy, for it is on David's throne that Jesus will sit in the coming kingdom (Luke 1:32).

So David did not sin by eating the bread, and Jesus did not sin by eating the grain. In fact, Jesus reminded the Pharisees that priests "profane" the Sabbath too; yet, they are "blameless" (Matt. 12:5). The priests had many duties on the holy days; a tremendous amount of work was involved. But it was spiritual work, and God had commanded them to do it. Therefore, they were without blame. And so was Jesus.

When Jesus went on to announce that He is, in fact, the "Lord of the Sabbath" (v. 8), He was really trying to get the Pharisees' attention. "It's decision day," He seemed to be saying. "I am the One who created the Sabbath. Will you follow Me, or your own, man-made traditions?" (Again, as we will see in more depth in chapter 5, there is no implication here that Jesus was doing away with, or even amending, the fourth commandment—or, for that matter, any other commandment.)

Matthew 12 continues:

> And, behold, there was a man which had his hand withered. And they asked him, saying, Is it lawful to heal on the sabbath days? that they might accuse him. And he said unto them, What man shall there be among you, that shall have one sheep, and if it fall into a pit on the sabbath day, will he not lay hold on it, and lift it out? How much then is a man better than a sheep? Wherefore it is lawful to do well on the sabbath days. Then saith he to the man, Stretch forth thine hand. And he stretched it forth; and it was restored whole, like as the other. Then the Pharisees went out, and held a council against him, how they might destroy him. But when Jesus knew it, he withdrew himself from thence: and great multitudes followed him, and he healed them all; And charged them that they should not make him known: That it might be fulfilled which was spoken by Esaias the prophet, saying, behold my servant, whom I have chosen; my beloved, in whom my soul is well pleased: I will put my spirit upon him, and he shall shew

judgment to the Gentiles. He shall not strive, nor cry; neither shall any man hear his voice in the streets. A bruised reed shall he not break, and smoking flax shall he not quench, till he send forth judgment unto victory. And in his name shall the Gentiles trust." (vv. 10–21)

As we begin to see here—chapter after chapter, verse after verse—Jesus was preaching and performing miracles, and the Pharisees were constantly challenging and rebuking Him. The pattern is clear: Jesus conducted His ministry; the Pharisees tried to foil Him every step of the way.

There is no prohibition in the Torah against healing anyone on the Sabbath. Search the Torah and you will not find an injunction from God against it. So Jesus was not breaking the law; He was fulfilling it—to the letter and in the spirit.

As Jesus went on to show that He was fulfilling not only the law, but also the prophets, He partially quoted Isaiah 42, where we read:

Behold my servant, whom I uphold; mine elect, in whom my soul delighteth; I have put my spirit upon him: he shall bring forth judgment to the Gentiles. He shall not cry, nor lift up, nor cause his voice to be heard in the street. A bruised reed shall he not break, and the smoking flax shall he not quench: he shall bring forth judgment unto truth. He shall not fail nor be discouraged, till he have set judgment in the earth: and the isles shall wait for his law. . . . I the LORD have called thee in righteousness, and will hold thine hand, and will keep thee, and give thee for a covenant of the people, for a light of the Gentiles. (Isaiah 42:1–6)

But the contest between Yeshua and the Pharisees continued. It's more than a pattern. It literally dominates the Gospels. Recognize and embrace its significance: Jesus wasn't trying to start a new religion. He was trying to clean up the old one:

Then was brought unto him one possessed with a devil, blind, and dumb: and he healed him, insomuch that the blind and dumb both spake and saw. And all the people were amazed, and said, Is not this the son of David? But when the Pharisees heard it, they said, This fellow doth not cast out devils, but by Beelzebub the prince of the devils. And Jesus knew their thoughts, and said unto them, Every kingdom divided against itself is brought to desolation; and every city or house divided against itself shall not stand: And if Satan cast out Satan, he is divided against himself; how shall then his kingdom stand? And if I by Beelzebub cast out devils, by whom do your children cast them out? therefore they shall be your judges. But if I cast out devils by the Spirit of God, then the kingdom of God is come unto you. Or else how can one enter into a strong man's house, and spoil his goods, except he first bind the strong man? and then he will spoil his house. He that is not with me is against me; and he that gathereth not with me scattereth abroad. Wherefore I say unto you, All manner of sin and blasphemy shall be forgiven unto men: but the blasphemy against the Holy Ghost shall not be forgiven unto men. And whosoever speaketh a word against the Son of man, it shall be forgiven him: but whosoever speaketh against the Holy Ghost, it shall not be forgiven him, neither in this world, neither in the world to come. Either make the tree good, and his fruit good; or else make the tree corrupt, and his fruit corrupt: for the tree is known by his fruit. O generation of vipers, how can ye, being evil, speak good things? for out of the abundance of the heart the mouth speaketh. A good man out of the good treasure of the heart bringeth forth good things: and an evil man out of the evil treasure bringeth forth evil things. But I say unto you, that every idle word that men shall speak, they shall give account thereof in the day of judgment. For by thy words thou shalt be justified, and by thy words thou shalt be condemned. (Matt. 12:22–37)

Can you believe the Pharisees actually accused Jesus of casting out demons through the power of Satan? Why were they so threatened by Him? Because He didn't come to them for consultation. He didn't act the way they thought the Messiah should act. They didn't recognize Him because of their own, man-made traditions and presuppositions—or, worse, they may have recognized Him but rejected Him because He threatened their lifestyle, their power, their wealth, their position. It was not the devil who was challenging Jesus—he gave up after forty days in the desert—it was the Pharisees, the religious establishment, men doing things the way men tend to do them—their own way.

Suddenly, the Pharisees changed their approach: "Then certain of the scribes and of the Pharisees answered, saying, Master, we would see a sign from thee" (Matt. 12:38). Keep in mind, Jesus had shown them a multitude of signs already. He'd healed all manner of illness—from blindness and deafness to demon possession. In turn, they had accused Him of violating the law and working miracles through the power of Satan. Now they "politely" ask Him for a sign:

> But he answered and said unto them, An evil and adulterous generation seeketh after a sign; and there shall no sign be given to it, but the sign of the prophet Jonas: For as Jonas was three days and three nights in the whale's belly; so shall the Son of man be three days and three nights in the heart of the earth. The men of Nineveh shall rise in judgment with this generation, and shall condemn it: because they repented at the preaching of Jonas; and, behold, a greater than Jonas is here. The queen of the south shall rise up in the judgment with this generation, and shall condemn it: for she came from the uttermost parts of the earth to hear the wisdom of Solomon; and, behold, a greater than Solomon is here. When the unclean spirit is gone out of a man, he walketh through dry places, seeking rest, and findeth none. Then he saith, I will return into my house from whence I came out; and when he is come, he findeth it empty, swept, and

garnished. Then goeth he, and taketh with himself seven other spirits more wicked than himself, and they enter in and dwell there: and the last state of that man is worse than the first. Even so shall it be also unto this wicked generation. (vv. 39–45)

The only answer is true and lasting repentance, He told them, again emphasizing that it is a narrow path that leads to redemption and His coming kingdom—to the restitution of all things.

But the Pharisees' pattern of condemnation and accusation continued: "Then came to Jesus scribes and Pharisees, which were of Jerusalem, saying, Why do thy disciples transgress the tradition of the elders? for they wash not their hands when they eat bread" (Matt. 15:1–2)?

Is there a Torah commandment about washing one's hands before eating? No there is not. But there was and is a Pharisee oral tradition about ritual washing of the hands before eating. It involved pouring a pitcher of water over one hand and then another. Orthodox Jews still do it today. But it's not a commandment. So Jesus answered them, "Why do *ye* also transgress the commandment of God by your *tradition*?" (v. 3, emphasis added).

Jesus emphasized His point a few verses later by quoting from the prophet Isaiah: "Ye hypocrites, well did Esaias prophesy of you, saying, This people draweth nigh unto me with their mouth, and honoureth me with their lips; but their heart is far from me. *But in vain they do worship me, teaching for doctrines the commandments of men*" (vv. 7–9, emphasis added).

Bingo! Do you see that? Jesus was calling them out, telling them exactly what they were doing wrong. Their grave sin? Teaching as doctrines the commandments of men.

This was a reference to Isaiah 29:13. Slightly different words, but the same meaning: "Wherefore the Lord said, Forasmuch as this people draw near me with their mouth, and with their lips do honour me, but have removed their heart far from me, *and their fear toward me is taught by the precept of men*" (emphasis added). Thus it was a fulfillment of prophecy that the children of Israel—including the Pharisees of Jesus' day—would reach this place of teaching for doctrines the commandments of men.

Some of this may seem redundant, but my goal here is to demonstrate the primacy of this point through the biblical repetition. There's a reason we see this pattern. God was making an important point—over and over again. And, as we will begin to see, it's a point that has profound application for us today. Notice the recurring conflict between Jesus' defense of the Torah and the Pharisees' commitment to their nonbiblical traditions. If this were not important, why is there so much of it?

By the way, we've only begun to scratch the surface. That's why I urge you to continue this study throughout all four gospels—looking for it whenever the Pharisees and Sadducees enter the picture.

This is not a contest about strict interpretation of God's commandments and a looser, more spiritualized interpretation offered by Jesus, as some pastors mistakenly teach because they don't know the Torah. You've got to study the beginning of the book to understand the end. Jesus never broke the law. He never *spiritualized* the commandments of God. He affirmed them again and again. In fact, as I'll demonstrate for you through the New Testament, He didn't *lower* the bar for His followers as far as the commandments of God go. He actually *raised* the bar for entering His kingdom.

We begin to see this in Matthew 19, when Jesus enters Judea, with great multitudes following Him and being healed. Enter the Pharisees, again:

> The Pharisees also came unto him, tempting him, and saying unto him, Is it lawful for a man to put away his wife for every cause?
>
> And he answered and said unto them, Have ye not read, that he which made them at the beginning made them male and female, And said, For this cause shall a man leave father and mother, and shall cleave to his wife: and they twain shall be one flesh? Wherefore they are no more twain, but one flesh. What

therefore God hath joined together, let not man put asunder.

They say unto him, Why did Moses then command to give a writing of divorcement, and to put her away?

He saith unto them, Moses because of the hardness of your hearts suffered you to put away your wives: but from the beginning it was not so. And I say unto you, whosoever shall put away his wife, except it be for fornication, and shall marry another, committeth adultery: and whoso marrieth her which is put away doth commit adultery. (Matt. 19:3–9)

Here Jesus was not only affirming the law of Moses, but imposing a *higher* standard for divorce and remarriage. Yet, over and over again, I have heard pastors teach that the law of Moses was *burdensome* and that Jesus freed us of that yoke. This dangerous misinterpretation of the Scriptures can lead people away from the narrow path of salvation and toward the broad way of destruction. But more on that in a later chapter.

In Matthew 21, Jesus enters Jerusalem, triumphantly riding a colt that had never been ridden, in fulfillment of Zechariah 9:9. Now He is about to confront a new level of religious authority and tradition in Israel—the priestly class:

And a very great multitude spread their garments in the way; others cut down branches from the trees, and strawed them in the way. And the multitudes that went before, and that followed, cried, saying, Hosanna to the son of David: blessed is he that cometh in the name of the Lord; hosanna in the highest. And when he was come into Jerusalem, all the city was moved, saying, Who is this? And the multitude said, This is Jesus the prophet of Nazareth of Galilee. And Jesus went into the temple of God, and cast out all them that sold and bought in the temple, and overthrew the tables of the moneychangers, and the seats of them that sold doves, and said unto them, It is written, My house shall be called the house of prayer; but ye have made it a den of thieves. (Matt. 21:8–13)

WHY I CALL JESUS "YESHUA"

Behold, God is my salvation; I will trust, and not be afraid
—ISAIAH 12:2

Yeshua is a variation of the name Yehoshuah, or in the more familiar, Greek-descended, anglicized form, Joshua. Jesus was almost certainly called Yeshua by His disciples. It was, and is, a name that denoted the power of salvation.

Imagine reading the Bible in Hebrew and coming to Exodus 15:2: "The LORD is my strength and song, and he is become my salvation." The word *salvation* in that verse would be pronounced "Yeshua." Notice how poignant and even prophetic that verse becomes by understanding the Hebrew behind that one word: "The LORD is my strength and song, and He is become my Yeshua."

"Yeshua" is a verbal derivative of the word *rescue*, or *deliver*, or *save*. Remember the old Jesus movement slogan "Jesus Saves." Indeed He does. But it's more than that. Jesus *is* salvation—and His very name tells us. Rich meaning is lost when we don't understand the Hebrew roots of our faith.

Matthew 1:21 says, "And she shall bring forth a son, and thou shalt call his name JESUS: for he shall save his people from their sins."

In Isaiah we read: "Therefore the Lord himself shall give you a sign; Behold, a virgin shall conceive, and bear a son, and shall call his name Immanuel" (Isa. 7:14). Why Immanuel? It means "God with us," which is exactly who Jesus is: God's Savior who came to live with us, deliver us, return to us and, ultimately, become our King.

There's more to the name "Jesus," and it has profoundly confused people.

Because we read Bible translations that were written in Hebrew and Greek, we see Jesus often referred to as Jesus Christ. "Christ" comes to us from the Greek word for Messiah. It is a title, not a name. He is Jesus *the* Christ. And that's why I have found it useful to refer to Jesus as Yeshua HaMashiach, translated Jesus the Messiah. It serves as a constant reminder to me of who Jesus, or Yeshua, really is—the promised Messiah of the Hebrew Scriptures.

This He did in fulfillment of a prophecy in Psalms: "Because for thy sake I have borne reproach; shame hath covered my face. I am become a stranger unto my brethren, and an alien unto my mother's children. For the zeal of thine house hath eaten me up; and the reproaches of them that reproached thee are fallen upon me" (Ps. 69:7–9).

After cleansing the temple, Jesus healed the blind and lame who had come: "And when the chief priests and scribes saw the wonderful things that he did, and the children crying in the temple, and saying, Hosanna to the son of David; they were sore displeased" (Matt. 21:14–15).

What? The Pharisees were *displeased* that He'd healed the sick and that the children of Israel recognized their Messiah? Why? Because they were not eagerly awaiting the Messiah. So they were not even willing to entertain the idea that He was or might be the Messiah.

Jesus left the temple and returned the next morning. And the conflict with the religious establishment heightened:

> And when he was come into the temple, the chief priests and the elders of the people came unto him as he was teaching, and said, By what authority doest thou these things? and who gave thee this authority? And Jesus answered and said unto them, I also will ask you one thing, which if ye tell me, I in like wise will tell you by what authority I do these things. The baptism of John, whence was it? from heaven, or of men? And they reasoned with themselves, saying, If we shall say, From heaven; he will say unto us, Why did ye not then believe him? But if we shall say, Of men; we fear the people; for all hold John as a prophet. And they answered Jesus, and said, We cannot tell. And he said unto them, Neither tell I you by what authority I do these things. (Matt. 21:23–27)

Jesus not only defied these religious leaders; He openly judged them with parables and a direct and personal warning: "The kingdom of God shall be taken from you, and given to a nation bringing forth the fruits thereof . . . And when the chief priests and Pharisees had heard his parables, they perceived that he spake of them. But when they sought to lay hands on him, they feared the multitude, because they took him for a prophet" (vv. 43, 45-46).

You know the rest of the story. Jesus was betrayed by one of His disciples, captured by the chief priests and Pharisees, tortured by Pontius Pilate, and crucified at the behest of the mob, to rise, victorious, on the third day. And in all that time, not once did Jesus ever suggest that He came for any other purpose but to teach, suffer, and die as an atonement for the sins of the world, fulfill the prophets, bring truth and light first to the lost sheep of the house of Israel and later to the Gentiles, and to lay the foundation for His coming kingdom and the restitution of all things.

This thoroughly Jewish God-man did not come to start a new religion. He came as the prophesied Jewish Messiah, a light to the whole world. And He came to rebuke the religious authorities who had hijacked Judaism, remaking it in their own image and in their own tradition—not God's.

Jesus didn't come because He or His Father had made some mistakes in the past and reforms were needed. Nor did He come to write new laws to replace old laws. On the contrary, what does Hebrews 13:8 say? "Jesus Christ the same yesterday, and to day, and for ever."

Too often, it seems, Christians opine that the rules of the Old Testament were established by the Father, Jehovah, in a world governed only by law, but then Jesus came along, "fulfilled" the law, and instituted a system of pure grace. If you have this perception, it's time to rethink it. It's a heresy. It's extrabiblical. It's a lie.

Jesus is eternal. It was He who created the heavens and the earth (see John 1:3, 10). It was also He who etched in stone the Ten Commandments with His finger (see Ex. 31:18). The Father and the Son are One (see John 10:38).

He didn't make any mistakes.

Instead, He orchestrated a big shift during the first century, opening up the opportunity for salvation and participation in the coming kingdom of God to vast numbers of Gentiles as well as Jews. How? Not by casting away the children of Israel, but by allowing Gentiles—those not sharing bloodlines with Abraham, Isaac, and Jacob—to be "grafted in" to the earlier, eternal covenant between God and His chosen people. Paul wrote, "I say then, Hath God cast away his people? God forbid. For I also am an Israelite, of the seed of Abraham, of the tribe of Benjamin. God hath not cast away his people which he foreknew" (Rom. 11:1–2).

This is an immensely important point—too often missed by Christian teachers and leaders today and over the last nineteen hundred years. There was always a remnant of true believers among the children of Israel, he explained—those who followed the "narrow path" rather than the broad path that leads to destruction. Even in the worst times of rebellion and apostasy, there remained a committed remnant. We see this in Elijah's time when Jehovah reserved seven thousand in Israel who had "not bowed unto Baal" and whose mouths had not "kissed him" (1 Kings 19:18).

"Even so then at this present time also there is a remnant according to the election of grace," explained Paul in Romans 11:5. He continued:

> I say then, Have they stumbled that they should fall? God forbid: but rather through their fall salvation is come unto the Gentiles, for to provoke them to jealousy. Now if the fall of them be the riches of the world, and the diminishing of them the riches of the Gentiles; how much more their fulness? . . . For if the firstfruit be holy, the lump is also holy: and if the root be holy, so are the branches. And if some of the branches be broken off, and thou, being a wild olive tree, wert grafted in among them, and with them partakest of the root and fatness of the olive tree; Boast not against the branches. But if thou boast, thou bearest not the root, but the root thee. Thou wilt say then, The branches were broken off, that I might be grafted in. Well; because of unbelief they

were broken off, and thou standest by faith. Be not highminded, but fear: For if God spared not the natural branches, take heed lest he also spare not thee. Behold therefore the goodness and severity of God: on them which fell, severity; but toward thee, goodness, if thou continue in his goodness: otherwise thou also shalt be cut off. And they also, if they abide not still in unbelief, shall be grafted in: for God is able to graft them in again. For if thou wert cut out of the olive tree which is wild by nature, and wert grafted contrary to nature into a good olive tree: how much more shall these, which be the natural branches, be grafted into their own olive tree? For I would not, brethren, that ye should be ignorant of this mystery, lest ye should be wise in your own conceits; that blindness in part is happened to Israel, until the fullness of the Gentiles be come in. And so all Israel shall be saved: as it is written, There shall come out of Sion the Deliverer, and shall turn away ungodliness from Jacob: For this is my covenant unto them, when I shall take away their sins. As concerning the gospel, they are enemies for your sakes: but as touching the election, they are beloved for the father's sakes. For the gifts and calling of God are without repentance. For as ye in times past have not believed God, yet have now obtained mercy through their unbelief: Even so have these also now not believed, that through your mercy they also may obtain mercy. For God hath concluded them all in unbelief, that he might have mercy upon all. (Rom. 11:11–12, 16–32)

Note how God's eternal covenant with Abraham and his line is in no way broken. Paul ensured here that all Israel will still be saved and that grafted in with the house of Israel are multitudes of Gentiles—not because they followed a new religion, but because they were adopted through grace into the house of Israel as grafted-in branches.

Remember when reading the New Testament that *all* of Jesus' early followers were Jewish, and following a Jewish Messiah. There was never any doubt among this remnant that salvation was of, through, and for the Jews. The question was, who else might enter the coming kingdom with them?

What did Jesus tell the Samaritan woman at the well? "Ye worship ye know not what: we know what we worship: for salvation is of the Jews" (John 4:22).

What did Paul say in Acts 13:26? "Men and brethren, children of the stock of Abraham, and whosoever among you feareth God, to you is the word of this salvation sent."

Who were the children of Israel, that they might be chosen of God? They were chosen to receive the oracles of the faith—to publish God's Word and to carry throughout the whole world the message of salvation (see Acts 7:38).

Were they left behind in the first or second century, cast aside, along with God's promise that they would see the coming kingdom ruled by an Anointed One from the lineage of David who would sit in judgment of the whole world and reign in Jerusalem? Did a new "church" inherit and maybe even abrogate those covenants? Did a new covenant replace the old, or is it simply a fulfillment of the old?

How were the rules of the game changed as to salvation?

All of these questions will be addressed in later chapters, though they all pertain directly to this idea within the Christian faith that Jesus came to start a new religion called "Christianity."

What does it mean to be a Christian?

As mentioned earlier, *Christ* is the Greek-derived English word for "Messiah," or "Anointed One." So a *Christian* is one who follows the Messiah. If more "Christians" understood that, the church would be better off. If they actually thought of themselves as followers of Messiah, they would better understand their relationship with God through Messiah Yeshua. Instead, we've lost touch with our Hebrew roots. Most Christians see themselves belonging to a new religion founded about two thousand years ago. They forget that all of the disciples were Jewish—including the Messiah, or "Christ," whom they follow as "Christians."

Whose Messiah was He? He was the promised Messiah to the

Jews. Yes, He is the Messiah to the non-Jews as well. But He came first for the Jews.

We might be closer to the truth if we thought of ourselves as "Messianics" rather than "Christians"—or at least if we understood why we use the term *Christian* and what it literally means. Messianic Jews today, like their first-century forebears, may be closer to the truth and a deeper understanding of who they are, what they believe, and what they represent than many other "Christians."

It is fundamentally an identity issue.

If you don't think this is important in understanding your faith, you are mistaken. It's not a small issue. Words mean things. They are critical for understanding.

In this chapter, we have explored the hostility between Jesus and the Pharisees, Sadducees, priests, and elders of first-century Israel. Why didn't they recognize Jesus as Messiah, Son of God, and heir to the throne of David?

They were blinded by a religion they themselves had created—not the faith of their fathers, and not the biblical faith of the Torah and the prophets. They had, over time, created their own religious system. They made their own rules—some of which were taken more seriously than Scripture. They followed their own man-made traditions—and missed their Messiah, because their hearts were hardened to the truth.

Today's Christians must understand this, embrace it, and pray about it, not only because it is critical to know what's going on when you are reading the Scriptures. There's also an important application for us in the twenty-first century as "Christians." Have you ever noticed the patterns we see in the Bible? The children of Israel know the Lord, the children of Israel know not the Lord. Revival comes, apostasy follows, and then judgment. The Bible is full of patterns like that. And they are there for a reason—to show us how we, too, can be deluded, tempted, and fallen. The risk is heightened by not learning the hard lessons through the experiences of the Jewish people.

Could it be that we have Pharisees among us today in Christianity? What would they look like?

Have many Christians been misled by false teachers in the church, who misrepresent the Word of God? Are these modern-day Pharisees making up their own rules based on tradition rather than the Bible? Do we listen more to "church fathers" of the second, third, or fourth centuries than we do the real church fathers—Peter, Paul, John, James, and the other Spirit-guided, first-century leaders?

More important, have we forgotten what's coming next? Do we even recognize the signs of the times Jesus warned us to be watching for so we would not be caught unawares at His Second Coming and the restitution of all things?

Remember, Jesus has given us stern and repeated warnings. Have we taken the cue?

2

WHAT DID THE FIRST-CENTURY FAITH LOOK LIKE?

And when they found them not, they drew Jason and certain brethren unto the rulers of the city, crying, These that have turned the world upside down are come hither also. —ACTS 17:6

WHAT'S GOING ON IN OUR WORLD TODAY?

It's on fire.

The map of the Middle East is being redrawn—in blood.

God's institution of marriage is being redefined by governments of men.

Being a man or a woman is simply a "state of mind," according to the prevailing ethos of the day.

Christians are being persecuted around the world.

The nation of Israel is under worldwide political, if not yet military, siege.

Anti-Semitism is on the rise again—just decades after the Holocaust.

The world is calling evil good and good evil.

Fifty-eight million unborn children have been sacrificed on the altars of Baal.[1]

Morality is being inverted. It's like living in an alternate universe. We've moved into Bizarro World—where up is down, left is right, and in is out.

Wrong is now right and right is now wrong.

It just takes a little time and a little reconditioning for people to invert their beliefs, discard ancient truths, adopt convenient lies and falsehoods.

It's easy when you remove God, the Author of right and wrong, from the equation and replace Him with a new, human-centered mythology.

While our once-Christian culture is rapidly being turned on its head, where has the Gentile church gone? Have any of you wondered where the "salt and light" are?

Are you as surprised as I am at how muted the opposition has been in this formerly Christian nation? It is as if our Christian leaders have been gagged, left speechless, kidnapped, or prematurely raptured.

These are unmistakable signs of the times—precisely those one would expect when reading the end-time prophecies of Matthew 24, Luke 21, and 2 Timothy 3:1–8.

We're living in times that require a deep and well-grounded faith. We are going to see a great falling away, potentially millions whose faith is not as solid as a rock. Our faith needs to be tested and true—like the faith of those in the first century.

It was nearly two thousand years ago that Jewish followers of Jesus the Messiah, or Yeshua Ha-Mashiach, turned the world upside down for God, launching the most important social and spiritual revolution in the history of humanity. It was that group of believers who in a radical way introduced the gospel to the world—including the Jewish world, the Gentile world, the pagan world, and the world of those with faith in the one true God.

Believers everywhere should be indebted to those Messianic Jews: Paul and Peter, John and Matthew, and all the rest of them. Every original disciple of Jesus was Jewish. And in the first century, these Messianic Jews spread the good news all over the known world as rapidly and effectively as it has ever been spread. They did it without radio, television, books, cars, planes, tracts—even without the Internet, for heaven's sake.

Think about that.

This is something most of the Christian world doesn't fully grasp or immediately appreciate. Most of the church today is ignorant of the fact that the first evangelists were all Jews. Many don't even think about Jesus in that context. Consequently, it has become too easy, as we've seen through history, to obscure the Hebrew roots of Christianity—to obliterate them, to twist them, to write them out of history, to demonize them, to revise them, to revile them. That's the only way vicious ideas like replacement theology—a topic we will explore in chapter 6—could ever gain a foothold among those who profess faith in Him.

And sadly, most Jews don't understand that what today is called "Christianity" is, or should be, simply the messianic, prophetic fulfillment of what the Tanakh, or "Old Testament," promised all along. They see it, and understandably so, as "another religion," a pagan one, that can be—and often has been throughout history—a personally threatening one.

Did you know Jesus never called His followers "Christians"? His apostles and early disciples never called each other "Christians." They knew each other as "brethren," "believers," "the faithful," "the elect," "the called," and "servants" of Messiah (see, for example, Acts 1:16; Rom. 1:6; Eph. 1:1; Phil. 1:1; Col. 3:12; 1 Tim. 4:12). The term

"Christians" was first used by pagans to describe the followers of Jesus.

It's not necessarily a bad name. After all, *Christ* is the Greek word for Messiah. So, in a sense, whether Christians realize it or not, they are actually calling themselves followers of Messiah—or, ironically, Messianics.

I'm not ethnically Jewish. In fact, I'm mostly ethnically Arab. I'm greatly indebted, though, to the Jews, who brought us their Messiah—revealed Him to us, spread His gospel the world over, and invited us to be grafted in to the promises and heritage of Abraham, Isaac, and Jacob. Today's Messianic Jewish movement bears witness to the reality of who the first-century believers were. I don't think it's a coincidence the movement is growing today, as we enter the end of the age and see the prophetic signs reaching a kind of climax—and, especially, now that the nation of Israel is back. It is also effectively teaching and inspiring other non-Jewish believers about the roots of their faith.

Likewise, as the Messianic Jewish movement takes on more prominence in God's last-days plans, there's a parallel movement growing among non-Jewish believers in Jesus. Over the last few decades, it seems, more and more followers of Jesus, or Yeshua, have begun exploring the Hebraic roots of their faith. This is a work of the Holy Spirit, or Ruach HaKodesh in Hebrew. And just as our spiritual forebears, those Messianic Jews, led the Yeshua Revolution in the first century, they will likely be at the vanguard of the Jesus Revolution that closes out the age and leads us to "the restitution of all things."

Jesus is coming back, and our role as on-fire believers in the Messiah—whether Messianic Jews or non-Jewish Christians who understand the roots of their faith—will expand before He returns. The expectations on us will be high. And we will be judged accordingly.

Jonathan Cahn, an anointed Messianic rabbi and author of the *New York Times* best seller *The Harbinger*, said something that resonated with me and struck me to the core a few years ago, when we were both speaking to a large group of Messianic believers: "Our time," he said of Messianic Jews, "is never when it's comfortable to be a believer. We don't get that. We only come along when it's radical to believe in Messiah. That's our time to take our place. Our movement is not about being comfortable; it's about being radical for God. The first Messianic believers were radical; they were revolutionaries; they were world-changers. And the last form of this faith is when it becomes radical again, and Jewish leaders must take your place in leadership as it was in the beginning."

I don't think it's a coincidence that Cahn and other Messianic teachers have taken a center-stage role in the church today. His profound and insightful teachings in *The Harbinger* and *The Mystery of the Shemitah* have made him one of the most sought-after speakers at churches, at conferences, on Christian TV and other media—even at the US Capitol and presidential inaugural prayer breakfasts.

What is he talking about when he says Messianic Jews need to take their place in leadership of the church?

As it was in the beginning, so it will be at the end.

Back in the first century, Cahn says, the movement was the head, not the tail, of those who called themselves "people of the way." And as we move closer to the end of the age, that's where this movement is going to be again—at the head, not the tail, because it is *still* "the way." Jesus is the one and only candidate in human history who qualified to be the Messiah, and you cannot separate Christianity from its Jewish roots—His roots—without distorting the very nature of where it came from and where it's going.

So, what was it like in the beginning of the age—in the first century?

In the book of Acts, we learn that the risen Jesus spent forty days with His followers. These formerly scared, despairing, and disillusioned Jewish men and women once again ate with their Lord, received wisdom from Him, and were empowered by the Holy Spirit to turn the world upside down for their God.

At first they had two things in common: they were Jews and they knew their Messiah. That's it. Nothing else. It was a small band of Galilean fishermen, His family members, some from Jerusalem who were convicted by His message and His miracles, and others who believed in their Scriptures deeply and saw its fulfillment in Him. There were only a few hundred who encountered the risen Jesus.

On that day of Pentecost, or Shavuot, as it is known in Hebrew, there were only about 120 disciples. Jews were coming to Jerusalem from neighboring lands for the biblical feast, as they were commanded to do every year. And when they heard the news of the risen Jesus, some three thousand became followers in the new Messianic fellowship.

This was Peter's message to them:

> Men and brethren, let me freely speak unto you of the patriarch David, that he is both dead and buried, and his sepulchre is with us unto this day. Therefore being a prophet, and knowing that God had sworn with an oath to him, that of the fruit of his loins, according to the flesh, he would raise up Christ to sit on his throne; He seeing this before spake of the resurrection of Christ, that his soul was not left in hell, neither his flesh did see corruption. This Jesus hath God raised up, whereof we all are witnesses. Therefore being by the right hand of God exalted, and having received of the Father the promise of the Holy Ghost, he hath shed forth this, which ye now see and hear. For David is not ascended into the heavens: but he saith himself, The Lord said unto my Lord, Sit thou on my right hand, Until I make thy foes thy footstool. Therefore let all the house of Israel know assuredly, that God hath made the same Jesus, whom ye have crucified, both Lord and Christ. (Acts 2:29–36)

Peter and the other disciples were empowered by the Spirit to speak with "tongues of fire," and each one present heard them in his own language. What were those three thousand new believers asked to do? Were they told to renounce their Jewish faith and become "Christians"? No, they were commanded to repent of their sins and follow the commandments in spirit and truth. They continued worshipping in the temple and in their synagogues outside of Jerusalem.

They worked many miracles, these Messianic Jews—giving sight to the blind, healing the sick, casting out demons, and even raising the dead, just as Jesus had.

Acts 2 tells us that "all that believed were together, and had all things common" (v. 44). They "sold their possessions and goods, and parted them to all men, as every man had need. And they, continuing daily with one accord in the temple, and breaking bread from house to house, did eat their meat with gladness and single-ness of heart, praising God, and having favour with all the people. And the Lord added to the church daily such as should be saved" (Acts 2:45–47).

It would be years before Peter and the rest of the disciples would even consider that the precious gift of salvation would be open to the "unclean" and uncircumcised Gentiles. It would be even longer before they saw non-Jews accept the Jewish Messiah. In the mean-time, they rocked their own, Jewish world.

One day, Peter and John walked up to the temple to worship and were met by a poor man crippled from birth and asking for money.

> Then Peter said, Silver and gold have I none; but such as I have give I thee: In the name of Jesus Christ of Nazareth rise up and walk. And he took him by the right hand, and lifted him up: and immediately his feet and ankle bones received strength. And he leaping up stood, and walked, and entered with them into the temple, walking, and leaping, and praising God. And all the people saw him walking and praising God: And they knew that it was he which sat for alms at the Beautiful gate of the temple: and they were filled with wonder and amazement at that which had happened unto him. And as the lame man which was healed held Peter and John, all the people ran together unto them in the porch that is called Solomon's, greatly wondering. And when Peter saw it, he answered unto the people, Ye men of Israel, why marvel ye at this? or why look ye so earnestly on us, as though

by our own power or holiness we had made this man to walk? The God of Abraham, and of Isaac, and of Jacob, the God of our fathers, hath glorified his Son Jesus; whom ye delivered up, and denied him in the presence of Pilate, when he was determined to let him go. But ye denied the Holy One and the Just, and desired a murderer to be granted unto you; and killed the Prince of life, whom God hath raised from the dead; whereof we are witnesses. And his name through faith in his name hath made this man strong, whom ye see and know: yea, the faith which is by him hath given him this perfect soundness in the presence of you all. And now, brethren, I wot that through ignorance ye did it, as did also your rulers. But those things, which God before had shewed by the mouth of all his prophets, that Christ should suffer, he hath so fulfilled. Repent ye therefore, and be converted, that your sins may be blotted out, when the *times of refreshing* shall come from the presence of the Lord. And he shall send Jesus Christ, which before was preached unto you: whom the heaven must receive until the times of *restitution of all things*, which God hath spoken by the mouth of all his holy prophets since the world began. (Acts 3:6–21, emphasis added).

This is what the first-century "church" was like. And don't be fooled by that word *church* in your Bible. Behind it is the same Greek word used for "synagogue." It doesn't imply a new religion was born. The disciples did not start meeting in "churches" as we think of them today. They continued meeting in the temple and in synagogues and in homes. And they did so, by the way, on the seventh-day Sabbath. There was no thought in their mind of changing the God-given, fourth-commandment edict to observe and honor the Sabbath. (More on this in chapter 5.)

For a long time they met and worshipped with non-Messianic Jews, until tensions caused them to be expelled. It didn't matter. Wherever they met, people flocked to hear the message and to witness astonishing miracles:

And by the hands of the apostles were many signs and wonders wrought among the people. And believers were the more added to the Lord, multitudes both of men and women. Insomuch that they brought forth the sick into the streets, and laid them on beds and couches, that at the least the shadow of Peter passing by might overshadow some of them. (Acts 5:12–15)

And to think: it started with a radical message about "times of refreshing" and "the restitution of all things." That's our destination as believers, a destination in the mind of God "since the world began" (Acts 3:21). Another five thousand joined the believers after Peter's message about "the restitution of all things."

If you want to get a better picture of what that first-century faith was like in the beginning, I implore you to read and absorb the entire book of Acts. This firsthand account by Luke is the best historical record we have of that time and the "works" of the apostles.

Works is often a dirty word in the church today. But it should not be so. Yet, because of error in the church many centuries ago, when people began confusing good works with finding salvation, the pendulum has swung the other direction—to the point that doing the good works of the Lord has, to many, become anathema. But while the Scriptures teach us that good works alone are useless in finding salvation, they also teach us that they are the visible and confirming fruit of salvation. Don't take my word for it. Read the book of James and see if you can reach any other conclusion. Faith without works is dead, the Messiah's once-skeptical brother wrote (James 2:20, 26).

What are the central differences between those early recountings of the gospel truth and what the "church" offers today? The first-century apostolic gospel

- was repentance driven

- did not promote a new creed, but rather, a gift of salvation that represented a seamless continuation of the prescription found from Genesis through Malachi

- affirmed all of the existing scriptures of that time, what we
  know as "the Old Testament"

- was empowered by the Holy Spirit, who had descended on
  believers in a dramatic way, giving them courage, boldness,
  insight, clarity, and unity

Contrast those characteristics with what you see in the twenty-
first-century church.

Do you realize what many churches are teaching and accepting
as truth today?

Repentance for sin is almost unheard-of in some corners of
today's church. In fact, sin itself— defined simply as "transgression of the law" (1 John 3:4)—is similarly unheard-of, because
the law, you see, has been "done away with," says this erring lot.

Some churches today preach that mere *acceptance* of the
reality of Jesus' work on the cross provides a kind of immuniza-
tion from sin. Let me straighten you out on that: Even the devil
himself accepts the reality of what He did on the cross.

Some even teach that Christians are incapable of sin and
shouldn't even concern themselves with transgressions of the
law. They believe that it was the law that was nailed to the cross,
rather than the sins from which they sorrowfully turned away.

Some in the church today see in the Old Testament merely
an antiquated, abrogated, discarded series of covenants between
God and man, rather than eternal laws and lessons as relevant
today as they were when they were written under the inspiration
of the Holy Spirit.

Do we want to return to the kind of faith that turned the
world upside down in the first century? If so, we need to think,
feel, breathe, pray, hear, speak, and do as the first-century, Messiah-
centric, Holy Spirit–driven believers did when their only Scriptures
were the Old Testament.

In short, we need to do what the Bible teaches, not what man
teaches. That was, after all, the grave error of the Pharisees, as we
saw in chapter 1.

Who today comes closest to that mark? Which group of believers has the best perspective on the harmony between the Old Testament and the Greek scriptures of the New Testament? Clearly, it is the heirs of the first-century believers—today's Messianic Jews. They recognize Yeshua as the fulfillment of all that was promised and foreshadowed in the Hebrew Scriptures. They see His finger etching the commandments in stone. They see Him as the Creator, the Word, the Light of the world, the Redeemer, and the King of kings, just as the apostle John did.

In short, they use the entire context of the Scriptures to shape their faith, their worldview, and their relationship with God.

It was the Messianic Jews who, with the leading of the Holy Spirit and the Word of God, spread the gospel so effectively after Jesus' ascension. They were the radicals who brought a revolutionary, fiery faith to their work. Later, because Jesus made it possible for Gentiles to find salvation through Him, others joined this other-worldly movement. Who were they? Cornelius was the first of these non-Jews to be "grafted in" to God's promises to Abraham and to the congregation of Israel *after* Jesus' ascension. That does not mean, of course, that no non-Jews were saved before that. There was always a pathway for Gentiles to become part of the house of Israel. Abraham himself, a onetime idol worshipper (see Josh. 24:2), found favor with the Lord. Ruth, a Moabite, joined the house of Israel and became part of the genealogical line of Jesus—as did Rahab. Even before that, some Egyptians joined the Israelites in the Exodus and thus became part of the congregation of Israel. And then, of course, there was Melchizedek, the mysterious high priest and king of Salem long before it became Jerusalem.

Remember: Israel was chosen as the nation to carry and preserve God's Word as a light to the Gentiles—meaning the whole world (Isa. 49:6). That is and was Israel's special responsibility.

Cornelius, the Roman centurion, an Italian in Caesarea, was chosen as God's vehicle to remind Peter and the other apostles of this mission. In Acts 10, we learn that Cornelius and his entire

And they shall turn away their ears from the truth, and shall be turned into fables. —2 TIMOTHY 4:4

Scripture speaks to us not only in specific, clear teachings of truth, instruction, prophecy, and wisdom. It also speaks to us in patterns.

In Exodus, Joshua, 1 and 2 Kings, 1 and 2 Chronicles, 1 and 2 Samuel, and other historical, prophetic, and wisdom books we see the pattern of the children of Israel walking with God and being blessed. We see them walk away from God and be disciplined through the removal of blessings—just as we would expect from reading God's instructions throughout the Torah.

Those patterns have as much meaning for us today as they did for the Israelites of old. Unfortunately, today we often read the New Testament with the idea that it is overthrowing the past, discarding its rules, or changing or rewriting them. As in the time of Jesus, we're guilty of making up our own rules and ignoring God's revelations of truth. But the entirety of Scripture is truth—for yesterday, today, and tomorrow.

In 2 Timothy 3 we're told, "The holy scriptures . . . are able to make thee wise unto salvation through faith which is in Christ. All scripture is given by inspiration of God, and is profitable for doctrine, for reproof, for correction, for instruction in righteousness" (vv. 15–16). Remember the holy Scripture Paul referred to was the Old Testament. He was endorsing it as true, valid, and applicable to believers after Jesus' death and resurrection and forevermore. He's telling us today to use the Old Testament Scriptures to ensure that we are in the truth, not falling into error, not following the commandments of men but only Holy Spirit–inspired teachings, backed by God's Word.

Any New Testament writings and doctrines must be measured by and consistent with the Old Testament Scriptures. There should be no contradictions between them. The patterns and truth were established long ago. The same God, the same Jesus who created the heavens and the earth, doesn't change His mind. He doesn't make mistakes. He doesn't rewrite the rules. He knows the end from the beginning.

Men's teachings aren't the standard—certainly not mine or anyone else's. The inerrant Word of God is the only standard that counts.

family worshipped the one true God, blessed the poor with alms, and prayed always. An angel appeared to him and beckoned him to dispatch men to Joppa and have them find Peter and summon him to Caesarea for instructions on what to do.

Meanwhile, as Cornelius's men were on their way, Peter was on his rooftop, praying.

> And he became very hungry, and would have eaten: but while they made ready, he fell into a trance, and saw heaven opened, and a certain vessel descending upon him, as it had been a great sheet knit at the four corners, and let down to the earth: wherein were all manner of fourfooted beasts of the earth, and wild beasts, and creeping things, and fowls of the air. And there came a voice to him, Rise, Peter; kill, and eat. But Peter said, Not so, Lord; for I have never eaten any thing that is common or unclean. And the voice spake unto him again the second time, What God hath cleansed, that call not thou common. This was done thrice: and the vessel was received up again into heaven. (Acts 10:10–16)

Today's Christians often use this passage as a message from the Lord that the biblical dietary laws have been overturned. But this can't be, because as you will see, Peter later interpreted the vision in another way entirely.

At the conclusion of his vision, while Peter "doubted in himself" about what the vision meant, "behold, the men which were sent from Cornelius had made enquiry for Simon's house, and stood before the gate, and called, and asked whether Simon, which was surnamed Peter, were lodged there. While Peter thought on the vision, the Spirit said unto him, Behold, three men seek thee. Arise therefore, and get thee down, and go with them, doubting nothing: for I have sent them" (Acts 10:17–19).

The true meaning of the vision quickly became clear as this delegation of non-Jews came to Peter's door. It was not the custom of the Jews at this time to have fellowship with non-Jews because they were considered "unclean." But the Spirit of God had clearly told Peter to do so.

> Then Peter went down to the men which were sent unto him from Cornelius; and said, Behold, I am he whom ye seek: what is the cause wherefore ye are come? And they said, Cornelius the centurion, a just man, and one that feareth God, and of good report among all the nation of the Jews, was warned from God by an holy angel to send for thee into his house, and to hear words of thee. Then called he them in, and lodged them. And on the morrow Peter went away with them, and certain brethren from Joppa accompanied him. (Acts 10:21–23)

What happened next is truly astonishing and reveals how God was opening up the non-Jewish world to the gospel and pouring out His Holy Spirit among non-Jewish believers in a major way.

As Peter and his delegation entered Caesarea, Cornelius and his large entourage of family and friends were waiting for them. When Peter entered his house, Cornelius greeted him, fell down at his feet, and worshipped him. But Peter picked him up and said: "Stand up; I myself also am a man" (Acts 10:26). Then, addressing the group that had assembled, "he said unto them, Ye know how that it is an unlawful thing for a man that is a Jew to keep company, or come unto one of another nation; but God hath shewed me that I should not call any man common or unclean. Therefore came I unto you without gainsaying, as soon as I was sent for: I ask therefore for what intent ye have sent for me?" (Acts 10:28–29).

Thus, Peter interpreted the vision God gave him in Joppa not as a change in the biblical dietary prohibition against eating unclean meats, but as a repudiation of an extrabiblical, man-made tradition of maintaining strict separation from men and women of other nations—or non-Israelis. It is without condemnation that I make this somewhat controversial suggestion: Christians who suggest that they are no longer prohibited from eating unclean meats will need to look for evidence elsewhere in Scripture. Peter's vision confirmed only that non-Jews are welcome into the congregation of Israel through repentance and adoption. But more on that later.

Peter went on to elaborate what he had learned from this experience: "Of a truth I perceive that God is no respecter of persons: But in every nation he that feareth him, and worketh righteousness, is accepted with him. The word which God sent unto the children of Israel, preaching peace by Jesus Christ: (he is Lord of all)" (Acts 10:34–36).

Peter provided a brief gospel message—perhaps the first delivered to a group of non-Jews—about the restitution of all things. And then the Holy Spirit fell on all who listened—Jew and non-Jew alike.

> And they of the circumcision which believed were astonished, as many as came with Peter, because that on the Gentiles also was poured out the gift of the Holy Ghost. For they heard them speak with tongues, and magnify God. Then answered Peter, Can any man forbid water, that these should not be baptized, which have received the Holy Ghost as well as we? And he commanded them to be baptized in the name of the Lord. Then prayed they him to tarry certain days. (Acts 10:45–48)

Thus those of us born outside the congregation of Israel were invited to join.

Controversies followed over many years. Were non-Jews to be circumcised? Were they subject to the other commandments of God? Which, if any, applied? But those issues are complex and detailed matters for another time. For now, let's continue with the first-century faith experience.

How did these non-Jews find their way into adoption into the house of Israel? They came in submission and for instruction after a heavenly messenger told Cornelius to seek out Peter. They didn't come demanding to be part of a new religion. They joined the Messianic Jews, who were, whenever possible, still worshipping in the temple and in synagogues. And the new believers were instructed to do likewise—learning the commandments and the Scriptures over time.

How do we know this?

Because it's in the Bible.

In Acts 15, there were disputes among the Messianic Jewish believers about what was required for the non-Jews to be saved. Some of the Pharisees who came to follow Jesus evidently brought some of their extra-legalistic ideas with them, insisting that the prerequisite to salvation was circumcision. Others said it was necessary to be in obedience to *all* the law, but how would the Gentiles know the law, not having been raised in it?

James, the brother of Jesus and the head of the Messianic Jewish believers in Jerusalem, had an answer: "My sentence is, that we trouble not them, which from among the Gentiles are turned to God: But that we write unto them, that they abstain from pollutions of idols, and from fornication, and from things strangled, and from blood. For Moses of old time hath in every city them that preach him, being read in the synagogues every sabbath day" (Acts 15:19–21).

This was the verdict: When Gentiles repented and became followers of Jesus, they would be commanded to turn away from all idolatry and sexual sin and to conform their diets with biblical law—though James did not specifically mention unclean meats.

But that was not the end of the journey to holiness for the new believers. As James concluded, they would have an opportunity over time to learn the entirety of the law to which they would be accountable because it would be preached to them weekly in the synagogues they attended each Sabbath.

This last verse is often neglected in Christian teaching today, but it's profound in its implications. It suggests that the Gentile believers would ultimately be responsible for knowing and following the law as they learned it over time. Even more interesting, they would be honoring the Sabbath from the start and be expected to attend Sabbath services in the synagogues—not Sunday services in churches.

Not to put too fine a point on it, but contrast that apostolic commandment with the behavior and expectations of the modern church: Do we learn the Torah? Are we expected to follow it? Is it taught as the law in churches? Do we observe the dietary laws and eat only what is defined as "clean"? Do we follow the Ten Commandments? Do we honor the Sabbath as the first-century believers did, from sundown Friday night to sundown Saturday night—abstaining from all work and worldly concerns?

I don't ask these questions with a holier-than-thou attitude. I ask them out of genuine concern for believers who may have been misled by human traditions rather than the commandments of God—just as the Pharisees in Jesus' time were.

Did something change in the first century that made believers unaccountable to God's commandments? Did God change His mind or His character, and suddenly the rules etched in stone on Mount Sinai were abrograted? Where is the scriptural evidence for this? We will explore these questions in more depth in succeeding chapters.

But I want to go back to who these new, Gentile believers were and what they did in the first century. They conformed with the teachings of the apostles. They conformed with what the Messianic Jews who led this spiritual revolution did. They became, in a very real sense, over time, conformed with the biblical laws that guided Messianic Judaism. That was the intent. That was the expectation.

And these Messianic non-Jews brought energy and vitality and excitement to the spiritual revolution that was shaking the known world to its very foundations.

That's interesting to me because something very similar is happening in the world today. There's a new phenomenon taking place in the world right now. I am evidence of it, and I am hardly alone. Non-Jewish Christians have begun to identify themselves more with Israel. They are observing Passover and Sukkot and Shabbat—or Sabbath.

This Israel-centric movement within the church comes in many forms. You can see it in numerous personalities—people like Mark Biltz, the discoverer of the blood moons phenomenon and a gifted teacher in what is often called the Hebraic roots movement. Other teachers include Bill Cloud, an itinerant Hebrew roots teacher, Ken Mentell, and dozens of others who are attempting to rediscover the power and truth of a first-century apostolic faith. Congregations are springing up all over the world—often meeting on the Sabbath, not Sunday. Some call this movement "Hebrew roots." Others call it "the Christian roots," acknowledging the undeniable fact that all early believers were Jews.

But the move of the Spirit is bigger than that. It comes in many different forms and practices. Some of the most notable prophecy teachers in the world today see the world the way the Bible does—in an Israel-centric way. It's hard not to if you study prophecy, because all of the yet-unfulfilled prophecies take us right back to Israel as the center of the world. Note Joel Richardson's terrific book with an amazing title: *When a Jew Rules the World.*

And, of course, the largest Messianic congregation in the United States and possibly the world is led by Rabbi Jonathan Cahn, who conducts two services every week—one on Shabbat and another on Sunday—to glorify the Lord, offer some of the richest teachings you will find anywhere, and bring together two movements under one Spirit-led house.

The key to both movements—Messianic Jewish and Messianic non-Jewish—is a love of the Jewish Messiah, Yeshua. These two movements recognize that the entire Bible makes a lot more sense when studied through the prism of Hebrew language, culture, and experience.

What does all this mean?

As it was in the beginning, so will it be at the end. As it was in the first century, so will it be in the last century before Jesus returns.

In the first century, Messianic Jews were the leaders of the movement. As we close out the age, they will necessarily return as leaders of the church to help prepare believers for the second coming of a very Jewish Messiah. And with them will be a remnant of Gentile Christians who identify more with the Messianics than they do with the Western Christian establishment, which operates more out of extrabiblical tradition than out of the unadulterated Word of God.

It is happening right before our eyes.

We're moving toward the day of restoration, "the restitution of all things," of which Jesus, His disciples, and all the prophets before them bore witness.

Bottom line: It's time for followers of Jesus to catch the fire of the first century. It's time to go deeper into the Scriptures and open ourselves up to a powerful outpouring of the Holy Spirit. And it's time to focus on the restitution of all things, a subject about which today's church knows little.

We're not there yet. Today the world is still on fire—just as it was in the first century. The early believers faced immense persecution. And today's believers are facing, once again, in terms of sheer numbers, what appears to be unprecedented affliction and oppression—even genocide.

It's to be expected:

"Yea, and all that will live godly in Christ Jesus shall suffer persecution." (2 Tim. 3:12)

"Blessed are they which are persecuted for righteousness' sake: for theirs is the kingdom of heaven." (Matt. 5:10)

"But and if ye suffer for righteousness' sake, happy are ye." (1 Peter 3:14)

The first century was the most exciting and fulfilling time of the last two thousand years, but it was also a time of immense suffering and tribulation for believers.

To persevere requires a radical faith.

Are you ready to explore what that means? Are you ready to go deeper into the Word to rediscover the radical roots that turned the world upside down? Are you willing to do it in obedience to God if He requires it?

If we believe this world, as we have known it, is heading to a climax, with something very new on the horizon, isn't it time to remove the scales from our eyes and get right with our Creator through sanctification in spirit and truth?

3

WHAT DOES IT MEAN TO BE A "CHRISTIAN" TODAY?

For if after they have escaped the pollutions of the world through the knowledge of the Lord and Saviour Jesus Christ, they are again entangled therein, and overcome, the latter end is worse with them than the beginning.
—2 PETER 2:20

HAVE YOU EVER WONDERED WHY a nation like the United States, where so many people attend Christian services weekly, is, by any standard, losing its Christian heritage and culture?

I don't think there's much mystery to it.

Are most Americans who call themselves
    Christians biblically literate?

How often do they read the Bible?

How many books of the Bible could they name,
    let alone explain the themes and content?

Are they equipped to explain the gospel to an unbeliever?

Can they defend their faith?

When others observe their lives, do they
    clearly see followers of Jesus?

Do they practice holiness?

Do they fellowship regularly with other believers?

How many put their faith in practice the way Jesus described?

How often do they pray?

Do they share their faith with nonbelievers?

Are they disciples?

Do they study the Word as the Bereans
    did? (See Acts 17:10–12) Or,

Do they get their notions of what the Bible is all about
    by listening to "teachers" and preachers? Are there
    good works associated with their faith that serve as
    evidence, or fruit, of their walk with the Lord?

In short, how many are making the kinds of sacrifices
    Jesus commanded His followers to make when He said,
    "Take up [your] cross . . . and follow me" (Luke 9:23)?

I was confronted with these thoughts when I used my position
at WND.com to launch a campaign to remind twenty-first-century
Americans about holiness, obedience to God, and the definition

of sin by posting copies of the Ten Commandments on billboards across the country.

While I fully expected to get heat from atheists, the American Civil Liberties Union, and the Freedom from Religion Foundation, I was shocked to receive angry denunciations from self-described "Christians."

Here are some examples of the "corrections" I received for reminding Americans about the commandments of God, along with the so-called scriptural evidence for them:

"The Law and Ten Commandments are inappropriate
    for those led by the Spirit, as the Law and Ten
    Commandments are of works, not faith (Gal. 3:12)."

"Those under the Law are under the curse of total
    and complete obedience (Gal. 3:10–12)."

"The Ten Commandments lead to condemnation
    and death (2 Cor. 3:7, 9)."

"The Ten Commandments and the Law incite
    coveting in the heart (Rom. 7:7–9)."

"The commandments lead to death, not life (Rom. 7:10)."

"The Law and the Commandments lead to the dominion
    of sin over us, resulting in bondage (Rom. 6:14)."

"The Law and Commandments served their purpose to
    preserve the lineage of Abraham to bring us to Christ so
    that we might be justified by faith (Gal. 4:23, 24)."

After posting copies of the Ten Commandments around the United States, I was told by one letter-writer: "You and WND are doing a disservice to God and your fellow man." This comment was reflective of many others I received. I was shocked.

In other words, people attending church and calling themselves believers in Jesus think the Ten Commandments are no longer valid, not for today or, worse yet, spiritually "dangerous." And some of them are quite zealous about this conviction.

Who is responsible for leading people to such conclusions? Are you, perhaps, one of them?

Ultimately, each of us is responsible for what we believe and for what we do with our lives. But there's a special place in judgment for so-called leaders of the church in the West for promoting such drivel—the notion that we serve a God who changed His mind about His rules or made a mistake when He issued them in the first place.

There are "Christian" teachers all over the country who are actually making such assertions. One of the most dangerous new theologies to have emerged in recent years was exposed by Michael Brown in his shocking book *Hyper-Grace*. The doctrine of "hyper-grace" is based largely on many of the out-of-context, misunderstood verses I just cited—passages that, interpreted incorrectly, stand in stark contradiction to the whole of the Bible and Jesus' own teachings. And this doctrine of men, not God, suggests, in its extreme form, that those who follow Jesus are no longer capable of sin. In fact, they shouldn't even think about the commandments of God any longer. They simply don't apply to believers after they repent once. This, of course, is heresy. It's voodoo theology.

Are these unusual presuppositions in the American church today? I fear they are not.

People don't want to be accountable for their sin—even those who call themselves Christians. One way of being unaccountable for sin is to deny it exists. That's what atheists do. That's what people who say the Bible is a fairy tale do. But increasingly, that's what too many who call themselves Christians do as well—often seizing on the teachings of contemporary pastors and authors who don't mind leading people to hell if it helps them build a popular and prosperous megachurch.

What's happening in the "church" now is that people are

embracing the preposterous notion that they are *incapable* of sinning because of their embrace of Jesus. But it's a false Jesus they are embracing. They are buying into the lie that they cannot sin because the law has been abolished. If there are no laws, you can't break any.

Could that be what the verses cited earlier suggest? Let's take a closer look at the scriptures used by those who find the Ten Commandments an anachronism, irrelevant, obsolete.

The first is Galatians 3:12: "And the law is not of faith: but, the man that doeth them shall live in them."

It's always a good idea to read the entire epistle from Paul for context. It's even better to read the whole Bible, written under the inspiration of the Holy Spirit, with the understanding that it is inerrant and consistent, with one overriding message: "Obey God and live well. Disobey God and perish." Another way to put it: "Repent of your *sin*," which, as noted earlier, is defined as "transgression of the law" (1 John 3:4).

To comprehend Paul's writings, which even Peter acknowledged were "hard to be understood" (2 Peter 3:16), it's important to know something about the cultural context of his words and what questions he was answering. Remember: this was a letter to the Galatians concerning controversies that had arisen in the community of believers. Sadly, too many pastors don't do much homework in that regard—or maybe the "light" is simply not in them. Yet, any confusion about what Paul was saying in Galatians about the law should have been resolved with certainty in 1994 in biblical scholar Martin Abegg's article in the November–December issue of *Biblical Archaeological Review*, titled "Paul, 'Works of the Law' and MMT." Abegg studied the original language found in the Dead Sea Scrolls and discovered, beyond any reasonable doubt, what Paul meant when he used the term "works of the law." It turns out the phrase Paul repeated throughout the letter refers not to the law of Moses but to rabbinical edicts in the Talmud—statutes involving things such as the bringing of Gentile corn into the temple, the presentation of Gentile offerings, and the cooking of sacrificial meat in unfit (impure) vessels. Paul never repudiated the Torah. On the contrary, he consistently affirmed it and practiced it. In fact, he wrote in Romans 3:31, "Do we then make void the law through faith? God forbid: yea, we establish the law."

So what Paul was saying in Galatians was not a new doctrine or some groundbreaking revelation he had received from the Holy Spirit that God had changed His mind about the law and the commandments. Instead, it was an affirmation of just what Jesus taught in all four gospels and a reiteration of His condemnation of what the Pharisees were doing—imposing man-made laws that often took precedence over God's commandments. (See chapter 1.) Jesus came not to abolish the law but to fulfill it, to live it perfectly, not so we wouldn't live according to the law, but as an example to us.

There's no distinction between what Paul taught and what Jesus taught. There cannot be, or His inspired words would simply not be a part of Scripture.

Next let's look at 2 Corinthians 3:7, 9: "But if the ministration of death, written and engraven in stones, was glorious, so that the children of Israel could not stedfastly behold the face of Moses for the glory of his countenance; which glory was to be done away . . . For if the ministration of condemnation be glory, much more doth the ministration of righteousness exceed in glory."

What was Paul talking about here? Was he saying something new? Was he suggesting the law of Moses was done away with? Paul was referring directly to the words of God in the Torah—Deuteronomy 18:15–18, to be precise:

> The LORD thy God will raise up unto thee a Prophet from the midst of thee, of thy brethren, like unto me [Moses]; unto him ye shall hearken; according to all that thou desiredst of the LORD thy God in Horeb in the day of the assembly, saying, Let me not hear again the voice of the LORD my God, neither let me see this great fire any more, that I die not. And the LORD said unto me, They have well spoken that which they have spoken. I will raise

them up a Prophet from among their brethren, like unto thee, and will put my words in his mouth; and he shall speak unto them all that I shall command him.

This was a reference to the greatest prophet—the Lord Jesus, who did all that and also said, "Till heaven and earth pass, one jot or tittle shall in no wise pass from the law, till all be fulfilled" (Matt. 5:18). What needed to happen before a jot or tittle of the law would pass? Heaven and earth needed to be gone. Are they gone? Do we have a new heaven and a new earth, as is promised in Revelation? No, we don't. Therefore, the law stands—every jot and tittle. You have Jesus' word on that.

Here's another one, Romans 7:7–10: "What shall we say then? Is the law sin? God forbid. Nay, I had not known sin, but by the law: for I had not known lust, except the law had said, Thou shalt not covet. But sin, taking occasion by the commandment, wrought in me all manner of concupiscence. For without the law sin was dead. For I was alive without the law once: but when the commandment came, sin revived, and I died. And the commandment, which was ordained to life, I found to be unto death."

Confused? Admittedly, Paul's words are not easy to grasp—especially out of context. So read on into the next two verses: "For sin, taking occasion by the commandment, deceived me, and by it slew me. Wherefore *the law is holy, and the commandment holy, and just, and good*" (vv. 11–12, emphasis added). Hello! Did you catch that? See, context is everything. Without it, grabbing a verse here and there and building a new doctrine around them can lead to exactly the opposite conclusion Paul was drawing. The New Testament is not in contradiction with the Old Testament. It simply provides more insight, or revelation, into the Hebrew Scriptures.

Then there's Romans 6:14: "For sin shall not have dominion over you: for ye are not under the law, but under grace."

I agree wholeheartedly. If you are living in a state of grace, sin does not have dominion over you. And what are Paul's very next words? "What then? shall we sin, because we are not under the law, but under grace? God forbid." Again, what is sin? The transgression of the law.

Another verse used by those who deem the law obsolete is Galatians 4:23–24, which says, "But he who was of the bondwoman was born after the flesh; but he of the freewoman was by promise. Which things are an allegory: for these are the two covenants; the one from the mount Sinai, which gendereth to bondage, which is Agar."

Allegory indeed. From such verses, sans context, false teachers are leading people astray. "The Law and commandments served their purpose to preserve the lineage of Abraham to bring us to Christ so that we might be justified by faith," they say. Justification was always by faith. Abraham himself was justified by faith. That is not just a New Testament doctrine found in Romans 1, Galatians 3, and Hebrews 10. It's found throughout the Old Testament, but most prominently in Habakkuk 2:4: "Behold, his soul which is lifted up is not upright in him: but the just shall live by his faith."

The truth, is we serve one God, who is the same yesterday, today, and tomorrow (see Mal. 3:6; Heb. 13:8). Jesus did not come to start a new religion. He came to save the world from sin. And remember: what He said in John 15:15 was the key: "If ye love me, keep my commandments."

Remember the Bereans, mentioned earlier, who "searched the scriptures daily, whether those things [they were being taught] were so" (Acts 17:11)? Which scriptures were they searching to determine if the apostles' teaching was true? The only Scriptures that existed at the time: the Old Testament. They served as the only written, scriptural litmus test there was in the first century. The Bereans knew there could be no conflict between truth and the Torah or the Tanakh. They knew the truth of the Old Testament was for eternity and could never be overthrown by anyone, not even Jesus.

In chapter 1, we explored Jesus' open conflict with the Pharisees, who were adding to the Word of God with the doctrines and commandments of men. We consider these Pharisees false teachers. Yet, there are equally pernicious doctrines being taught by modern-day Pharisees in the church today. They descend from the bizarre notion that God's character in the Old Testament somehow changed in the New Testament. Is that possible?

Not according to Scripture. Jesus Christ, who created the world (Eph. 3:9), is "the same yesterday, and to day, and for ever" (Heb. 13:8).

Another strange and unscriptural doctrine popular within the church today is the notion that you are saved forever the day you "take Jesus into your heart as your Lord and Savior."

Consider then the unambiguous words of Peter: "For if after they have escaped the pollutions of the world through the knowledge of the Lord and Saviour Jesus Christ, they are again entangled therein, and overcome, the latter end is worse with them than the beginning. For it had been better for them not to have known the way of righteousness, than, after they have known it, to turn from the holy commandment delivered unto them" (2 Peter 2:20–21).

Do you want to stake your eternal life on the once-saved-always-saved "doctrine," which simply lacks scriptural support?

Peter's clear warning that it would be better for a person never to have known the truth than to fall into unrepentant sin again strongly suggests that repentance is more than a onetime event in our lives. We see it through the body of Scripture, Old Testament and New.

There's a prevalent misunderstanding throughout the church that "salvation" through the embrace of Jesus the Atoner is the fulfillment of the spiritual journey. In fact, it is the very beginning. Discipleship, holiness, steadfastness, and life-changing and enduring commitment that bear fruit are the hallmarks and testimony of salvation.

What is driving the church in such a wayward direction?

Have you noticed how the church is conforming to the world to attract people to the pews? Has the church become a business, as the temple did in Jesus' time?

Why would the church conform to a world that is growing darker by the day? Aren't God's people supposed to be set apart?

Aren't we supposed to be salt and light in a dying, decaying world? Aren't we to be *in* the world but not *of* it (see John 17:16)? "Wherein in time *past* ye walked according to the course of this world, according to the prince of the power of the air, the spirit that now worketh in the children of disobedience," we see in Ephesians 2:2 (emphasis added).

Look at America today. Too many people just don't find any meaning in life. They're like dead men walking. It's no wonder. We are told from the youngest age in state-run schools that humans are merely the result of billions of years of evolution from lower life-forms and random mutations. There is no Creator God who loves us and to whom we are accountable, and no laws higher than those government imposes on us. No sin. No ultimate, objective moral code. In fact, humans are a blight on the planet. It would be better off without us—or at least with a lot fewer of us polluting the air with carbon dioxide and overheating the earth.

Furthermore, prayer and Bible reading are prohibited, but explicit instructions on how to have promiscuous sex without consequences are mandated.

Abortion is subsidized, while adoption is prohibitively expensive—in the unlikely event you can find a child to adopt.

Increasingly, the state its sticking its nose into what we eat, what we say, how we raise our children—even our thoughts. That's what so-called hate crimes are all about.

Government is fine with pornography. But purity and abstinence are discouraged.

In other words, right is wrong, up is down, black is white, and left is right.

And we sit here and wonder why people are killing themselves.

This is not the gospel.

Jesus and His apostles did not tell us to accommodate the world and to live like it. They commanded us to be "salt and light" to the world by being set apart from it.

Is that what we see today when we look at the church?

Jesus said in Luke 20:25, "Render therefore unto Caesar the things which be Caesar's, and unto God the things which be God's." Was He telling us to render our children or our own lives to Caesar and to the ways of the world? Was He telling us to put our faith and hope in Caesar? In other words, are we to make government the ultimate authority in our lives?

I think not.

When government replaces God, people's lives become empty. We become subjects of the state, rather than citizens endowed by our Creator with certain inalienable rights—among those being life, liberty, and the pursuit of happiness. Man's laws will never live up to the perfection of God's laws.

We are not to add to or take away from God's laws. Jesus judged the Pharisees guilty of adding to the law. Some in the church today are guilty of taking away from God's laws.

So, what's the answer? Followers of Jesus need to discover, or rediscover, why He created us, how much He loves us, and what it is He requires of us. When we figure this out and we are truly repentant for straying from His commandments, He offers us salvation by grace—and much more. But we cannot continue whoring after other gods and living the worldly life. We each are commanded to pick up our cross and follow Him, dying to our old life.

This is not the "cheap grace" gospel being preached in too many churches.[1]

We're all going to be judged individually in the Day of the Lord. We know what that standard of judgment is. If Jesus is truly the Lord of our lives, we live forever. We rule with Him for a thousand years in the millennial kingdom, and our spirits live on in a new heaven and new earth after that. But if we are not in covenant with God through that atoning sacrifice, we are eternally separated from God.

Let's look at Jesus' parable of the talents for an illustration:

For the kingdom of heaven is as a man travelling into a far country, who called his own servants, and delivered unto them his goods. And unto one he gave five talents, to another two, and to another one; to every man according to his several ability; and straightway took his journey. Then he that had received the five talents went and traded with the same, and made them other five talents. And likewise he that had received two, he also gained other two. But he that had received one went and digged in the earth, and hid his lord's money. After a long time the lord of those servants cometh, and reckoneth with them. And so he that had received five talents came and brought other five talents, saying, Lord, thou deliveredst unto me five talents: behold, I have gained beside them five talents more. His lord said unto him, Well done, thou good and faithful servant: thou hast been faithful over a few things, I will make thee ruler over many things: enter thou into the joy of thy lord. He also that had received two talents came and said, Lord, thou deliveredst unto me two talents: behold, I have gained two other talents beside them. His lord said unto him, Well done, good and faithful servant; thou hast been faithful over a few things, I will make thee ruler over many things: enter thou into the joy of thy lord. Then he which had received the one talent came and said, Lord, I knew thee that thou art an hard man, reaping where thou hast not sown, and gathering where thou hast not strawed: And I was afraid, and went and hid thy talent in the earth: lo, there thou hast that is thine. His lord answered and said unto him, Thou wicked and slothful servant, thou knewest that I reap where I sowed not, and gather where I have not strawed: Thou oughtest therefore to have put my money to the exchangers, and then at my coming I should have received mine own with usury. Take therefore the talent from him, and give it unto him which hath ten talents. For unto every one that hath shall be given, and he shall have abundance: but from him that hath not shall be taken away even that which he hath. And cast ye the unprofitable servant into outer darkness: there shall be weeping and gnashing of teeth. (Matt. 25:14–30)

THE RESTITUTION OF ALL THINGS

This is a picture of the kingdom to come, in which we will see "the restitution of all things." Is it what we expect? Who is that "man" traveling into a far kingdom before His return? Are we living up to His expectations? What *does* He expect from us while He is away, just a onetime "confession of faith"? How will we be judged when He returns? Are we doing His work? Are we being profitable servants?

On a personal basis, ask yourself the questions raised in this parable:

- With how many talents have you been gifted?

- What have you done with them?

- Have you been obedient to Messiah?

- Have you truly, independently searched the Scriptures to determine what God requires of you?

- Are you obeying His commandments, or have you allowed yourself to be convinced they are no longer valid?

- Have you accepted the teaching that all you have to do to ensure your eternal destiny is to "take Jesus into your heart" once and for all, and nothing else is required of you?

- In the kingdom to come, will you be rewarded for your obedience—or cast into outer darkness?

Time's running out. The signs are everywhere.

God is sitting on His throne in heaven, but He's about to act.

The world as we have known it throughout our lifetimes is going to change dramatically and forever. A certain date is set. I don't pretend to know when that day or hour will come, but I believe it is near—very near.

Why?

Let's look at some Scripture:

"This know also, that in the last days perilous times shall come. For men shall be lovers of their own selves, covetous, boasters, proud, blasphemers, disobedient to parents, unthankful, unholy, without natural affection, trucebreakers, false accusers, incontinent, fierce, despisers of those that are good, Traitors, heady, high-minded, lovers of pleasures more than lovers of God; Having a form of godliness, but denying the power thereof: from such turn away." (2 Tim. 3:1–5)

"For the time will come when they will not endure sound doctrine; but after their own lusts shall they heap to themselves teachers, having itching ears; And they shall turn away their ears from the truth, and shall be turned unto fables." (2 Tim. 4:3-4)

Is there any more apropos description of the time in which we live than this?

Turn on the television and you will see the evidence.

Read the news and you will see it.

Visit your neighborhood school and you will see it.

Worse yet, attend many churches in America and you will see it.

What abounds in our world today is sin, pride, and spiritual darkness. And it's getting worse every day. It's palpable. The handwriting is on the wall.

There's a growing divide between the ways of the world and the wisdom and truth of God's Word. And this is exactly what the Bible tells us will happen before the end.

The reigning ethos of the age is self-esteem or self-love. The notion of self-love as an ideal was popularized in 1956 by psychologist Erich Fromm, who postulated that loving oneself is different from being egocentric. He suggested that loving oneself means caring about oneself, taking responsibility for oneself, respecting oneself, and knowing oneself. Further, to be able to truly love another person, one needs first to love oneself. Sounds reasonable—even righteous—by human standards.

But it's not what God's Word tells us.

In Deuteronomy 6:5, we're instructed to "love the LORD thy God with all thine heart, and with all thy soul, and with all thy might." Jesus reaffirmed this: "The first of all the commandments is, . . . And thou shalt love the Lord thy God with all thy heart, and with all thy soul, and with all thy mind, and with all thy strength: this is the first commandment. And the second is like, namely this, Thou shalt love thy neighbour as thyself. There is none other commandment greater than these" (Mark 12:29–31).

Loving ourselves is not the secret to loving others. Loving God is.

The self-love/self-esteem model is the gospel of man, not the gospel of the kingdom. In fact, Jesus tells us, "Whosoever will come after me, let him deny himself, and take up his cross, and follow me" (Mark 8:34).

The gospel is not about us. It's about Jesus and His monumental sacrifice to atone for our sins, if we will accept that sacrifice through repentance—which means turning away from sin, not once but forever.

That's not to suggest we will not fall short of the mark and sin again. But new sins need to be atoned for through a penitent heart. Scripture warns about habitual sin (see Heb. 10:26–31).

There are, indeed, responsibilities that come with forgiveness and salvation. This is not to be confused with "works." There are no works we can do to be saved. There are, however, responsibilities: denial of self and taking up the cross.

Followers of Jesus are to be salt and light unto the world:

> Ye are the salt of the earth: but if the salt have lost his savour, wherewith shall it be salted? it is thenceforth good for nothing, but to be cast out, and to be trodden under foot of men. Ye are the light of the world. A city that is set on an hill cannot be hid. Neither do men light a candle, and put it under a bushel, but on a candlestick; and it giveth light unto all that are in the house. Let your light so shine before men. (Matt. 5:13–16)

Self-love and self-esteem are inextricably linked with pride. In this age, pride is celebrated.

But not in God's Word. Proverbs 16:18 tells us that "pride goeth before destruction, and an haughty spirit before a fall."

It's not just true of individuals. It's true of nations too. In Ezekiel 30:6 we read, "Thus saith the LORD; they also that uphold Egypt shall fall; and the pride of her power shall come down: from the tower of Syene shall they fall in it by the sword, saith the Lord GOD."

Even ancient Israel, the nation God chose to be a beacon of light to the whole world, the people He set apart and the land to which He committed the holy oracles, fell because of the sin of pride, as we learn in Hosea: "And the pride of Israel doth testify to his face: therefore shall Israel and Ephraim fall in their iniquity: Judah also shall fall with them" (5:5).

Even the elect can be "lifted up with pride" and "fall into the condemnation of the devil" (1 Tim. 3:6).

Satan himself fell from heaven because of the sin of pride:

> How art thou fallen from heaven, O Lucifer, son of the morning! how art thou cut down to the ground, which didst weaken the nations! For thou hast said in thine heart, I will ascend into heaven, I will exalt my throne above the stars of God: I will sit also upon the mount of the congregation, in the sides of the north: I will ascend above the heights of the clouds; I will be like the most High. Yet thou shalt be brought down to hell, to the sides of the pit. They that see thee shall narrowly look upon thee, and consider thee, saying, Is this the man that made the earth to tremble, that did shake kingdoms; That made the world as a wilderness, and destroyed the cities thereof; that opened not the house of his prisoners? (Isa. 14:12–17)

With some of the most profound words he ever wrote, Bob Dylan nailed it in his song, "Gotta Serve Somebody," explaining it's really a choice between the King of kings or the prince of this world.

"JESUS WEPT"

Jesus wept. —JOHN 11:35

It's the shortest verse in the Bible. But it may be the most profound and telling. It is poignant and especially relevant to the theme of this book.

There are only two occasions in the Bible where we are told Jesus wept, and both times when Jesus wept, He wept for *His people*, because they were blind to the truth (John 11:35; Luke 19:41). Both occasions come just before His passion in the garden of Gethsemane.

In the first recorded instance of Jesus weeping, His friend Lazarus had died and had been in his tomb for four days. Jesus was overcome by the suffering of Lazarus's sisters, Mary and Martha. But he also recognized that in raising his friend Lazarus, He was sealing His fate—His purpose for coming. And though He prayed that those present—who were about to see a great miracle—would believe that the Father had sent Him (John 11:42), He recognized that some would turn more strongly against Him, which is exactly what happened. It was indeed a turning point in Jesus' ministry. He could no longer walk openly among the people.

The second time Scripture was recorded in Luke 19:41–44 where the disciple tells us Jesus wept was when He approached Jerusalem in the days before His crucifixion and gazed over the city. Again, He wept, not for Himself, but for His people—too many of whom failed to recognize the time of His visitation—and for the suffering and death that would befall them.

Jesus wept both times for those who persecuted Him—the Pharisees, who had added to the law through their man-made traditions—a practice that blinded them to the truth and His saving grace.

If the church today is guilty of the same sin as the Pharisees—adding to, subtracting from, and twisting the Scriptures, His commandments, His teachings, and His Torah—we must ask ourselves:

Is Jesus weeping for us?

Will *we* recognize Him at the time of His next visitation?

Will it be as we envision it?

Are we any more prepared for His coming than were the generation of His previous visitation?

That's the choice each of us earth must make. Whom are we going to serve? There are only two choices—the God of Abraham, Isaac, and Jacob, or the No. 1 adversary, the deceiver, the tempter—Satan.

It's really that simple.

And time is running out. At any given moment, any of us could breathe our last breath. That's been true since man's fall. But there's another reason time's running out—not just for each of us, but for all of humanity.

Since the fall of Lucifer, he has literally been "the prince of this world." But he has been judged and is about to be cast out of this world just as he was cast out of heaven. What happens then?

Everyone who has ever lived will be judged along with him. Whom did they serve? Did they serve the Lord or did they serve the devil?

Nations, too, will be judged.

And Jesus will rule as King over the entire earth for a thousand years. This is "the restitution of all things."

To most of the world, this sounds like a fairy tale.

The world is full of scoffers today. They are found in the citadels of political power and in positions of powerlessness and despair. They include both people of great wealth and the poor. They are found in the media, in Hollywood, and in all of the major cultural institutions of our day. They are even found in churches and synagogues, in both the pews and the pulpit.

But all of this is part of the script. It was all predicted with great accuracy. Just read 2 Peter 3:

> There shall come in the last days scoffers, walking after their own lusts, and saying, Where is the promise of his coming? for since the fathers fell asleep, all things continue as they were from the beginning of the creation. For this they willingly are ignorant of, that by the word of God the heavens were of old, and the earth standing out of the water and in the water: whereby the

world that then was, being overflowed with water, perished: but the heavens and the earth, which are now, by the same word are kept in store, reserved unto fire against the day of judgment and perdition of ungodly men. But, beloved, be not ignorant of this one thing, that one day is with the Lord as a thousand years, and a thousand years as one day. The Lord is not slack concerning his promise, as some men count slackness; but is longsuffering to us-ward, not willing that any should perish, but that all should come to repentance. But the day of the Lord will come as a thief in the night; in the which the heavens shall pass away with a great noise, and the elements shall melt with fervent heat, the earth also and the works that are therein shall be burned up. (vv. 3–10)

What's the solution? How does one escape certain death? How do we prepare for this coming cataclysm that leads to "the restitution of all things"? I'll deal with that question in more depth later in this book, but here's an important clue from Peter: "Ye therefore, beloved, seeing ye know these things before, beware lest ye also, being led away with the error of the wicked, fall from your own stedfastness. But grow in grace, and in the knowledge of our Lord and Saviour Jesus Christ" (2 Peter 3:17–18).

Can believers be led astray? Can we fall victim to the error of the wicked? Yes, says Peter. So we are commanded not only to remain steadfast but to grow stronger. Salvation is only the beginning of the journey. We're responsible for much more.

The clock is ticking. History is reaching its climax. The whole world is heading into the most perilous time since the Flood.

The choice is yours, and simple—death or eternal life.

Whom are you going to serve? There's no neutral ground. As Jesus said, "He that is not with me is against me" (Matt. 12:30).

I don't know about you, but I want to be *with* him. It's not enough to just get saved. There are too many people sitting in churches or walking around on the street who believe they are saved because at one point in their lives they said some magic words and "accepted Jesus into their hearts." That's not enough. We have to make Him Lord of our lives.

If you want the full blessings of the kingdom, you have got to be obedient and pursue holiness in your life. You've got to reject the ways of the world and follow Jesus with a 100 percent, sold-out commitment.

Is that you?

In John 3 we're told, "He that believeth on [Jesus] is not condemned: but he that believeth not is condemned already, because he hath not believed in the name of the only begotten Son of God. And this is the condemnation, that light is come into the world, and men loved darkness rather than light, because their deeds were evil. For every one that doeth evil hateth the light, neither cometh to the light, lest his deeds should be reproved." (vv. 18–20).

The question is, will we be judged by simple "belief"? Or by conduct that affirms that belief? According to John, it's by our conduct: we are not to *do* evil because our *deeds* will be reproved. Are you doing evil?

It's found in 2 Chronicles 7:14: "If my people, which are called by my name, shall humble themselves, and pray, and seek my face, and turn from their wicked ways; then will I hear from heaven, and will forgive their sin, and will heal their land." What does that mean? It really wasn't until I read Jonathan Cahn's *The Harbinger* that I got it.

The context of this familiar passage is Solomon's dedication of the temple. God manifested a strong presence and spoke to Israel's king. He offered that His people, His holy nation, would inevitably stray from God in the future. They would suffer as a result, but their chastisement would be designed to bring them back to the Creator.

God promised that if *His people* would do four things, He would in turn do three things. If those "called by His name" would (1) humble themselves, (2) pray, (3) seek His face, and (4) turn from their sin, He would (1) hear their prayers, (2) forgive their sin, and (3) heal their land.

If you want God to heal our land, follow the prescription. Don't wait for others to do so. Encourage them, but don't wait. If His people don't follow the prescription, judgment will follow.

Think about this and pray about it. If we don't approach God in humility, our prayers could fall on deaf ears. We have to be serious about this prescription and follow it to the letter.

The solutions to our nation's problems are not to be found in politics. They are to be found in getting right with God. And believers hold the secret for that—if only we can discern the truth and the power that resides in us by studying the Scriptures with the guidance of the Holy Spirit.

Of course, without a recognition that believers hold a higher responsibility to biblical standards, not a lower one, it's unlikely they will tap into God's prescription of repentance.

Why do I say believers have a higher standard to uphold the law than do those in the world? Because Jesus Himself said so. In Matthew 5, Jesus said:

> Ye [believers] are the salt of the earth: but if the salt have lost his savour, wherewith shall it be salted? it is thenceforth good for nothing, but to be cast out, and to be trodden under foot of men. . . .
>
> Think not that I am come to destroy the law, or the prophets: I am not come to destroy, but to fulfil. For verily I say unto you, Till heaven and earth pass, one jot or one tittle shall in no wise pass from the law, till all be fulfilled. Whosoever therefore shall break one of these least commandments, and shall teach men so, he shall be called the least in the kingdom of heaven: but whosoever shall do and teach them, the same shall be called great in the kingdom of heaven. For I say unto you, That except your righteousness shall exceed the righteousness of the scribes and Pharisees, ye shall in no case enter into the kingdom of heaven. Ye have heard that it was said of them of old time, Thou shalt not kill; and whosoever shall kill shall be in danger of the judgment: But I say unto you, That whosoever is angry with his brother without a cause shall be in danger of the judgment: and

whosoever shall say to his brother, Raca, shall be in danger of the council: but whosoever shall say, Thou fool, shall be in danger of hell fire. (Matt. 5:13–22)

Does that sound like believers have a free pass when it comes to the transgression of the law, or that Jesus has annulled the law and lowered the bar for us so we can skate into the kingdom? No. Listen to how He expects His followers to behave:

Ye have heard that it was said by them of old time, Thou shalt not commit adultery: But I say unto you, That whosoever looketh on a woman to lust after her hath committed adultery with her already in his heart. And if thy right eye offend thee, pluck it out, and cast it from thee: for it is profitable for thee that one of thy members should perish, and not that thy whole body should be cast into hell. And if thy right hand offend thee, cut it off, and cast it from thee: for it is profitable for thee that one of thy members should perish, and not that thy whole body should be cast into hell. It hath been said, Whosoever shall put away his wife, let him give her a writing of divorcement: But I say unto you, that whosoever shall put away his wife, saving for the cause of fornication, causeth her to commit adultery: and whosoever shall marry her that is divorced committeth adultery. (Matt. 5:27–32)

Those are tough words, but we must obey them. Jesus said, "If ye love me, keep my commandments" (John 14:15). And by the way, *which* commandments are we to keep? The ones He Himself delivered to Moses on Mount Sinai—etched in stone with His own finger. There are no other commandments—except those in the imaginations of men.

4

WASN'T THE LAW NAILED TO THE CROSS?

But we know that the law is good, if a man use it lawfully; Knowing this, that the law is not made for a righteous man, but for the lawless and disobedient, for the ungodly and for sinners, for unholy and profane, for murderers of fathers and murderers of mothers, for manslayers, For whoremongers, for them that defile themselves with mankind, for menstealers, for liars, for perjured persons, and if there be any other thing that is contrary to sound doctrine; according to the glorious gospel of the blessed God, which was committed to my trust. —1 TIMOTHY 1:8-11

HAVE YOU NOTICED WE LIVE in an age of lawlessness?

It's true for the world—increasingly so. But it's also true for much of what we call the "church."

Tell me if you've heard any of the following statements from Christian leaders and pastors, followed by an enthusiastic, maybe even knee-jerk, "Amen!"

- "The law was nailed to the cross."

- "The age of the law has been replaced by the age of grace."

- "We are no longer burdened by the law, which was overturned by grace."

Are these proclamations true? Are they legitimate, Bible-backed doctrine? If not, what are the implications of such teachings?

There's a spirit of antinomianism rampant through the institutions of believers. It's been gaining ground for a long time—at least the last nineteen hundred years. But it is reaching something of a crescendo within "Christianity" with ideas such as "hyper-grace," as covered in the last chapter. Is it possible that the church has fallen into deep error with regard to the role of the law in our lives today?

I'm not referring to the temporal laws of men, but rather, to the unchanging law of God—namely, what we learn about in the Old Testament.

Can the church make mistakes, or is it infallible? We know from both history and the Bible that it *can* make mistakes. Just read Revelation 1–3 if you have any doubts.

Revelation 2:5 says, "Remember therefore from whence thou art fallen, and repent, and do the first works; or else I will come unto thee quickly, and will remove thy candlestick out of his place, except thou repent." These were hard words directed at the church. This shows that it's not only individual believers who fall short. The institutions of believers do also.

So allow me to challenge your assumptions, the beliefs you have that come from teachers who "tickle your ears" with what you like to hear.

Is it possible that most of today's "Christians" and the institutions they belong to are in error when it comes to their responsibility to the Law of Moses? We all see through a glass, darkly (1 Cor. 13:12). No one has a monopoly on truth.

I don't expect everyone reading this to agree with everything

I say. I am not seeking affirmation or approval. My role with this message is to challenge conclusions you may have reached about our heavenly Father that are based on something other than the clear instruction of the Bible.

This is not a lecture. I do not consider myself the greatest biblical scholar or the best teacher. I'm just a student of the Bible and of history, and an observer of what is going on in our world today. And I try to understand what is happening through the lens of truth: the revelation we receive through the Bible and the leading of the Holy Spirit.

I share these observations reluctantly, because too few are doing so. This entire book is written in that spirit. I hope to challenge you with plenty of material to think about and pray about—to prick your consciences, maybe, in a way that will open your hearts to the Holy Spirit's leading on a whole new level. In the meantime, as I said earlier, don't believe anything I say just because I say it. Check everything I say against the Word of God.

To my comfort, nothing I will tell you will hurt you in your walk with Jesus. Everything I say is meant to deepen your walk with Him. It is birthed from my desire to share with you what I believe is most lacking in our world today—actual obedience to Jesus, the one true God. Having said that, let's move on with our study in this chapter.

Most of the problems we face in the world today result from lawlessness. That may be very obvious to you. After all, the world's trouble is sin, and sin is, by definition, the transgression of the law.

There are two ways to transgress the law:

1. by disobeying it, whether consciously or unconsciously (remember the old saying, "Ignorance of the law is no excuse)

2. by writing our own spiritual laws or allowing others to do it for us (this was the grave sin of the Pharisees, discussed in chapter 1)

One of the clichés you will hear in our society today over and over is, "You can't legislate morality." (Maybe you've even said it.)

The next time you hear someone say this, I want you to remember what I am about to tell you. It's very important. Every single law or regulation or edict of government is the reflection of someone's sense of morality. Whether it's a speed limit designed to save lives or a change in tax law designed to bring about "fairness," all laws are all the result of someone, some lawmaker, some politician, attempting to impose his or her morality on the rest of us. (If you can find even one that reflects something *other* than someone's idea of morality, I'd really like to hear about it.) So, in fact, someone's sense of morality is the *only* thing people can ever legislate.

You need to challenge that ridiculous comment every time you hear it. It is dangerous, because if they hear it enough, people will start to accept it. Unfortunately, we have people in both major parties today making this assertion as if there were some substance behind it. You might as well be saying, "You can't tell people not to speed" or, "You can't regulate food safety" or, "You can't legislate economic policy."

The purpose of that cliché is to keep people of faith out of politics. It's just that simple. It's to keep people of faith outside of public policy and debate—outside the public square. If you are a believer, then the people around you don't want you involved in shaping the law. They don't want you passing laws that stop the killing of the most innocent human life, or that preserve marriage as an institution between one man and one woman. It's perfectly OK for them, however, to pass laws to kill babies in the womb or to redefine marriage as anything they deem fit.

If you can't legislate morality, then the entire Western civilization comes tumbling down because it is based on the moral law of the Judeo-Christian Bible. God was the first one to legislate morality.

At first, He kept it very simple. His very first law was, "Of every tree of the garden thou mayest freely eat: but of the tree of the knowledge of good and evil, thou shalt not eat of it: for in the day that thou eatest thereof thou shalt surely die" (Gen. 2:16–17).

That was the whole law in the garden of Eden. We call it the

Edenic covenant. And it got messed up when Satan tempted Eve to doubt the truth of God's one and only commandment to man.

Next we have the Adamic covenant in Genesis 3. And later, the Noahic covenant of Genesis 9. And later still the Abrahamic covenant. These are all pretty simple and straightforward. And each new covenant builds upon the others. In other words, the Adamic covenant, which spells out simply our salvation plan (obey and live), is not scrapped in favor of the Noahic covenant. Nor is the Noahic covenant, promising that the earth will never again be destroyed by a flood, overturned or delegitimized by the Abrahamic.

That's because, as we all know, God is the same yesterday, today, and tomorrow. He doesn't make mistakes.

Likewise, when the Mosaic covenant was given in the book of Exodus, it was actually a fulfillment of the Abrahamic and built on the others, setting the stage for the next major covenant, the Davidic, which established the genealogical line through which Jesus would be born and eventually reign supreme over the entire world at the time of "the restitution of all things."

But all through those early covenants, from the very first and right up to today, an overlooked phenomenon was taking place: man, in addition to rebelling against God's law, has been adding his own laws on top of God's law.

We see it in the garden when Eve tells the serpent, "We may eat of the fruit of the trees of the garden: but of the fruit of the tree which is in the midst of the garden, God hath said, Ye shall not eat of it, neither shall ye touch it, lest ye die" (Gen. 3:3).

When did God say, "Neither shall ye touch it"? He didn't. She added that.

And it's been that way ever since. Man adds to God's laws, even while disobeying God's laws.

After Moses came down from Mount Horeb with God's laws, etched by God Himself in stone, he found that the people had built a golden calf idol to worship. In anger, Moses broke the stone tablets. But then, fearing God's wrath on the people, he went back up the mountain to talk to God, pleading with Him to be merciful and to give them a second chance.

God did so, for Moses' sake. "And the LORD said unto Moses, Hew thee two tables of stone like unto the first: and I will write upon these tables *the words that were in the first tables,* which thou brakest" (Ex. 34:1, emphasis added). Notice He did not change the laws. God etched the *same* laws on the second set of tables.

These were meant to be laws for God's people *forever.*

But didn't Jesus fulfill the law? Doesn't that mean His followers were free of the burden of obedience to the law? Didn't the age of grace render the law obsolete?

Many Christians today have rejected the very clear teaching Jesus brought to the world two thousand years ago about the Torah. They now think of God's perfect and just laws as oppressive, something they have been freed from observing. Nowhere in the New Testament did Yeshua repudiate the Torah. Far from it. It was the basis of most of His teaching. He affirmed it over and over again. Neither did any of the New Testament writers reject the Torah in whole or in part. All they did was affirm it.

Following are some scriptures that prove this point. First, hear Jesus:

> Think not that I am come to destroy the law, or the prophets: I am not come to destroy, but to fulfil. For verily I say unto you, Till heaven and earth pass, one jot or one tittle shall in no wise pass from the law, till all be fulfilled. (Matt. 5:17–18)

> Therefore all things whatsoever ye would that men should do to you, do ye even so to them: for this is the law and the prophets. (Matt. 7:12)

> Master, which is the great commandment in the law? Jesus said unto him, Thou shalt love the Lord thy God with all thy heart, and with all thy soul, and with all thy mind. This is the first and great commandment. And the second is like unto it, Thou shalt

love thy neighbour as thyself. On these two commandments hang all the law and the prophets. (Matt. 22:36–40)

And, behold, a certain lawyer stood up, and tempted him, saying, Master, what shall I do to inherit eternal life? He said unto him, What is written in the law? how readest thou? And he answering said, Thou shalt love the Lord thy God with all thy heart, and with all thy soul, and with all thy strength, and with all thy mind; and thy neighbour as thyself. And he said unto him, Thou hast answered right: this do, and thou shalt live. (Luke 10:25–28)

And it is easier for heaven and earth to pass, than one tittle of the law to fail. (Luke 16:17)

Now hear the apostles:

Do we then make void the law through faith? God forbid: yea, we establish the law. (Rom. 3:31)

What shall we say then? Is the law sin? God forbid. Nay, I had not known sin, but by the law: for I had not known lust, except the law had said, Thou shalt not covet. . . . Wherefore the law is holy, and the commandment holy, and just, and good. (Rom. 7:7, 12)

That the righteousness of the law might be fulfilled in us, who walk not after the flesh, but after the Spirit. (Rom. 8:4)

Now I praise you, brethren, that ye . . . keep the ordinances, as I delivered them to you. (1 Cor. 11:2)

Whosoever committeth sin transgresseth also the law: for sin is the transgression of the law. (1 John 3:4)

Am I suggesting to you that we must obey every Torah law without fail to be saved? Of course not. This is not a salvation issue. This is an obedience issue. Repentance has always been the prescription God gave people for when they fell short of the mark.

Why was David a man after God's own heart? Not because he never sinned. But because he sought God's forgiveness when he did.

It has become quite fashionable in Christian circles to suggest that the law is dead, that the law itself—not sin—has been nailed to the cross. We hear what a terrible burden the law was. I know, because the Bible tells me so, that no man is justified by the law, only by faith. But God gave us the law and He told us, over and over again, it was forever. It's the one and only standard by which He judges our behavior, our conduct, our lives.

To be charitable, the confusion over the role of the law in our lives today comes from a misunderstanding of Jesus' confrontations with the Pharisees. This is ground well covered in chapter 1, but let's examine the Scripture more closely:

> Then came to Jesus scribes and Pharisees, which were of Jeru-salem, saying, Why do thy disciples transgress the tradition of the elders? for they wash not their hands when they eat bread. But he answered and said unto them, Why do ye also transgress the commandment of God by your tradition? For God commanded, saying, Honour thy father and mother: and, He that curseth father or mother, let him die the death. But ye say, Whosoever shall say to his father or his mother, It is a gift, by whatsoever thou mightest be profited by me; and honour not his father or his mother, he shall be free. Thus have ye made the commandment of God of none effect by your tradition. Ye hypocrites, well did Esaias prophesy of you, saying, This people draweth nigh unto me with their mouth, and honoureth me with their lips; but their heart is far from me. But in vain they do worship me, teaching for doctrines the commandments of men. (Matt. 15:1–9)

What was this all about? Were the Pharisees really concerned about the disciples' hygiene?

No. This was about the Pharisees' oral tradition; they taught that *ritual* hand washing was required before eating. It wasn't about cleanliness. It was about man-made laws of the rabbis, found still today in the Talmud, the Mishnah, and the Midrash. The Pharisees believed these oral laws were actually passed down from Moses—and had all the weight of the Torah.

Can you see why Jesus was so upset with them?

Read the entirety of Matthew 23 for a clear picture of what I am telling you. We tend to think today that the Pharisees were simply "hypocrites"—not practicing what they preached. But there's something much bigger that most of us miss. Jesus said, "The scribes and the Pharisees sit in Moses' seat: All therefore whatsoever they bid you observe, that observe and do; but do not ye after their works: for they say, and do not. For they bind heavy burdens and grievous to be borne, and lay them on men's shoulders; but they themselves will not move them with one of their fingers" (vv. 2–4) In other words, listen to the Pharisees when they "sit on Moses' seat," that is, when they are instructing from God's law, the Torah. But don't follow their tedious man-made laws and traditions. See the difference? Jesus was not judging His *own* laws as a grievous burden. He was clearly condemning man's foolish rubrics.

Unfortunately, many Christians today use these' verses to rationalize their misguided view that we believers are no longer subject to God's laws. I hear this all the time. This dangerous teaching pervades the church. Never did Jesus repudiate the Torah. He repudiated *only* those pharisaical, manufactured rules and regulations that touched every aspect of the life of the religious Jews of His time—and still encumbers them today.

I love 1 Timothy 1:8. It says, "But we know that the law is good, if a man use it lawfully." What does that mean? Obviously, that the law can be used *un*lawfully. That's what the Pharisees were doing, by adding to it. And today's "Pharisees"—both in government and in the church—are still doing it, to our hurt.

But it is *God's* commandments—no one else's—that we are to keep, and they are "for ever" commandments:

And when there had been much disputing, Peter rose up, and said unto them, Men and brethren, ye know how that a good while ago God made choice among us, that the Gentiles by my mouth should hear the word of the gospel, and believe. And God, which knoweth the hearts, bare them witness, giving them the Holy Ghost, even as he did unto us; And put no difference between us and them, purifying their hearts by faith. Now therefore why tempt ye God, to put a yoke upon the neck of the disciples, which neither our fathers nor we were able to bear? But we believe that through the grace of the Lord Jesus Christ we shall be saved, even as they." Acts 15:7–11

Remember: these are "forever" commandments:

Thou shalt keep therefore his statutes, and his commandments, which I command thee this day, . . . for ever. (Deut. 4:40)

Observe and hear all these words which I command thee, that it may go well with thee, and with thy children after thee for ever, when thou doest that which is good and right in the sight of the LORD thy God. (Deut. 12:28)

The works of his hands are verity and judgment; all his commandments are sure. They stand fast for ever and ever. (Ps. 111:7–8)

I know that, whatsoever God doeth [his decrees, which are the works of His heart], it shall be for ever: nothing can be put to it, nor any thing taken from it: and God doeth it, that men should fear before him. (Eccl. 3:14)

As for me, this is my covenant with them, saith the LORD . . . My words which I have put in thy mouth, shall not depart out of thy mouth, nor out of the mouth of thy seed, nor out of the mouth of thy seed's seed, saith the LORD, from henceforth and for ever. (Isa. 59:21)

If ye love me, keep my commandments. —JOHN 14:15

Recently, a well-intended pastor sent me a long article he had written about whether the Shemitah, the biblical sabbath-year principle, could possibly be affecting our world today, as Messianic rabbi Jonathan Cahn has suggested in his popular books *The Harbinger* and *The Mystery of the Shemitah*. "Is it true that an Old Testament, Jewish farming regulation could be the catalyst for worldwide judgment or blessings at this time?" he asked. "And, if so, why? Didn't the apostle Paul teach us in Colossians 2:14 that all such ordinances were nailed to the cross?"

First of all, the shemitah principle is much more than a Jewish farming regulation. It's part of the sabbath cycle. Every week ends with a day of rest. Ezekiel calls this cycle a sign between God and His people (Ezek. 20). Most Christians today would say they believe in a Sabbath in some form—even if it is observed on a different day and in a different way than originally observed. It's a day on which God calls "all flesh"—not just Jews—to come before Him for worship (Isa. 66).

Likewise, every year ends with a week of rest.

Furthermore, the shemitah affected the economy of the nation of Israel. In addition to the restriction on planting and reaping during the shemitah cycle, there was an economic release of debts.

Finally, the shemitah pattern also affected the entire world, not just Israel, as we can see with the Babylonian and Persian empires. One empire fell and another arose. Israel's seventy-year captivity as punishment for the unobserved shemitahs in Israel took place so that the children of Israel could return to their land right on schedule. In other words, the shemitah ordered world events beyond Israel.

So the real question is whether the shemitah cycle could still be impacting global events. Based on the overwhelming evidence Jonathan Cahn presents in *The Mystery of the Shemitah*, it is.

So let's look at Colossians 2:14 and see what it says about the Torah being nailed to the cross. We'll include verse 13, for context: "And you, being dead in your sins and the uncircumcision of your flesh, hath he quickened together with him, having forgiven you all trespasses; *blotting out the handwriting of ordinances that was against us, which was contrary to us, and took it out of the way, nailing it to his cross"* (emphasis added).

Is this suggesting the law of God was nailed to the cross at Jesus' death? Or does it say that sin was nailed to the cross at Jesus' death? I would suggest it is the latter.

I love the King James Version, but almost every other Bible translation interprets Paul's words as I do—that the *indictments* of believers, the *charges* against them, the *legal indebtedness* of believers, these are what were dropped and nailed to the cross at Jesus' death, rather than the law itself, which Scripture consistently characterizes as eternal and good.

I would further suggest that any other interpretation of Paul's words would be in absolute contradiction to the words of Jesus, the other apostles, and even Paul himself in other passages of Scripture. (See, for example, Matt. 5:17–18; 19:17; Rom. 3:31; 7:12; Gal. 3:10; John 14:15; 1 John 2:3–4; 3:4; 5:3; 2 John 1:6; Rev. 22:14.)

So, is the law dead?

Of course not. It's alive and well. But obedience to the law does not bring about salvation. That comes by grace through repentance for your transgressions of the law. If the law were dead, repentance would be unnecessary. Even for the believer, the rules of engagement are the same. When a believer stumbles and sins, sincere repentance is required. A believer doesn't have immunity from sin, only the Holy Spirit's help in combating temptation.

Most Christians would agree with this statement: "God is the same yesterday, today, and tomorrow." It's not an exact scriptural quotation, but it's true and faithful to Scripture (see Hebrews 13:8). God's character didn't change when Jesus came. In fact, Jesus was a perfect reflection of God the Father. He didn't come to abolish the law He had Himself written with His finger in tablets of stone. He came to fulfill the law. "For verily I say unto you, till heaven and earth pass, one jot or one tittle shall in no wise pass from the law, till all be fulfilled," He said (Matt. 5:18).

Have heaven and earth passed? No.

Has all been fulfilled? No.

Has the restoration of all things occurred? No.

Therefore, according to Jesus Himself, not even the smallest commandment has passed from the law. Not even, I would add, those seemingly archaic laws regarding the Sabbath and shemitah cycles.

Could things have changed when Jesus came or after He was risen? Check out these New Testament verses:

Whosoever therefore shall break one of these least commandments, and shall teach men so, he shall be called the least in the kingdom of heaven: but whosoever shall do and teach them, the same shall be called great in the kingdom of heaven. (Matt. 5:19)

If ye love me, keep my commandments. (John 14:15)

He that hath my commandments, and keepeth them, he it is that loveth me: and he that loveth me shall be loved of my Father, and I will love him, and will manifest myself to him. (John 14:21)

If ye keep my commandments, ye shall abide in my love; even as I have kept my Father's commandments [the Torah], and abide in his love. (John 15:10)

And hereby we do know that we know him, if we keep his commandments. He that saith, I know him, and keepeth not his commandments, is a liar, and the truth is not in him. (1 John 2:3–4)

For this is the love of God, that we keep his commandments: and his commandments are not grievous. (1 John 5:3)

And the dragon was wroth with the woman, and went to make war with the remnant of her seed, which keep the commandments of God, and have the testimony of Jesus Christ. (Rev. 12:17)

Here is the patience of the saints: here are they that keep the commandments of God, and the faith of Jesus. (Rev. 14:12)

Blessed are they that do his commandments, that they may have right to the tree of life, and may enter in through the gates into the city. (Rev. 22:14)

You must ignore a lot of very clear Scripture—Old Testament and New—to conclude that Torah law no longer applies to believers in Jesus. And you have to cling to a very few misused scriptures to make that point.

This is a seeming contradiction that most of today's church does not wish to examine. Most pastors would prefer to cling to answers based in tradition rather than in biblical context and Berean-like study. Certainly, much of the rejection of the Torah, as it applies to Christians, began with a quite appropriate rejection of pharisaical traditions. Sadly, in the second, third, and fourth centuries, after the all-Jewish apostles were gone, this degenerated into rejection of anything "Jewish" or "Hebrew," if you will. (More on that in chapter 7.)

So let me ask you: Do you believe in the Ten Commandments? Do you believe you are obligated, as a Christian, to do your best to live by them—not as a matter of salvation, mind you, but as a matter of obedience to the God of the universe and His Son, Jesus? Do you believe that if you break one of the Ten Commandments today, you need to repent of that transgression of the law? If so, it may surprise you that much of the church in America today no longer accepts that even the *Ten Commandments* applies to them, based on teachings that are not only unsupported by the Bible but are repeatedly contradicted in both testaments. That's what is being taught to many of our kids growing up in the church!

Look: Jesus came to give us a way to escape death—the penalty of the law. He clearly stated He did not come to overturn the law. In fact, when He returns to preside over His millennial kingdom, the Torah will be the law of the land:

> Thus saith the LORD, Keep ye judgment, and do justice: for my salvation is near to come, and my righteousness to be revealed. Blessed is the man that doeth this, and the son of man that layeth hold on it; that keepeth the sabbath from polluting it, and keepeth his hand from doing any evil. Neither let the son of the stranger, that hath joined himself to the LORD, speak, saying,

The LORD hath utterly separated me from his people: neither let the eunuch say, Behold, I am a dry tree. For thus saith the LORD unto the eunuchs that keep my sabbaths, and choose the things that please me, and take hold of my covenant; Even unto them will I give in mine house and within my walls a place and a name better than of sons and of daughters: I will give them an everlasting name, that shall not be cut off. Also the sons of the stranger, that join themselves to the LORD, to serve him, and to love the name of the LORD, to be his servants, every one that keepeth the sabbath from polluting it, and taketh hold of my covenant; even them will I bring to my holy mountain, and make them joyful in my house of prayer: their burnt offerings and their sacrifices shall be accepted upon mine altar; for mine house shall be called an house of prayer for all people. (Isa. 56:1–7)

This is clearly a millennial kingdom prophecy, speaking of the time of "the restitution of all things"—when we will observe the Sabbath and abide by the Torah.

So, if the law was important before Jesus came, *and* it was important to Jesus during His earthly ministry, *and* it was important in the first-century apostolic era, *and* it's going to be important again after His return, shouldn't those of us who love the Lord and want to be obedient to His will be doing our best to observe it today? Just asking.

How are we not in compliance with the law? How have modern American Christians become scofflaws? Not to indict anyone, but ask yourself:

- Why are we not observing the Sabbath? How did an hour or two of Sunday worship replace a twenty-four-hour observance, beginning Friday at sundown and ending at sundown Saturday?

- Why do we celebrate Christmas and Easter but not Passover and the Feast of Trumpets? Could it be that human tradition is as important to us today as it was to the Pharisees of old?

By raising these questions, I hope to interest you in looking at the Scriptures in ways you have never looked at them before. It could mean a much deeper and more authentic walk in faith than you have previously experienced, because too many in the church today equate righteousness solely with the acceptance of Jesus—putting all personal responsibility out of the picture. That is not at all biblical.

Does it make sense to you that Jesus and the apostles observed the biblical feasts and the Sabbath throughout their lives, then suddenly these observances were mysteriously done away without any biblical reference?

The law is not done away with. It is not dead. The law is eternal. Yes, it was fulfilled in Yeshua, but so was righteousness fulfilled in Him. Is righteousness something we should no longer strive to attain just because Jesus fulfilled it?

We're saved by grace, not by works (Eph. 2:8–9). But that's not the end of the story. That's the beginning. We're supposed to walk in His paths of righteousness. Grace is a second chance to do just that.

Most are familiar with the first part of Proverbs 29:18: "Where there is no vision, the people perish . . ." But there is no period at the end of that well-known and widely quoted scripture. The rest of the verse says: "but he that keepeth the law, happy is he." Similarly, you've likely heard, "My people are destroyed for lack of knowledge: because thou has rejected knowledge, I will also reject thee" (Hos. 4:6). But what is "knowledge"? It is defined in the very same verse: "seeing thou has forgotten *the law of thy God*, I will also forget thy children" (emphasis added).

What is knowledge? It's the law of God. And if you forget it, God will forget you.

The prophet Jeremiah saw this happen in his time. He said of Israel, "Her gates are sunk into the ground; he hath destroyed and broken her bars: her king and her princes are among the Gentiles: the law is no more; her prophets also find no vision from the LORD" (Lam. 2:9).

Today, even many professing Christians dismiss the law, claiming it was somehow "nailed to the cross," with their Savior, Jesus, when it was actually their sins, their indictments, that were forgiven through the blood shed on the cross. To do this, you've got to allegorize a lot more unambiguous Scripture about the importance and permanence of the law. Wouldn't it be better to say, "Hmm . . . A few verses in the New Testament seem to suggest that the law is dead. Was another meaning intended?"

Indeed there is, for God's eternal law is not a burden; it is a blessing.

"So shall I keep thy law continually for ever and ever," David wrote in Psalm 119. "And take not the truth utterly out of my mouth; for I have hoped in thy judgments. So shall I keep thy law continually for ever and ever" (vv. 42–45).

Forever and ever. That is God's intent for His law.

No, Christians *don't* earn their salvation through their works. But our repentance—necessary for our redemption—should be evidenced by works: "For as the body without the spirit is dead, so faith without works is dead also" (James 2:26). Works, then, are the confirmation of our faith. They're how we measure whether we are actually walking in the Spirit.

But didn't Paul say these works of the law were "nailed to the cross"?

Let's take a careful look at that passage in Colossians 2:

Beware lest any man spoil you through philosophy and vain deceit, *after the tradition of men*, after the rudiments of the world, and not after Christ. For in him dwelleth all the fulness of the Godhead bodily. And ye are complete in him, which is the head of all principality and power: In whom also ye are circumcised with the circumcision made without hands, in putting off the body of the sins of the flesh by the circumcision of Christ: Buried with him in baptism, wherein also ye are risen with him through the faith of the operation of God, who hath raised him from the dead. And you, being dead in your sins and the uncircumcision of your flesh, hath he quickened together with him, having forgiven you all trespasses; *blotting out the handwriting of ordinances that was against us*, which was contrary to us, and took it out of the way, nailing it to his cross; And having spoiled principalities and powers, he made a shew of them openly, triumphing over them in it. Let no man therefore judge you in meat, or in drink, or in respect of an holyday, or of the new moon, or of the sabbath days: which are a shadow of things to come; but the body is of Christ. . . . Wherefore if ye be dead with Christ from the rudiments of the world, why, as though living in the world, are ye subject to ordinances, (Touch not; taste not; handle not; which all are to perish with the using;) *after the commandments and doctrines of men?* (vv. 8–22, emphasis added)

Paul framed the entire context of this passage with two phrases that explain what he was warning the church about: "the tradition of men, at the beginning"; and "the commandments and doctrines of men," at the end. One simply cannot comprehend the message without noting those two warnings.

And as to what was "nailed to the cross," Paul said it was "the handwriting of ordinances that was against us." He was clearly not talking about God's law here. He was referring to that of which he warned both at the beginning and the end of his message: "the tradition of men" and "the commandments and doctrines of men"—in other words, the Pharisees.

And the spirit of the Pharisees was still alive and well in the apostolic era, as we saw in chapter 2, where we learned that in Acts 10, Peter was reluctant to welcome non-Jews into his house. Was sitting at a table with Gentiles a violation of the Torah? No, only of the Oral Law of the Jews.

Tradition, not Scripture. This is where the confusion continues to this day.

Worse, while embracing such man-made tradition, they have also embraced the antinomianism we have been discussing, which says that under this current "dispensation of grace," the Old Testament law is no longer applicable.

For instance, today, much of the church sees Acts 10 as overturning the Torah's dietary laws, rather than the way Peter himself understood it—that we are not bound to the man-made traditions of the Pharisees.

But the confusion is sometimes willful. Man has always tried to escape the consequences of God's law. It's the entire story of the Bible—Old Testament and New. It's the history of man as told through Scripture. The escape comes in two ways—ignoring or revising God's law and adding to it.

Paul's writings are most often cited by those who claim that God's laws no longer apply, but they can do so only by taking passages out of context. In Romans 3:31, he makes this clear when he writes: "Do we then make void the law through faith? God forbid: yea, we establish the law." In other words, we are justified, saved, and redeemed not through any act of our own, but purely by the atoning sacrifice of Jesus. Once that happens, however, we "establish the law," not discard it.

I believe this spirit of antinomianism is at work in our civil society, too.

For instance, what is happening in American society today? After Christians grew comfortable with the idea of forgetting God's law, they grew comfortable with the idea of forgetting the very meaning of the founding documents of their country—especially the limitations they placed on government. The Founders had warned that they would always be inadequate for the preservation of liberty of any people not grounded in the morality of the Bible.

And that's where we are today in this age of lawlessness—a time when even the clear, concise words of the Declaration of Independence, which created the nation, and the unambiguous text of the Constitution, which defined how it would work, are allegorized to mean whatever we want them to mean. And just as the Pharisees did, we've added so many burdensome, man-made laws on top of that framework that it has become impossible for people to obey them all—even to know them all.

There is little question that there is more contempt for the law than ever before—be it God's statutes or America's basic creed.

While we despise and discount the most fundamental commandments of God and the foundational law of America, we embrace thousands of man-made regulations and codes that do violence to both—and to our individual liberties.

That's true lawlessness.

What breeds this contempt for the law—especially God's commandments? After all, even hardened atheists and agnostics, who put their faith in modernity, science, and human traditions, readily acknowledge that there are eternal laws about which they can do nothing but accept.

Everyone, for instance, believes there are scientific laws. There are laws of physics, and the law of gravity. We may not fully understand them, but there's no denying them.

The question is, if they are laws, who wrote them?

This is a question no scientist, no nonbeliever, no skeptic can answer, yet they respect these laws—but not God's laws.

The foundations are indeed trembling—and crumbling. That's what happens when the guardrails are gone, when every man does what is right in his own eyes. That's what happens when laws aren't lawful and lawful laws aren't obeyed.

But this is to be expected—if indeed we are living in the last days.

The signs are all around us. Let's revisit a passage we looked at earlier, in chapter 3:

> This know also, that in the last days perilous times shall come. For men shall be lovers of their own selves, covetous, boasters, proud, blasphemers, disobedient to parents, unthankful, unholy, without natural affection, trucebreakers, false accusers, incontinent, fierce, despisers of those that are good, traitors, heady, highminded, lovers of pleasures more than lovers of God; having

a form of godliness, but denying the power thereof: from such turn away. For of this sort are they which creep into houses, and lead captive silly women laden with sins, led away with divers lusts, ever learning, and never able to come to the knowledge of the truth. (2 Tim. 3:1–7)

We're living in perilous times, all right.

Has there ever been a moment in history when the love of self has been more obvious? If you don't think so, look at the titles of some of the popular books of our day: *Loving Yourself: The Mastery of Being Your Own Person*; *Loving Yourself: Four Steps to a Happier You*; *Love Yourself: The Secret Key to Transforming Your Life*. You get the idea.

And covetousness? American political leaders and movements who accuse the rich of "greed" are calling for their "supreme authority"— government—to redistribute the wealth "fairly" and "equitably" (by force, if necessary). But in reality, at the heart of such crusades is covetousness of other people's property and a desire for power.

Boastfulness? Pride? Have you noticed how pride—one of the great sins of the Bible—has become a virtue in the world today?

What about blasphemy? It's all around us, but even Christians had better be careful with this one, because if our operating spiritual assumptions are based on man's traditions rather than the Word of God, we will be in the same boat as the Pharisees.

"Unholy"? The word itself is really a synonym for lawlessness, because if sin is the transgression of the law, and holiness is set apart from the world and its sin, there's a strong connection here. This is really the heart of my message.

"Without natural affection, trucebreakers, false accusers, incontinent, despisers of those that are good": we have examples of people like this all around us. And "traitors, heady, highminded, lovers of pleasures more than lovers of God"? It doesn't take much imagination to recognize that all over our world today.

Then there's this interesting verse: "Having a form of godliness, but denying the power thereof." What does this mean? To whom does this refer? Could it be those who call themselves Christians but think that being a "Christian" begins and ends with reciting some words about accepting Jesus into our hearts one day, and being free from the consequences of sin thereafter?

Here's the bottom line: there are potentially millions of Americans who think they're saved who may not be. There are millions more who may be saved but are missing out on so much in eternity because they have a form of godliness but don't allow godliness to rule over their lives. They live in a carnal or, put another way, lawless state. This shouldn't be good enough for the church—who is meant to be the spotless "bride of Messiah" (see Eph. 5:27). Christians must return to godliness if they are to provide the salt and light necessary to bring our nation and our world back to God, back to a culture of lawfulness—the only environment in which self-governance can long endure.

5

WHY DON'T WE OBSERVE
THE SABBATH ANYMORE?

And it shall come to pass, that from one new moon to another, and from one sabbath to another, shall all flesh come to worship before me, saith the LORD.
—ISAIAH 66:23

THE TITLE QUESTION OF THIS CHAPTER represents a key turning point in my own journey of faith and biblical exploration that led not only to this book, but to deeper questioning of teachings based more on the traditions of men than the express will of God.

This subject is a tough one for people. It was a tough one for me. I had been a churchgoing believer for decades when the question began to haunt me. The explanations of pastors and the wisest teachers I knew fell short of persuasiveness and support from the Word of God.

If the Ten Commandments are still for today, then what about the fourth—interestingly, the longest of all?

In the appendix, I have included a comprehensive list of all Scripture—Old Testament and New—dealing with the seventh-day Sabbath. In it you will not find a single rationale for the idea that the apostles ceased to honor and keep the seventh-day Sabbath in the first century.

There are a few verses cited by those who attempt to make a biblical case that the apostles abandoned the seventh-day Sabbath—or that they determined it was unnecessary for Gentile followers of Jesus to do so. All four gospels, for instance, note that it was on the first day of the week that Mary Magdalene ventured to Jesus' tomb to find He had risen. Of course, this was to be expected, since she and the other followers of Jesus had been observing the Sabbath.

Much, too, has been made of the fact that Jesus rose on the first day of the week; therefore, His followers determined to worship on that day henceforth. First of all, we don't know that Jesus actually rose on the first day of the week. What we know is that His followers first *encountered* Him in His risen state on that day. He could have risen earlier—on the Sabbath. But second, there is no biblical evidence that such a profound change in observance actually took place; we have strong scriptural proof to demonstrate it did not.

The apostles and their followers continued to observe the Sabbath as they did before Jesus came, while He was alive, and after His resurrection.

Wouldn't it make sense that such a profound change in God's commandments would be equally profound in its obviousness? Wouldn't it be stated explicitly so there would be no room for confusion?

Here are the four passages the church most often cites to suggest the seventh-day Sabbath has been abandoned:

- Then the same day at evening, being the first day of the week, when the doors were shut where the disciples were assembled for fear of the Jews, came Jesus and stood in the midst, and saith unto them, Peace be unto you. And when he had so said, he shewed unto them his hands and his side. Then were the disciples glad, when they saw the Lord. Then said Jesus to them again, Peace be unto you: as my Father hath sent me, even so send I you. (John 20:19–21)

- And upon the first day of the week, when the disciples came together to break bread, Paul preached unto them, ready to depart on the morrow; and continued his speech until midnight. And there were many lights in the upper chamber, where they were gathered together. And there sat in a window a certain young man named Eutychus, being fallen into a deep sleep: and as Paul was long preaching, he sunk down with sleep, and fell down from the third loft, and was taken up dead. And Paul went down, and fell on him, and embracing him said, Trouble not yourselves; for his life is in him. When he therefore was come up again, and had broken bread, and eaten, and talked a long while, even till break of day, so he departed. And they brought the young man alive, and were not a little comforted. (Acts 20:7–11)

- Now concerning the collection for the saints, as I have given order to the churches of Galatia, even so do ye. Upon the first day of the week let every one of you lay by him in store, as God hath prospered him, that there be no gatherings when I come. (1 Cor. 16:1–2)

- I was in the Spirit on the Lord's day, and heard behind me a great voice, as of a trumpet . . . (Rev. 1:10)

Let's look at these one by one.
In John 20, was the apostle describing the first Sunday-go-to-

meeting gathering? No, this was the same day that Mary and the other women found the resurrected Jesus near the garden tomb. The apostles were gathered behind locked doors for fear of the Pharisees who had put the Messiah to death a few days earlier. There is scriptural suggestion of a new day of worship here.

What about Acts 20? Was *this* the first Sunday service? Doubtful indeed. The first day of the week on God's calendar begins when the sun sets, ending the Sabbath. More likely this was a nighttime gathering immediately following the Sabbath, perhaps even the continuation of a sabbath service. We know it was dark, because "there were many lights in the upper chamber," and Paul spoke until midnight.

What about 1 Corinthians 16? Could this have been the first Sunday service, complete with the collection basket being passed? No. Paul was simply writing ahead of time, asking that the collection for the persecuted believers in Jerusalem be taken up on the first day of the week, because it would be inappropriate to do so on the Sabbath. It was considered work since, back then, believers didn't donate money; they donated goods, which had to be stored for travel.

And Revelation 1:10? While some Christians have referred to Sunday as "the Lord's Day" since as early as the third century, it was not known that way in the first century, when John wrote Revelation. It could just as easily have meant the Sabbath. There is no historical association whatsoever between "the Lord's day" and the first day of the week.

Lastly, a scripture I listed earlier, Hebrews 4, is sometimes cited by those arguing that Sunday became the new Sabbath in the apostolic era. However, it suggests just the opposite—that if the Sabbath had changed, Jesus would have mentioned it: "For if Jesus had given them rest, then would he not afterward have spoken of another day" (v. 8). But Jesus never spoke of another day. Wouldn't He have noted such a profound change?

But there's much more to consider than some possibly ambiguous verses. God Himself clearly stated that His Sabbath is forever (Gen. 2:2–3). It didn't start with the giving of the law by Moses. It began on the seventh day of creation.

Leviticus 23 tells us the seventh-day Sabbath is the first of the "feasts of the LORD," as opposed to the feasts of the Jews. It states that they are *for ever*.

Isaiah 56 shows that the Lord's feasts are for the "sons of the stranger," or Gentile followers of God, too (see vv. 2, 6–7). It also strongly hints that the Sabbath will be observed in the millennial kingdom of God, when the Messiah rules from Jerusalem (see vv. 6ff).

Isaiah 66:23 is a prophecy about the millennial kingdom and eternity thereafter. What does it say about the Sabbath? "And it shall come to pass, that from one new moon to another, and from one sabbath to another, shall all flesh come to worship before me, saith the LORD."

So, are we to believe that God intended that the Sabbath be observed from Creation through the resurrection of Jesus, then forgotten for the next many centuries, only to be reinstituted when He returned? That stretches credulity, does it not? Is that what we are meant to take away from the totality of Scripture? Scripture is not to be interpreted out of context. What does the entirety of Scripture say about the seventh-day Sabbath? If you have any doubts, let me suggest reading all the verses that deal with Sabbath and the seventh day, conveniently listed in the appendix.

So what accounts for the fact that so many Christians, now and throughout the last seventeen hundred years, have observed a very different kind of Sabbath on a different day—now often referred to as "the Lord's day"?

Some argue that when Jesus declared Himself "Lord of the Sabbath" in the Synoptic Gospels, He was setting the stage for the overturning the seventh day for another.

Of course, Jesus is also Lord of all creation. He's the Word. He's God. He was not breaking the Sabbath when He healed the sick on that day. Nowhere in the Torah does it ever suggest that healing was a violation of the Sabbath. Again, the Pharisees charged Him with breaking the Sabbath based on the Oral Law—traditions of men. They had effectively added laws to God's. According to Jesus (see Matt. 23:4), these were "heavy burdens" laid upon men, not the perfect laws of God, designed to be loved and obeyed. The Sabbath is never described as a "burden" in the Bible. Instead, it's a "delight" (Isa. 58:13).

Besides, as noted in chapter 1, Jesus, in His role as Messiah, could not break any law. If He had, He could not have been the perfect sacrifice for the sins of the world. So He did not "destroy" a single law; He fulfilled the whole law.

But let's get down to basics here. Just beneath the surface of modern Christianity is a conviction that the God of the Old Testament and the God of the New Testament had different characters. Some even suggest that the God of the Old Testament was the Father and the God of the New Testament was the Son.

But that's not what the Bible says at all. First of all, it clearly says that the Father and Son are one, and that they are unchanging in character:

I and my Father are one. (John 10:30)

In the beginning was the Word, and the Word was with God, and the Word was God. The same was in the beginning with God. All things were made by him; and without him was not any thing made that was made. (John: 1:1–3)

Jesus Christ the same yesterday, and to day, and for ever. (Heb. 13:8)

God doesn't change His mind. In fact, if Jesus was in the beginning with God and made all things, what we know about the character of God we know from man's experience with Jesus.

So how did the seventh-day Sabbath move to Sunday?

One thing is certain, as stated earlier, there is no biblical or historical evidence that it happened or was even suggested by either

Jesus or the apostles of the first-century apostolic age. So if *not* in the first century, when the apostles were alive and building the faith of the risen Messiah, then when?

It's clearly an extrabiblical development.

That's not to say it's a mystery. If the answer is not to be found in the Bible, there are many historical clues that can help piece together the puzzle. However, the questions remain: Is man's replacement of God's Sabbath ever justified? Wouldn't this once again be a case of human traditions supplanting God's commandments? Wouldn't that be repeating the great error of the Pharisees that we learn about throughout the Gospels (see chapter 1)?

Let's take a look at what we do know about the shift from Sabbath to Sunday.

Most researchers and scholars who have looked at the question agree it could not have happened before AD 70, the year the temple was destroyed. Passages throughout the New Testament books show that temple worship and activity were taking place before its destruction. Acts 2:46, for instance, tells us, "And they, continuing daily with one accord in the temple, and breaking bread from house to house, did eat their meat with gladness and singleness of heart."

What changed with the destruction of the temple?

First, of course, the temple was gone. It could no longer serve as the principal meeting place in Jerusalem and the heart and soul of the Messianic faith, with James, the brother of Jesus, as its leader.

Second, though there were tensions between the Messianic Jews and the non-Messianic Jews, epitomized by Saul's harassment of believers, we know that the Jerusalem assembly maintained relations with the Pharisees and Sadducees of their day. Many of them, including many priests, had become followers of Jesus (see Acts 6:7).

Third, history suggests that the Messianic Jews living in Jerusalem fled the city before its destruction, as they remembered Jesus' warning about the "abomination of desolation" (see Matt. 24:15).

But did this split with the majority of Jews result in a change of traditions on Sabbath keeping? There is no evidence to suggest it did. In fact, two historians—Eusebius (260–340) and Epiphanius (315–403)—both wrote that the church of Jerusalem through the siege of Hadrian in AD 135 consisted entirely of Messianic Jews and was administered by fifteen bishops of the "circumcision." Eusebius also reported that many were "zealous to insist on the literal observance of the law." Epiphanius noted critically that the group known as "the Nazarenes" "were characterized by their tenacious attachment to Jewish observances." He even called them "heretics" for following the law and the seventh-day Sabbath—just as the apostles and seemingly all first-century believers did. Note the time period: at least sixty-five years *after* the fall of the temple and the destruction of Jerusalem.[1]

Another development is worth noting. Around AD 80, after the fall of the temple, rabbinical authorities in Israel instituted in synagogue services, within what was known as *Shemoneth Esrei*, a "prayer" designed to smoke out any Messianic Jews present. It was actually a malediction, or "curse" that all participants were expected to recite: "May the apostate have not any hope and may the empire of pride be uprooted promptly in our days. May the Nazarenes and the Minim perish in an instant, may they all be erased from the book of life, that they may not be counted among the righteous. Blessed be Thou, O God, who bringest down the proud."[2] (This malediction was the only "test" the Jews could institute to separate themselves, as the Messianic believers conducted themselves in every other way as Jews—observing the Sabbath, keeping the Torah, but perhaps not the man-made traditions of the Oral Law that Jesus, and eventually the other apostles, opposed.)

This suggests that, at least until this period, Messianic Jews were still attending Shabbat services among non-Messianic Jews, just as they were at the time of the apostles, as recorded in Acts and other epistles.

As non-Messianic Jews began separating themselves in services from Messianic Jews—which, at this time, comprised the vast majority of followers of Jesus in Israel—the "Christians" would have needed to organize their own Sabbath services.

Coinciding with the sacking of Jerusalem, Hadrian changed the name of Jerusalem to *Aelia Capitolina*, after the Roman emperor Aelius Adrian. After wiping out much of the Jewish population (the Roman historian Tacitus put the estimate at six hundred thousand deaths), forbidding the rest to return to the city under penalty of death, and prohibiting Sabbath worship, he brought in new inhabitants—Gentiles. He also brought in non-Jews to run what had been a very Jewish church in Jerusalem. He apparently made no distinction between Messianic Jews and non-Messianic Jews, so the church of Jerusalem was now headed by Marcus.

This is among the first evidence of anti-Semitism's impact on the development of the early church. Still, it is unknown whether the new Roman-sponsored church in Jerusalem adopted Sunday worship at that time. There is no credible historical evidence to suggest it did through the end of the second century.

Yet, the stage was set.

Non-Messianic Jews were showing open hostility to worship with Messianic Jews, while Messianic Jews—for all intents and purposes the only "Christians" in Israel—were facing the same kind of persecution from Rome as the Pharisees and Sadducees.

What about outside of Israel?

By the latter part of the first century, the new Messianic faith, spearheaded by the thoroughly Jewish apostles, was attracting more and more interest from non-Jews—especially in Rome.

Reading Paul's letter to the Romans, especially chapters 11 and 16, suggests Paul may have been writing to a church that was, by then, predominantly non-Jewish. By AD 49, Emperor Claudius had "expelled the Jews from Rome since they rioted constantly at the instigation of *Chrestus*," according to the historian Suetonius. "Chrestus" is thought by some to be an erroneous transcription of Christ. Aquila and Priscilla were among the Jews banished, which suggests that Roman authorities made no distinction between Messianic Jewish followers of Jesus.[3]

Fourteen years later, however, Nero "fastened the guilt [for arson] and inflicted the most exquisite tortures on a class hated for their abomination, called Christians by the populace," according to Tacitus.[4]

But as the Jewish revolts in Israel continued, the tide turned against all Jews in Rome. By the second century, Roman Christians began differentiating themselves from their Jewish ancestors in an attempt to reconcile with the empire. While Hadrian "reserved his severity for the Jews . . . he felt himself attracted to, with sympathy for Christianity," according to historian Marcel Simon.[5]

Meanwhile, the second century marked an upsurge in the publication of anti-Jewish literature by "Christian writers," as we will see in chapter 7. Not coincidentally with this popular condemnation of the Jews in Rome came condemnation of the Sabbath—and the push for Sunday worship.

Justin Martyr is a good case study. He lived from AD 100 to 165, teaching and writing in Rome. For him, the Sabbath was a temporary ordinance, derived from Moses, which God did not intend to be kept literally, for He Himself "does not stop controlling the movement of the universe on that day." Instead, Justin wrote in his famous *Dialogue with Trypho*, "O, He imposed it on the Jews as a mark to single them out for punishment they so well deserved for their infidelities."

Not surprisingly, for some Roman Christians the seventh day, once a day of feasting and joy, became a day of fasting and mourning. Interestingly, that idea originated with Marcion, later expelled from the church of Rome for his dualistic-Gnostic teachings.

Nevertheless, by the time of Pope Sylvester, from 314 to 335, the Sabbath fast, through a new tradition of man, had become for many a matter of religious doctrine, as had Sunday worship:

> If every Sunday is to be observed joyfully by the Christians on account of the resurrection then every Sabbath on account of the burial is to be regarded in execration of the Jews (*execratione*

Judaeorum). In fact all the disciples of the Lord had a lamentation on the Sabbath, bewailing the buried Lord, and gladness
prevailed for the exulting Jews. But sadness reigned for the
fasting apostles. In like manner we are sad with the saddened
by the burial of the Lord, if we want to rejoice with them in the
day of the Lord's resurrection. In fact, it is not proper to observe,
because of Jewish customs, the consumption of food (*destructions
ciborium*) and the ceremonies of the Jews.[6]

Does this sound familiar after reading chapter 1? Just like the
Pharisees of Jesus' time, fourth-century Christians were, in effect,
changing and adding to the law of God.

As we will see, the historical and biblical evidence is overwhelming that this is how the Sabbath moved to Sunday—not
through any act or new revelation of God, but by new traditions
of men.

Perhaps the most persuasive and documented work on this
subject was done by the late Samuele Bacchiocchi, the first non-
Catholic to graduate from the Pontifical Gregorian University in
Rome. He received a gold medal from Pope Paul VI for earning the
academic distinction of summa cum laude. Bacchiocchi had unprecedented access to historical files in the Vatican for his scholarly book
From Sabbath to Sunday in 1977, the first book ever published by
the Pontifical Gregorian University Press by a non-Catholic with the
Catholic imprimatur. It establishes that the change from Saturday
to Sunday began to occur approximately a century after Jesus' death,
with active leadership from the church of Rome.

The change began in earnest during the time of Ignatius, the
bishop of Antioch at the time of Trajan (AD 98–117). Ignatius
argued, according to the writings of Irenaeus, "against the Judaizing tendencies of his territory, which not far geographically from
Palestine, had suffered the influences of the synagogue and of the
Judeo-Christians."[7]

At this point we see the first efforts to separate Judaism from

Christianity: "For if we are still practicing Judaism, we admit that we have not received God's favor. For the most divine prophets lived in accordance with Jesus Christ," wrote Ignatius. He added:

> It is wrong to talk about Jesus Christ and live like the Jews. For Christianity did not believe in Judaism but Judaism in Christianity.
>
> Let us therefore no longer keep the Sabbath after the Jewish manner, and rejoice in days of idleness. . . . But let every one of you keep the Sabbath in a spiritual manner, rejoicing in the meditation on the law, not in the relaxation of the body, admiring the workmanship of God, and not eating things prepared the day before, nor using lukewarm drinks, nor walking within prescribed space, nor finding delight in dancing and plaudits which has no sense in them.[8]

This plea strongly suggests that, at the time of this writing, many Christians were still following the examples of Jesus and the apostles and that the separation of Christianity from Judaism was still in progress and not complete—especially outside of Rome.

Why Sunday worship rather than another day of the week?

As early as the first century, Rome was dominated by a pagan sun cult. It's not difficult to imagine that a nascent, budding faith arising out of biblical, Judaic roots could be influenced by the empire's culture—perhaps even subsumed in a form of syncretism.

The pagan sun worshippers of Rome venerated Sunday. They also venerated December 25, the apparent birthday of the Sumerian sun god, Tammuz, referenced once in the Bible in Ezekiel 8:

> Then he brought me to the door of the gate of the LORD's house which was toward the north; and, behold, there sat women weeping for Tammuz. Then said he unto me, Hast thou seen this, O son of man? turn thee yet again, and thou shalt see greater abominations than these. And he brought me into the inner court of the LORD's house, and, behold, at the door of the temple of the LORD, between the porch and the altar, were about five and twenty men, with their backs toward the temple of the

LORD, and their faces toward the east; and they worshipped the sun toward the east. (vv. 14–16)

Apparently, in Ezekiel's time, some in Israel had fallen under the spell of this pagan sun god born on December 25, who had died and was mourned by his followers. But the Hebrew Scriptures specifically condemn sun worship (see Deut. 4:19; 17:3; and Jer. 8:2).

Could it be that the new, emerging Christian faith of the first, second, and third centuries fell victim to the same mistakes at the very moment it was separating from its Jewish roots?

Consider the words of Eusebius, one of the early "church fathers," in his commentary on Psalm 91:

> The Logo has transferred by the New Alliance the celebration of the Sabbath to the rising of the light. He has given us a type of the true rest in the saving day of the Lord, the first day of the light. . . . In this day of light, first day and true day of the sun, when we gather after the interval of six days, we celebrate the holy and spiritual Sabbaths. . . . All things whatsoever that were prescribed for the Sabbath, we have transferred them to the Lord's day, as being more authoritative and more highly regarded and first in rank, and more honorable than the Jewish Sabbath. In fact, it is on this day, of the creation of the world that God said: "Let there be light and there was light." It is also on this day that the Sun of Justice has arisen for our souls.[9]

When it comes to the question of how Christianity moved from Sabbath to Sunday worship, one thing is clear. There was always resistance to it from biblical purists. As late as the fourth century, that opposition to new traditions was still around.

Influenced by rising anti-Semitism, the Council of Antioch in AD 341 prohibited Christians from celebrating Passover with Jews. Twenty-three years later, while Constantine was emperor, the Council of Laodicea determined it would be illegal—by force of Roman law—for either Jews or Christians to observe the seventh-day Sabbath.

The edict (Canon 29) that came out of that council was clear: "Christians shall not Judaize and be idle on Saturday, but shall work on that day; but the Lord's day they shall especially honor, and, as being Christians, shall, if possible, do no work on that day. If, however, they are found Judaizing, that shall be shut out from Christ."[10]

While Constantine was known as the emperor who converted to Christianity, there is ample historical evidence he may have done so more to bring unity to the empire than out of spiritual conviction. He had previously been a sun-worshipping pagan—and there are indications he never left that grounding.

In AD 321, Constantine put what could be called the world's first "blue laws" in place: "On the venerable day of the Sun let the magistrates and people residing in cities rest, and let all workshops be closed. In the country however persons engaged in agriculture may freely and lawfully continue their pursuits because it often happens that another day is not suitable for gain-sowing or vine planting; lest by neglecting the proper moment for such operations the bounty of heaven should be lost."

The abandonment of the seventh-day Sabbath can be attributed historically and biblically to several factors:

- a spirit of anti-Semitism within the church and the division this caused within a faith with deep Hebrew roots (more on this in chapter 7)

- the rise of ancient pagan sun-worshipping cults and the convenience of syncretism within the Roman Empire for the purpose of unity

- the power of the Roman state to enforce such edicts as Constantine's

- the willingness of the Roman church to both change the Sabbath to another day and justify this counterbiblical sleight of hand with Scripture

[O]n the seventh day God ended his work which he had made; and he rested on the seventh day from all his work which he had made. And God blessed the seventh day, and sanctified it. —GENESIS 2:2–3

There have been many calendars throughout history. Our current calendar uses a seven-day week, which doesn't divide well into the lunar cycle. One complete lunar phase cycle is 29 days, 12 hours, 44 minutes, and 3 seconds. A year— it takes for the earth to revolve around the sun—equals 365.25 of our days, which explains the leap-year phenomenon every four years on the currently accepted Julian calendar.

So what accounts for the universal acceptance of the seven-day week?

On the surface, it bears no relationship to either the earth's rotations, the moon's cycles, or the earth's revolutions around the sun. So, other than relatively brief efforts to tamper with it, why, throughout history, has the seven-day week been observed so consistently? Could it be because God ordained it, just as His Word tells us in Genesis?

Is it possible this is actually evidence of the Genesis account of creation—a legacy God left us that points directly to Him?

After searching out other calendars or explanations for a seven-day week, I found none. Various ancient civilizations had inexplicably decided to follow a seven-day week system—many of which ended with a holy day, but none considered the obvious explanation for such a calendar: God's Word.

The seven-day week has also defied all attempts at man's rebellion against it.

The original Julian calendar in Rome was established on an eight-day week. But it was abandoned as the empire expanded and ran smack into cultures that all operated on the seven-day cycle.

In 1793, the atheistic leaders of the French Revolution took a stab at ridding themselves of the seven-day week, substituting three ten-day "decades." It never caught on and was abandoned in 1802.

In 1929 the atheistic Soviet Union tried a five-day week, with one day of rest, with citizens assigned different days to keep the factories running efficiently all the time. Due to the chaos the system created, it was revised in 1932 to a six-day week. Eight years later, the Soviets were back on the seven-day cycle.

In 1936 the League of Nations solicited proposals for world calendar reform and considered almost two hundred different schemes, many of which rearranged the week. Yet the seven-day week remains.

Some suggest the custom began with Moses, who committed the Genesis creation account to writing. But there is plenty of historical and biblical evidence to suggest the seven-day week ending in a day of rest was being observed around the world before Moses's time.

But the testimony of the seven-day week's ties to creation testimony is strongest in the legacy of the names of the last day of the week throughout so many nations, as still reflected in their languages today.

William Mead Jones (1818–1895) was an American preacher, abolitionist, and missionary to Haiti and Palestine. During part of his life, Jones worked for ten years for the British Museum on a work he published called "A Chart of the Week," a table comprising the names of the days of the week in 160 languages. In every one of these languages, the days of the week appear in the same order, and in 108 of them the last day of the week is called either "Seventh Day," "Sabbath," or "Rest Day."

Jones's thesis was that the Sabbath was first given to humankind at the end of the creation week, which fixed the seven-day weekly cycle on a global basis. He further surmised that the ancient world had known of the seventh-day Sabbath.

His study of the world's languages bolstered his theory. Following is his list of ancient languages that memorialized their culture's knowledge of the seventh-day Sabbath in their names for the last day of the seven-day week.

Abyssinian	Dayak (Borneo)	Maba (central Africa)
Ancient Syriac	Hebrew	Osmanlian (Turkey)
Armenian (Armenia)	Hindustani	Pahlavi (ancient Persian)
Babylonian Syriac	Kazan Tatar (East Russia)	
Chaldee Syriac (Kurdistan, Urumia, Persia)	Latin (Italy)	Teda (central Africa)
		Wolof (Senegambia, West Africa)
	Lusatian (Saxony)	
Coptic (Egypt)		And many more.

Even Socrates noted in his *Ecclesiastical History*, book 5, chapter 22 that the entire known world at his time, with the exception of Rome and Alexandria, observed the seventh day of the week as a day of rest. Might there be something significant about the nature of the seven-day week?

For a complete list of languages and the Chart of the Week, go to www.sabbathtruth.com/portals/20/documents/chart-of-the-week.pdf.

Where does all that leave true "Bereans" in the twenty-first century? Do we too follow the traditions of men, the great sin of the Pharisees that Jesus condemned throughout the Gospels? Or do we who believe the Bible is the true and inerrant Word of God consider prayerfully the possibility that what the Bible says about the Sabbath and the other holy days of Leviticus 23 is true—that they are appointed times for Him to meet with His people *forever*?

If God's commandments were in place before Jesus, during His earthly reign (when He fulfilled them), and in the first-century apostolic age—and will be in place again when He returns—shouldn't we be observing them today?

Consider this prophetic verse, which deals specifically with the coming kingdom on earth:

> And it shall come to pass, that from one new moon to another, and from one sabbath to another, shall all flesh come to worship before me, saith the LORD. (Isa. 66:23)

Do you believe the Bible?

Do you believe in prophecy?

Do you believe Jesus is coming back?

If you believe in the coming kingdom and it is your blessed hope, or, as Peter called it, "the restitution of all things," then this is your future.

You will be observing the Sabbath. Everyone will. And by all accounts, the Torah will be our instruction manual. Maybe it's time to start rehearsing now.

6

HOW EARLY DID REPLACEMENT THEOLOGY BEGIN?

Woe be unto the pastors that destroy and scatter the sheep of my pasture! saith the Lord. —JEREMIAH 23:1

IN THIS CHAPTER WE WILL DISCUSS what has become a very hot topic in the church today: replacement theology, the concept that God's promises to and covenants with the Jewish people have been abrogated and passed on to a new people of a new faith: Christians.

It comes in many forms, some more abhorrent than others, and it is the primary reason Jews and Christians today generally look at one another as belonging to two different religions. It's also one of the main reasons for the rampant, global anti-Semitism over the last two thousand years.

How early did it begin?

Astonishingly, there is clear evidence of it in the Bible, in the New Testament, while the Jewish apostles were still alive. In fact, history strongly suggests the apostles themselves were victimized by anti-Jewish bigotry stirred by the birth of replacement theology in the first century.

We find a shocking example in 3 John, where we read about a historically obscure figure by the name of Diotrephes:

> I wrote unto the church: but Diotrephes, who loveth to have the preeminence among them, receiveth us not. Wherefore, if I come, I will remember his deeds which he doeth, prating against us with malicious words: and not content therewith, neither doth he himself receive the brethren, and forbiddeth them that would, and casteth them out of the church.
>
> Beloved, follow not that which is evil, but that which is good. He that doeth good is of God: but he that doeth evil hath not seen God. (vv. 9–11)

We don't know a lot about who Diotrephes was. But all we need to know is revealed in this short book of the Bible. His name means "nourished by Jupiter" or "nourished by Zeus." That's kind of a strange name for a first-century believer. He was obviously not a Jew. His name suggests he was Greek. In the first century, it was common for new Gentile believers with pagan names that glorified other gods to change them. Diotrephes did not do this. He kept his pagan name, which glorifies a pagan Greek god.

We also know that Diotrephes spoke maliciously against the inspired Jewish apostolic leadership and refused to welcome Messianic Jewish believers into his assembly. In fact, he threw them out!

Just to underscore the incredible historical lesson given here: the apostle John, or Yochanan, a Jewish disciple, *was not welcome in a Christian church.*

Clearly, according to John, Diotrephes was evil and did not know God. Yet he held a position of power and influence in the first-century church.

This is compelling scriptural evidence that within one generation of Jesus' death and resurrection, the spirit of replacement theology was already active in the church. Imagine that! Even John, the "disciple whom Jesus loved" (see John 20:2; 21:7, 20), was unwelcome in a church within one lifetime after Jesus.

By AD 150, Justin Martyr had written his *Dialogue with Trypho*, an antinomian and arrogant screed that blamed the Jews as a race for rejecting Jesus and asserted that the promises to Israel were now promises to the church. Justin demonstrated in this writing both a profound knowledge of the Scriptures and yet such profound distortions as this:

> We too, would observe your circumcision of the flesh, your Sabbath days, and in a word, all your festivals, if we were not aware of the reason why they were imposed upon you, namely, because of your sins and the hardness of heart. The custom of circumcising the flesh, handed down from Abraham, was given to you as a distinguishing mark, to set you off from other nations and from us Christians. The purpose of this was that you and only you might suffer the afflictions that are now justly yours; that only your land be desolated, and your cities ruined by fire, that the fruits of your land be eaten by strangers before your very eyes; that not one of you be permitted to enter your city of Jerusalem. Your circumcision of the flesh is the only mark by which you can certainly be distinguished from other men . . . As I stated before it was by reason of your sins and the sins of your fathers that, among other precepts, God imposed upon you the observance of the Sabbath as a mark.

Now, having read that quotation from this "church father," ask yourself:

- Did Jesus ever suggest that circumcision, the Sabbath, and the festivals—all of which He practiced and observed—had been overthrown as institutions for the future?

- Did any of the apostles suggest any such thing as they were practicing and observing all of them?

- Doesn't this suggest that something happened to drive a wedge between the original, first-century messianic faith begun by Jewish believers and the very Gentile followers who were given an opportunity to be grafted into the eternal promises and covenants God made with the house of Israel?

Let's take a brief stroll through church history in the years following *Dialogue*.

The next phase of replacement theology came a few decades later with a man named Origen, whose life spanned the middle of the second century and into the third. He is often referred to as a "church father," a "scholar," and "an early Christian theologian."[1] Born in Alexandria, where he lived for the first half of his life, he was indeed a prolific writer in multiple branches of theology, including textual criticism, biblical exegesis, and hermeneutics; philosophical theology; preaching; and spirituality written in Greek. He was eventually anathemized at the Second Council of Constantinople, meaning he was repudiated, denounced as a heretic, and cursed.[2]

Why?

Unlike many so-called church fathers, Origen's teachings directly contradicted those attributed to the apostles, notably Paul and John. He taught such heretical ideas as the preexistence of souls; the final reconciliation of all creatures, including perhaps even Satan; and the subordination of God the Son to God the Father. The Greek historian Eusebius even reported that Origen, misinterpreting Matthew 19:12, castrated himself.[3] Origen was also a zealous proponent of abandoning the Sabbath and the Torah.

Here's a quote from Origen: "We may thus assert in utter confidence that the Jews will not return to their earlier situation, for they have committed the most abominable of crimes, in forming this conspiracy against the Savior of the human race . . . hence the city where Jesus suffered was necessarily destroyed, the Jewish nation was driven from its country, and another people was called by God to the blessed election."[4]

While Origen was discredited and condemned by some in the church, his teachings about replacement theology took hold in the church—and are, in one form or another, still with us today.

By the middle of the fourth century, another revered "church father," Augustine, wrote: "How hateful to me are the enemies of your Scripture! How I wish that you would slay them [the Jews] with your two-edged sword, so that there should be none to oppose your word! Gladly would I have them die to themselves and live to you!"[5]

Things got worse by the latter part of the fourth century with the rise of John Chrysostom, who condemned as heretics and worse those followers of Jesus who kept God's commandments, because they were tinged with Jewish history and culture.

"What is this disease?" Chrysostom thundered. "The festivals of the pitiful and miserable Jews are soon to march upon us one after the other and in quick succession: The Feast of Trumpets, the Feast of Tabernacles, the fasts (Day of Atonement). There are many in our ranks who say they think as we do. Yet some of those are going to watch the festivals and others will join the Jews in keeping their feasts and observing their fasts. I wish to drive this perverse custom from the church right now. . . . But now that the Jewish festivals are close by and at the very door, if I should fail to cure those who are sick with the Judaizing disease . . . [they] may partake in the Jews' transgressions."[6]

That's how the express observation of the law was redefined as transgression of the law.

Flash forward to the sixteenth century and you have the "the great reformer" Martin Luther writing:

What then shall we Christians do with this damned, rejected race of Jews? Since they live among us and we know about their lying and blasphemy and cursing, we can not tolerate them if we do not wish to share in their lies, curses, and blasphemy. In this way we cannot quench the inextinguishable fire of divine rage nor convert the Jews. We must prayerfully and reverentially practice a merciful severity. Perhaps we may save a few from the fire and flames [of hell]. We must not seek vengeance. They are surely being punished a thousand times more than we might wish them. Let me give you my honest advice. . . . their synagogues should be set on fire, and whatever does not burn up should be covered or spread over with dirt so that no one may ever be able to see a cinder or stone of it. And this ought to be done for the honor of God and of Christianity in order that God may see that we are Christians, and that we have not wittingly tolerated or approved of such public lying, cursing, and blaspheming of His Son and His Christians.[7]

John Calvin wrote of the Jews: "Their rotten and unbending stiffneckedness deserves that they be oppressed unendingly and without measure or end and that they die in their misery without the pity of anyone."[8]

How did the church drift so far so quickly and so convincingly from its Hebrew roots? And how did it last so long—even through the Reformation? More important, what are the spiritual implications and ramifications of this historical revisionism for the church that survives today?

A faith founded on the sacrificial and atoning work of a Jewish Messiah was twisted into a faith that not only condemned the Jews, but hijacked their covenant promises.

It's simply a history too few Christians understand. It still impacts many of their theological precepts. But it's a phenomenon that runs contrary to the entirety of Scripture—especially when you look to what the Word says about the future.

You simply can't believe God is through with Israel and believe in the literal fulfillment of Scripture because not only is every historical aspect of the Bible Jewish, but so is the future tense, the as-yet unfulfilled prophecies of Jesus' return and what those prophecies say about the coming millennial kingdom.

Are we supposed to believe that's all allegory?

How did it all come to this?

Perhaps it's time for Christians to put aside the traditions and customs they inherited from their "church fathers" and get back to *sola Scriptura*, as the Reformation tried to do but fell short.

The keys to unlocking the truth are found in Jesus' own words in the Gospels.

Did He come to undo His Father's work? God forbid! Just as Jesus repudiated the traditions of men continually throughout all four gospels, He also spoke continually of His Father in heaven, reflecting, as it were, His perfect, divine, eternal, and unchanging will. Here are just a few select verses from Matthew to make the point:

> Let your light so shine before men, that they may see your good works, and glorify your Father which is in heaven. (Matt. 5:16)

> . . . that ye may be the children of your Father which is in heaven: for he maketh his sun to rise on the evil and on the good, and sendeth rain on the just and on the unjust. . . . Be ye therefore perfect, even as your Father which is in heaven is perfect. (Matt. 5:45, 48)

> For if ye forgive men their trespasses, your heavenly Father will also forgive you: But if ye forgive not men their trespasses, neither will your Father forgive your trespasses. (Matt. 6:14–15)

> Not every one that saith unto me, Lord, Lord, shall enter into the kingdom of heaven; but he that doeth the will of my Father which is in heaven. (Matt. 7:21)

Whosoever therefore shall confess me before men, him will I confess also before my Father which is in heaven. But whosoever shall deny me before men, him will I also deny before my Father which is in heaven. (Matt. 10:32–33)

For whosoever shall do the will of my Father which is in heaven, the same is my brother, and sister, and mother. (Matt. 12:50)

But he answered and said, Every plant, which my heavenly Father hath not planted, shall be rooted up. (Matt. 15:13)

For the Son of man shall come in the glory of his Father with his angels; and then he shall reward every man according to his works. (Matt. 16:27)

In reading these verses, can one possibly conclude that there is any disagreement between the Father and the Son, or that Jesus came to do something different from what He knew to be His Father's will? So *did* He come to change direction, start a new belief system, or prescribe a new set of rules or a paradigm shift concerning salvation and eternal life?

Those are some of the questions we should be asking as we read Scripture with fresh eyes, unprejudiced by the modern-day teachings and traditions of men.

What we see in Jesus' own words affirms everything found in the Old Testament, the only Scriptures that existed at His time. It is impossible to find in the New Testament even one example of Jesus or any of His apostles repudiating what came before. Instead, every New Testament writer built on the foundation of the Torah and the rest of the Hebrew Scriptures. There are no deviations, no revisions. In fact, the apostles demanded to be judged on what they said and wrote by the standard of the Tanakh.

So, the real church fathers are Jesus, Peter, Paul, Matthew, Mark, Luke, John, James, and Jude, all having written under the inspiration of the Holy Spirit. We needn't look beyond them for doctrine.

HOW WE "LOST" PASSOVER

Let the children of Israel also keep the passover at his appointed
season . . . according to all the rites of it, and according to all the
ceremonies thereof, shall ye keep it. —NUMBERS 9:2–3

Most Christians around the world celebrate the resurrection of Jesus on
Easter—an ancient pagan holiday, but it wasn't always this way.

Jesus was crucified and rose from the dead during Passover week, also
known as the Feast of Unleavened Bread. So why don't Christians observe
Jesus' death and resurrection when they actually happened?

Most of the church today does not observe Passover week because of
anti-Semitism.

Jesus observed Passover. Likewise, Passover continued to be celebrated
by His apostles and all of His early disciples throughout their lives. In Acts
20, Luke related that he and Paul "sailed away from Philippi after the days
of unleavened bread, and came unto them to Troas in five days; where
we abode seven days" (v. 6). The Feast of Unleavened Bread—alternately
known as Passover, is a seven-day observance. In 1 Corinthians 5, Paul
wrote concerning Passover: "Purge out therefore the old leaven, that ye
may be a new lump, as ye are unleavened. For even Christ our passover is
sacrificed for us: therefore let us keep the feast, not with old leaven, neither
with the leaven of malice and wickedness; but with the unleavened bread
of sincerity and truth" (vv. 7–8). In fact, the resurrection was observed
around Passover week for hundreds of years after Jesus' death by many if
not most in the church—and it is still observed by a small minority today.

Passover is not really a "Jewish holiday." It's one of the feasts of the
Lord—our Lord. It's a very important observance, a very biblical one, an
appointed time that we, all God's children, were commanded to mark as
a "holy convocation" forever, "throughout [our] generations."

The reason we think of Passover as a "Jewish holiday" is because Jews
have been, since the early part of the fourth century, pretty much the
only people who have kept this commandment. That's when the Roman
emperor Constantine, concerned more for the unity of his empire than

for God's Word, forsook Passover and coerced other followers of Jesus to observe Easter because it was more convenient, and so that the church would have "nothing in common with the Jews," whom he blamed for Jesus' death.

The Council of Nicea in AD 325 declared:

When the question relative to the sacred festival of Easter arose, it was universally thought that it would be convenient that all should keep the feast on one day . . . It was declared particularly unworthy for this, the holiest of all festivals, to follow the custom of the Jews, who have soiled their hands with the most fearful of crimes . . . In unanimously adopting this mode, we desire, dearest brethren, to separate ourselves from the detestable company of the Jews, for it is truly shameful for us to hear them boast that without their direction we could not keep this feast . . . They do not possess the truth in this Easter question; a Divine Providence wills that this custom should be rectified and regulated in a uniform way; and everyone, I hope, will agree upon this point. As, on the one hand, it is our duty not to have anything in common with the murderers of our Lord; and as, on the other, the custom now followed by the Churches of the West, of the South and of the North, and by some of those of the East, is the most acceptable . . . You should consider not only that the number of churches in these provinces make a majority, but also that it is right we should have nothing in common with the Jews.

Following this fateful decision, the Roman Empire began to persecute those who, like Jesus and His apostles, observed Passover throughout their lives.

There's much more to this history that is well recorded. You are not likely to hear it in your churches on Easter Sunday because, sadly, most Christians follow the tradition of men rather than the Word of God. I don't contest that we are to live by faith and in the Spirit. But we are not to be deceived either. We are not to follow man-made traditions at the expense of what we can learn from the Scriptures.

Might not some of the "doctrines" and traditions we have inherited from our "church fathers" be *corruptions* of the truth, as the Pharisees' traditions were? Indeed, the Bible warns of this: "Woe be unto the pastors that destroy and scatter the sheep of my pasture!" the Lord said, as far back as Jeremiah's time (Jer. 23:1). And what did Jesus Himself tell us? "Beware of false prophets, which come to you in sheep's clothing, but inwardly they are ravening wolves" (Matt. 7:15). Peter added, "But there were false prophets also among the people, even as there shall be false teachers among you, who privily shall bring in damnable heresies, even denying the Lord that bought them, and bring upon themselves swift destruction" (2 Peter 2:1). And finally, John warned, "Beloved, believe not every spirit, but try the spirits whether they are of God: because many false prophets are gone out into the world" (1 John 4:1).

So the question is, are we learning the lessons Jesus and His apostles taught, or are we repeating the errors they exposed?

Can the true church of Jesus be anything but followers of the Father?

By the way, just what *is* the "church"? Is it a new institution, or a continuation of those set apart from the beginning?

The word *church* as it appears in the Bible is the exact same word as *synagogue*, meaning the assembly. So, has God really forsaken the Jews, or has He only chastened them, as He did so frequently throughout Scripture because He called them to be a people set apart?

What is the foundation of the Christian inheritance in the kingdom if not the one first described in Exodus 19:6? "And ye shall be unto me a kingdom of priests, and an holy nation. These are the words which thou shalt speak unto the children of Israel." Indeed, we are those *grafted* into the coming kingdom of the children of Israel—a kingdom of priests, a holy nation—saved only through the sacrificial atonement of Jesus.

Let's look at what Paul taught about that in Romans: "Boast not against the branches. But if thou boast, thou bearest not the root, but the root thee. Thou wilt say then, The branches were broken off, that I might be grafted in. Well; because of unbelief they were broken off, and thou standest by faith. Be not highminded, but fear" (11:18–20). Evidently, by the first century, some Gentile believers were claiming superiority over non-Messianic Jews. Paul warned them not to boast but to "fear."

Fear what?

"For if God spared not the natural branches, take heed lest he also spare not thee. Behold therefore the goodness and severity of God: on them which fell, severity; but toward thee, goodness, if thou continue in his goodness: otherwise thou also shalt be cut off" (vv. 21–22). In other words, a failure to be both informed and humble concerning unbelieving Israel could very well result in believing Gentile Christians being "cut off" from God.

That's right. True Christians *are* grafted into a tree of life because of their faith in the Jewish Messiah and obedience to His command-ments. *But* we are subject to the same fate as the branches cut off if we lose our humility and "boast" against them.

What is our fate if we remain true to our faith?

It's the same fate as the Jews who do so and are redeemed through Jesus' blood sacrifice.

Paul's words in Romans 11 are unambiguous. But elsewhere they are not always so— especially when they are interpreted outside the context of his specific audience and the message he was trying to convey to them.

Indeed, there are some "hard sayings" in Paul's letters. But nothing Paul wrote can be interpreted as contradicting other Scripture.

As the historical divide between the Gentile church and the Jews, both Messianic and non-Messianic, grew wider in the second, third, and fourth centuries, the church began laying the foundation for their replacement theology precisely on scattered, out-of-context scriptures— often citing Paul. And according to D. Thomas Lan-caster, author and director of education for the Torah-based ministry First Fruits of Zion, "Paul's compiled letters, when read outside of their original context, provided ample justification for that disassociation. The emerging Christian movement read Paul's arguments for the *inclusion* of Gentiles in the kingdom backward to imply the *exclusion* of Torah."⁹

Well said. But there was even more official anti-Semitism involved in the parting of the ways between Jews and Christians beginning in the latter part of the first century through the Middle Ages and even to the current day, when we see entire Christian denominations participating in boycotts and divestments from Israel.

Right after the destruction of the second temple in AD 70, the Roman Empire instituted a two-denarii tax on Jews, called *fiscus Judaicus*, initially imposed by Emperor Vespasian in retaliation for the First Jewish–Roman War. Romano-Jewish historian Josephus wrote that the tax was imposed on all Jews throughout the empire, not just on those who took part in the revolt against Rome. Worse, though their temple was destroyed, the Jews were forced to pay this tax in place of the levy they had once paid for temple upkeep. To add spiritual insult to injury, the new tax was to go to the temple of Jupiter Capitolinus, the main center of pagan Roman religion. Only Jews who had abandoned their religion were exempt from paying it. But worst of all, while the tithe paid in the temple of Jerusalem was required only of adult men ages twenty to fifty, the *fiscus Judaicus* was also demanded of women, children, the elderly, and even Jewish slaves. You can imagine that Messianic Jews might claim to belong to another faith to avoid this tax, though we don't have any historical evidence of that.

In spite of the tax, the Roman Empire's Christian population—both Jewish and Gentile—was exploding in the latter part of the first century. When Domitian became emperor in AD 81, many Christians, at least in their religious observances, were hard to distinguish from Jews; most were likely still observing the Sabbath and feasts. For this reason, perhaps, the emperor further began to exact the *fiscus Judaicus* from those who concealed that they were Jews, and even from those who simply *observed Jewish customs*. The historian Suetonius noted that Roman officials once examined a ninety-year-old to see if he was circumcised.[10]

It didn't take long for Christians to petition the emperor for an exemption to the tax by claiming they weren't Jews.

Domitian was murdered in AD 96 and his successor, Nerva, relaxed the rules of collection to impact only those who openly practiced Judaism. Nonetheless, *fiscus Judaicus* remained in effect for more than two hundred years.

Meanwhile, in 313, Constantine the Great, who claimed to be a convert to Christianity, approved the Edict of Milan, which ended official persecution of Christians. Later during his reign, the official Roman Church and state became one—with Constantine weighing in on church matters and the church influencing matters of governance.

By 321, Constantine had decreed that Christians and Roman sun worshippers should be united in observing the venerable day of the sun, or Sunday.

In 325, Constantine convened the First Council of Nicea, where it was decided to separate the date of Easter from the Jewish Passover. Constantine's official decree stated:

> It was . . . declared improper to follow the custom of the Jews in the celebration of this holy festival, because, their hands having been stained with crime, the minds of these wretched men are necessarily blinded . . . Let us, then, have nothing in common with the Jews, who are our adversaries . . . Let us . . . studiously [avoid] all contact with that evil way . . . For how can they entertain right views on any point who, after having compassed the death of the Lord, being out of their minds, are guided not by sound reason, but by an unrestrained passion, wherever their innate madness carries them . . . Lest your pure minds should appear to share in the customs of a people so utterly depraved . . . [t]herefore, this irregularity must be corrected, in order that we may no more have any thing in common with those parricides and the murderers of our Lord . . . no single point in common with the perjury of the Jews.[11]

Following the reign of Constantine, the Roman Empire continued to push Sunday worship exclusively—even to the point of forbidding "idleness" on Saturday.

The church-state union thus did more to divide Christianity from its Jewish roots than probably any other factor, enforcing, as it were, an official version of anti-Semitism.

Meanwhile, coinciding with a new wave of European anti-Semitism, the *fiscus Judaicus* made a return in 1342 under a new name during the reign of Emperor Louis IV the Bavarian, who ordered all Jews above age twelve and possessing twenty guldens to pay one gulden annually for protection. The practice was justified on the grounds that the emperor, as legal successor of the Roman emperors, was the rightful recipient of the temple tax that Jews paid to the Romans after the destruction of the second temple. Again, adding spiritual insult to injury, the tax was collected on Christmas Day.

Persecution of Jews continued century after century, with pogroms in Russia, Germany, and Poland, and further crusades throughout Europe.

In 1290, England expelled the Jews on an auspicious day in Jewish history—the ninth of Av, the date both the first and the second temples were destroyed.

In 1306, France expelled the Jews two days before the ninth of Av on the Hebrew calendar.

In 1492, Spain expelled the Jews on the tenth of Av.

In 1941, German SS commander Heinrich Himmler received formal approval from the Nazi Party for the "Final Solution" on the ninth of Av, launching the Holocaust in which nearly one-third of the world's Jewish population perished.

No people in history have faced such persecution over thousands of years. And no people have emerged from those attempts at annihilation victorious—back in their own homeland in the twenty-first century.

The Christian church, throughout that history, has too often played the role of bystander—or persecutor.

How could that have happened, given Christianity's Jewish roots—with the worship of a *Jewish* Messiah as the Son of God, and all of its early adherents being Jewish?

It could happen only because Christians did not understand their own Good Book; they neither read nor comprehended the front of that book.

Today's churches spend most of their study of the Bible in the Epistles. Most of the rest of the time is divided between the Gospels, Acts, and the Psalms, with some dabbling in the Prophets. Is that generally your experience in Bible study?

If so, let me bluntly suggest it's the wrong approach. We need to understand the front of the book to understand the back of the book.

Keep in mind, when Jesus and the apostles were teaching, the only Scriptures known were the Hebrew Scriptures, or Tanakh. Jesus said they testified of Him (John 5:39)—and indeed they do.

After the resurrection, Jesus spent a day with two believers on their way to Emmaus, going through the Scriptures and how they pointed to Him (see Luke 24).

Yes, it's all about Jesus.

- He is the Creator of the world. (John 1:3)

- He's the Redeemer of the world. (Isa. 54:5)

- He's the coming King of the world. (Ps. 2:28)

But His coming kingdom may hold some real surprises for the twenty-first-century believer. Even Jesus Himself—that is, Yeshua—may look and sound unfamiliar. After all, the generation that witnessed His first coming didn't recognize Him or the time of His visitation. I wonder how many Christians in the world today will have the same problem.

Their expectations may be wrong: they may be expecting another Jesus—a Gentile Jesus, or one who behaves as He did during His first visitation, instead of the Israel-centric Messiah who will come as a conquering King. There are all kinds of possibilities for shock and awe when Jesus returns, especially for those not steeped in the prophetic scriptures—the very ones that point to Him and that exquisitely detail His expectations for His coming kingdom. These are the ones we ignore on Sunday and in Bible studies.

When we look at the prophetic scriptures about Christ's kingdom, it is unmistakable that the land of Israel, reborn in 1948, will once again be the center of everything:

> Judgment will come to the nations that spoiled Israel, which remains, in the future tense, "the apple of [God's] eye." (Zech. 2:8)

> Jesus will return to the Mount of Olives in Jerusalem. (Zech. 14:4)

> His future global kingdom will be finally restored in Jerusalem. (Zech. 14:9–11)

> The entire world will be required to observe the Feast of Tabernacles. Those who refuse will have no rain. (Zech. 4:16–19)

> The very basis for the judgment of the nations will be how they treated the nation of Israel. (Zech. 12:9)

> The nation that doesn't serve Israel will be utterly wasted. (Isa. 60:12)

> The fulfillment of the new covenant takes place in Israel. (Jer. 31)

One would need to allegorize a tremendous amount of Scripture to deny the centrality of Israel to the restitution of all things that God promises to believers—through His covenants with Israel.

1

ARE WE LIVING IN THE NEW COVENANT TODAY?

Behold, the days come, saith the LORD, that I will make a new covenant with the house of Israel, and with the house of Judah. —JEREMIAH 31:31

ASK MOST CHRISTIANS TODAY whether we are living in new covenant times and the answer will undoubtedly be an emphatic "yes." That's what most of us have been told by our pastors and priests: We're not beholden to old covenants of the past, since the death and resurrection of Messiah overturned the law. Now we believers live in the Spirit, rather than under the bondage of the law.

That's what we hear, and it tickles our ears . . . but is it true? If so, where is the evidence for these assertions as our world appears to be falling deeper into the morass of sin, violence, and hopelessness?

We first learn of the coming new covenant in Jeremiah 31, a beautiful passage that speaks directly of the coming kingdom and "the restitution of all things," spoken of by all the prophets. It begins with God declaring that He will be the God of all the families of Israel, "and they shall be my people" (v. 1). Speaking through Jeremiah, God declares that He has loved Israel "with an everlasting love" (v. 3). It is that love which caused Him to draw all of His people back to the land promised to them in His covenant with Abraham.

The chapter goes on to speak of a time of overwhelming joy and celebration in Israel, with music and dancing. There will be such wonder in Jerusalem, where the King is present, that those returning from captivity in foreign lands, including some who were alienated from His commandments, will say, "Arise ye, and let us go up to Zion unto the LORD our God" (v. 6).

The chapter continues:

> For thus saith the LORD; Sing with gladness for Jacob, and shout among the chief of the nations: publish ye, praise ye, and say, O LORD, save thy people, the remnant of Israel. Behold, I will bring them from the north country, and gather them from the coasts of the earth, and with them the blind and the lame, the woman with child and her that travaileth with child together: a great company shall return thither. They shall come with weeping, and with supplications will I lead them: I will cause them to walk by the rivers of waters in a straight way, wherein they shall not stumble: for I am a father to Israel, and Ephraim is my firstborn. Hear the word of the LORD, O ye nations, and declare it in the isles afar off, and say, He that scattered Israel will gather him, and keep him, as a shepherd doth his flock. For the LORD hath redeemed Jacob, and ransomed him from the hand of him that was stronger than he. Therefore they shall come and sing in the

height of Zion, and shall flow together to the goodness of the LORD, for wheat, and for wine, and for oil, and for the young of the flock and of the herd: and their soul shall be as a watered garden; and they shall not sorrow any more at all. Then shall the virgin rejoice in the dance, both young men and old together: for I will turn their mourning into joy, and will comfort them, and make them rejoice from their sorrow. And I will satiate the soul of the priests with fatness, and my people shall be satisfied with my goodness, saith the LORD. (vv. 7–14)

These passages are among the most ecstatically cheerful in all the Bible. Why? Because they describe a time that all the prophets of old pointed to—the restitution of all things, the kingdom of God on earth, with its capital in Jerusalem. Seldom do we read words like these from the prophet Jeremiah, who is best known as "the weeping prophet," the bearer of so much bad news for Israel.

In verse 15, the celebration is momentarily broken because "a voice was heard in Ramah, lamentation, and bitter weeping; Rahel weeping for her children refused to be comforted for her children, because they were not." This verse is considered to be a prophecy foreshadowing Herod's slaughter of all male children in and around Bethlehem a few years after the birth of Jesus in an attempt to slay the future King of the Jews. But it is quickly followed with this reassurance: "Thus saith the LORD; Refrain thy voice from weeping, and thine eyes from tears: for thy work shall be rewarded, saith the LORD; and they shall come again from the land of the enemy" (v. 16).

Even the tribe of Ephraim—dispersed so long ago from the Northern Kingdom for chasing after other gods—will return. "Is Ephraim my dear son? is he a pleasant child? for since I spake against him, I do earnestly remember him still . . . I will surely have mercy upon him, saith the LORD" (v. 20).

All is forgiven. God still loves His people. He cannot even see their sin anymore, but welcomes them back to their own borders as a "virgin" bride. He calls their revived nation a "habitation of justice, and mountain of holiness" (v. 23).

Jeremiah awakened from this pleasant dream and saw a time of abundance in agriculture and livestock.

And then came the big news. And notice the announcement is relevant to the new, future kingdom, where Jesus will preside over the affairs of the entire earth from Jerusalem.

It's the news of the beginning of the new covenant:

> Behold, the days come, saith the LORD, that I will make a new covenant with the house of Israel, and with the house of Judah: Not according to the covenant that I made with their fathers in the day that I took them by the hand to bring them out of the land of Egypt; which my covenant they brake, although I was an husband unto them, saith the LORD: But this shall be the covenant that I will make with the house of Israel; after those days, saith the LORD, I will put my law in their inward parts, and write it in their hearts; and will be their God, and they shall be my people. And they shall teach no more every man his neighbour, and every man his brother, saying, Know the LORD: for they shall all know me, from the least of them unto the greatest of them, saith the LORD: for I will forgive their iniquity, and I will remember their sin no more. (Jer. 31:31–34)

First note with whom this new covenant is made: the "house of Israel" and the "house of Judah." Fortunately, as Gentile believers in Jesus, we are spiritually grafted into those houses, so it's a promise for us too.

And what's "new" about this new covenant? It's something that surely hasn't happened yet. God promises that He will put His law in our "inward parts," and "write it in [our] hearts." And there will be no need to teach our neighbors or family members how to know the Lord, because *everyone* will know the Lord.

If you believe you are already living in the new covenant, you must ask yourself:

Do I really have the law written in my heart?

Have we been able to stop teaching the Torah today
  because everyone knows the Lord?

This is a revolutionary new covenant—something we have not seen and experienced yet. It's a kingdom promise—like many more that will be revealed to you in the ensuing chapters.

I get goose bumps when I read this passage, and you, as a fellow believer in Jesus, should too.

Notice also the Lord's absolute pledge in the next three verses:

Thus saith the LORD, which giveth the sun for a light by day, and the ordinances of the moon and of the stars for a light by night, which divideth the sea when the waves thereof roar; the LORD of hosts is his name: If those ordinances depart from before me, saith the LORD, then the seed of Israel also shall cease from being a nation before me for ever. Thus saith the LORD; if heaven above can be measured, and the foundations of the earth searched out beneath, I will also cast off all the seed of Israel for all that they have done, saith the LORD.

What is He saying here?

God is telling us that His law is not dead—and it won't be dead in the coming kingdom, when it is written in our hearts. In fact, it would be more likely for Him to forsake Israel than to render His law obsolete. It's forever.

That's the new covenant.

The only bad news is, we're not there yet. It's a solemn promise for the future, though, along with the return of the Messiah.

Until then, we have much work to do.

I know Christians don't like to hear the word *work*. Their salvation is through grace, not works, they are quick to tell you. And that's true, as we discussed in chapter 4. But according to James, the brother of Jesus, faith, if it hath not works, is dead, being alone. Yea, a man may say, Thou hast faith, and I have works: shew me thy faith without thy works, and I will shew thee my faith by my works. Thou believest that there is one God; thou doest well: the devils also believe, and tremble. But wilt thou know, O vain man, that faith without works is dead? Was not Abraham our father justified by works, when he had offered Isaac his son upon the altar? Seest thou how faith wrought with his works, and by works was faith made perfect? And the scripture was fulfilled which saith, Abraham believed God, and it was imputed unto him for righteousness: and he was called the Friend of God. Ye see then how that by works a man is justified, and not by faith only. Likewise also was not Rahab the harlot justified by works, when she had received the messengers, and had sent them out another way? For as the body without the spirit is dead, so faith without works is dead also. (James 2:17–26)

So what "works" must we do?

We need to pursue righteousness—even if our pursuit is imperfect because God's law is not yet written in our hearts.

Remember: salvation is by grace, through faith, but salvation is not the endgame. It's only the beginning. With salvation comes responsibility, accountability, and an ongoing spirit of repentance.

This is not a message much of today's church wants to hear. But it's a message it needs to hear.

This is the message of Paul, too, in Hebrews 8, where he repeats Jeremiah 31:31 almost word for word:

For finding fault with [the first covenant], he saith, Behold, the days come, saith the Lord, when I will make a new covenant with the house of Israel and with the house of Judah: Not according to the covenant that I made with their fathers in the day when I took them by the hand to lead them out of the land of Egypt; because they continued not in my covenant, and I regarded them not, saith the Lord. For this is the covenant that I will make with the house of Israel after those days, saith the Lord; I will put my laws into their mind, and write them in their hearts: and I will be to them a God, and they shall be to me a people: And they shall not teach every man his neighbour, and every man his brother, saying, Know the Lord: for all shall know me, from the least to the greatest. For I will be merciful to their unrighteousness, and their sins and their iniquities will I remember no more. In that he saith, A new covenant, he hath made the first old. Now that which decayeth and waxeth old is ready to vanish away. (vv. 8–13)

Notice that Paul agreed that the new covenant had not yet come. Instead, he looked forward to its coming because it spells redemption for His beloved Israel and a new day for the entire world.

It's important for Christians to understand this not our world today. Jesus is not yet reigning over the world from Jerusalem. The lamb has not yet lain down with the wolf (see Isa. 11:6). Satan is not yet bound. We live in a world of preparation for that kingdom and that new covenant. And the temptations we face today are very real. Without donning spiritual armor, we are no match for the challenges we face.

In fact, I would make the case that the church is not providing the kind of salt and light in the world that it is charged with offering. Not only is our world more Godless and lawless than perhaps ever before, but the church isn't much better. As believers, we're charged with being *in* the world but not *of* it (see Rom. 12:2). In reality, many believers are very much "*of* the world" (see John 17:6). We're not prepared to contend with our culture, to challenge it, and to be beacons of truth. Unfortunately, we're disengaged in the most tumultuous time in history, with the kingdom so near.

How many of us are truly living for God with all our hearts, minds, and souls? Are we *really* prepared for spiritual combat—or, like the ancient children of Israel, are we whoring after other gods?

Does that sound harsh? Sorry, but God calls us to be a holy people:

Follow peace with all men, and holiness, without which no man shall see the Lord. (Heb. 12:14)

But as he which hath called you is holy, so be ye holy in all manner of conversation; because it is written, Be ye holy; for I am holy. (1 Peter 1:15–16)

But ye are a chosen generation, a royal priesthood, an holy nation, a peculiar people; that ye should shew forth the praises of him who hath called you out of darkness into his marvellous light. (1 Peter 2:9)

We can be a holy people only if we obey God's commandments. If we believe they are null and void, we cannot even attempt to please God in our holiness. *Holy* implies being "set apart." Are we setting ourselves apart from nonbelievers? Can your neighbor distinguish you from a nonbeliever? If not, then maybe you're not so "peculiar" after all.

Let's look at what the Bible tells us about this pattern of straying from holiness. In Exodus 34, Moses intervenes with God to forgive the sins of his people, saying, "If now I have found grace in thy sight, O Lord, let my Lord, I pray thee, go among us; for it is a stiffnecked people; and pardon our iniquity and our sin, and take us for thine inheritance" (v. 9).

So, God made a covenant: "Before all thy people I will do marvels, such as have not been done in all the earth, nor in any nation: and all the people among which thou art shall see the work of the Lord: for it is a terrible thing that I will do with thee" (v. 10). *But* it came with a condition:

Observe thou that which I command thee this day: . . . Take heed to thyself, lest thou make a covenant with the inhabitants of the land whither thou goest, lest it be for a snare in the midst of thee: But ye shall destroy their altars, break their images, and cut down their groves: For thou shalt worship no other god: for the Lord, whose name is Jealous, is a jealous God: Lest thou make a covenant with the inhabitants of the land, and they go a whoring after their gods, and do sacrifice unto their gods, and one call thee, and thou eat of his sacrifice; And thou take of their daughters unto thy sons, and their daughters go a whoring after their gods, and make thy sons go a whoring after their gods. (vv. 11–16)

What happened? God kept His commitment, but the children of Israel did not destroy the altars, break the images, or cut down the groves. They did not set themselves apart. Instead, they went "whoring" after other gods.

In Numbers 15, God commanded Moses:

Speak unto the children of Israel, and bid them that they make them fringes in the borders of their garments throughout their generations, and that they put upon the fringe of the borders a ribband of blue: And it shall be unto you for a fringe, that ye may look upon it, and remember all the commandments of the LORD, and *do them*; and that ye seek not after your own heart and your own eyes, after which ye use to go a whoring: that ye may remember, and do all my commandments, and be holy unto your God. (vv. 38–40, emphasis added)

In other words, they were to be "set apart." What do *we* do as God's people to set us apart and to remind ourselves to do all of His commandments? Or, do we pretend those commandments do not apply to us anymore? If so, how *do* we aspire to holiness?

In Judges, we learn that in the generation following Joshua, the people once again turned away from obeying God's commandments: "And yet they would not hearken unto their judges, but they went a whoring after other gods, and bowed themselves unto them: they turned quickly out of the way which their fathers walked in, obeying the commandments of the LORD; but they did not so" (2:17).

What are we doing as believers today to ensure that our children are also set apart? Do we send them to public schools, where they are forced to use restrooms with the opposite sex and are taught that they are nothing more than the products of millions of years of evolution and that the worst sin they can commit is to leave a large carbon footprint?

Or are we seeking holiness through obedience?

You have likely read about the heroics of Gideon through his obedience to God. Yet, in Judges 8, we learn that "as soon as Gideon was dead," the "children of Israel turned again, and went a whoring after Baalim, and made Baalberith their god. And the children of Israel remembered not the LORD their God, who had delivered them out of the hands of all their enemies on every side: Neither shewed they kindness to the house of Jerubbaal, namely, Gideon, according to all the goodness which he had shewed unto Israel" (vv. 33–35).

Over and over again, we see the same pattern. In 1 Chronicles 5, immediately after winning a war against the their enemies the Hagarites, God's people "transgressed" against Him and "went a whoring after the gods of the people of the land, whom God destroyed before them" (v. 25).

Psalm 106 tells the same story:

They did not destroy the nations, concerning whom the LORD commanded them: but were mingled among the heathen, and learned their works. And they served their idols: which were a snare unto them. *Yea, they sacrificed their sons and their daughters unto devils, and shed innocent blood, even the blood of their sons and of their daughters, whom they sacrificed unto the idols of Canaan: and the land was polluted with blood.* Thus were they defiled with their own works, and went a whoring with their own inventions. Therefore was the wrath of the LORD kindled against his people, insomuch that he abhorred his own inheritance. And he gave them into the hand of the heathen; and they that hated them ruled over them. Their enemies also oppressed them, and they were brought into subjection under their hand. Many times did he deliver them; but they provoked him with their counsel, and were brought low for their iniquity. (vv. 34–43, emphasis added)

For the LORD will have mercy on Jacob, and will yet choose Israel, and set them in their own land —ISAIAH 14:1

I find it both disturbing and perplexing when I meet Christians who suggest that Israel has no significance or connection to their faith. If that's true, then they don't really understand their own faith, or at least don't know where it's grounded.

Let's examine the biblical case for the Jews' return to their homeland, which is not only predicted in the Bible; it is mandated. Without the following fulfilled prophecies, the Christian faith itself is neutered:

> For the LORD will have mercy on Jacob, and will yet choose Israel, and set them in their own land: and the strangers shall be joined with them, and they shall cleave to the house of Jacob. . . . and the house of Israel shall possess them in the land of the LORD for servants and handmaids. (Isa. 14:1–2)

> As a shepherd seeketh out his flock in the day that he is among his sheep that are scattered; so will I seek out my sheep, and will deliver them out of all places where they have been scattered in the cloudy and dark day. And I will . . . bring them to their own land, and feed them upon the mountains of Israel by the rivers, and in all the inhabited places of the country. (Eze. 34:12–13)

> For the children of Israel shall abide many days without a king. . . . Afterward shall the children of Israel return, and seek the LORD their God, and David their king; and shall fear the LORD and his goodness in the latter days. (Hos. 3:4–5)

> And I will bring again the captivity of my people of Israel, and they shall build the waste cities, and inhabit them. . . . And I will plant them upon their land, and they shall no more be pulled up out of their land which I have given them, saith the LORD thy God. (Amos 9:14–15)

But upon mount Zion shall be deliverance, and there shall be holiness; and the house of Jacob shall possess their possessions. (Obad. 1:17)

Behold, at that time I will undo all that afflict thee: and I will save her that halteth, and gather her that was driven out. . . . At that time will I bring you again, even in the time that I gather you. (Zeph. 3:19–20)

Thus saith the LORD of hosts; Behold, I will save my people from the east country, and from the west country; And I will bring them, and they shall dwell in the midst of Jerusalem: and they shall be my people, and I will be their God, in truth and in righteousness. (Zech. 8:7–8)

Our salvation comes through the promises to the Jews. Remember: When Jesus returns, it will be to Israel (Zech. 14:4). What's more, *all* of Israel will be saved (Rom. 11:26).

What we see today in the state of Israel is another necessary fulfill-ment—a spectacular one, indeed—for the return of the Messiah. What we see in Jesus is the personal fulfillment of all that the prophets foretold regarding salvation—what Peter called "the restitution of all things."

Are there lessons here for us today? Should we not be learning from ancient Israel, setting our sights higher than they did? Or, do we, too, think that we can live like heathen and still be blessed by God? Are we also "sacrificing" our children, and in far greater numbers than did those punished by God in Israel?

Clearly, we're not yet living in the new covenant. The Holy Torah commandments are not yet written in our hearts. So we have to use our heads. We need to learn from the experience of the children of Israel so as not to repeat their errors, going whoring after other gods, and defiling ourselves with our own "inventions."

Allow me to unpack this a little more precisely: If we don't understand something as important to the Christian faith as the new covenant—what it means, who it's for, how we benefit from it, and when and where it takes effect—we could be making other big mistakes too about our place in God's coming kingdom.

Look at this passage from Jeremiah:

O Lord, my strength, and my fortress, and my refuge in the day of affliction, the Gentiles shall come unto thee from the ends of the earth, and shall say, *Surely our fathers have inherited lies, vanity, and things wherein there is no profit* (Jer. 16:19)

Who had inherited lies? The Gentiles. They were deceived. These Gentiles, some of whom probably thought of themselves as followers of God, were guilty of the *same* sins as were God's chosen people who had too often done what was wise in their *own* eyes, adding to God's laws and misinterpreting His word.

The same is happening today. As a result, the church has played a disgraceful role in creating deceptive doctrines such as replacement theology—leading many Gentile believers to actually persecute God's chosen people.

This verse from Jeremiah is one for Christians to study and pray about. Might it also apply to those who embrace replacement theology, who think they are living in new covenant times prematurely, and who boast about their place in God's economy? Is it possible, this time, that *we* are the ones who have "inherited lies"?

I think this is a verse for Christians to study and pray about. Is it possible, this time, that *we* are the ones who "inherited lies"?

I can speak only for myself, but as someone born into a nominal Christian faith who grew into one that was serious, committed, even zealous: yes, I inherited lies.

Have you?

8

WHAT IS THE GREATEST MIRACLE IN HISTORY?

Therefore, behold, the days come, saith the Lord, that it shall no more be said, The Lord liveth, that brought up the children of Israel out of the land of Egypt; But, The Lord liveth, that brought up the children of Israel from the land of the north, and from all the lands whither he had driven them: and I will bring them again into their land that I gave unto their fathers.
—JEREMIAH 16:14–15

I'VE ALWAYS BEEN A BIG FAN of Mark Twain, and the two of us have some things in common—besides being writers.

In 1866, when he was still known by his given name of Samuel L. Clemens, Mark Twain got his first big professional writing break when the owners of the *Sacramento Union*, which Twain described as "a great and influential daily journal," sent him to Hawaii to write four articles a month for twenty dollars apiece.

Those articles are credited with turning Twain into a journalistic star, so much so that when he returned to California, he found himself to be "about the best known man on the Pacific Coast."

One hundred twenty-four years later, I was hired as the editor in chief of the *Sacramento Union*, which was then the oldest daily west of the Mississippi. When I first walked into the lobby of the paper, I was greeted by a massive bronze bust of Twain with an inscription that recounted the story in his own words.

I spent only two years running the paper, but virtually every *Sacramento Union* history, long or short, mentions two people prominently: Twain and me.

We both became well-known because of our work there—he for his dispatches from Hawaii, or the Sandwich Islands, as they were called back then, and me for attempting to rejuvenate a failing newspaper in the capital of the largest state with a strong Judeo-Christian worldview.

But a year after Twain got his job at the *Sacramento Union*, he did something remarkable. He literally fulfilled a Bible prophecy on a visit to the Holy Land.

In his book *The Innocents Abroad*, Twain wrote that he found Israel to be "a desolate country whose soil is rich enough, but is given over wholly to weeds . . . a silent mournful expanse . . . a desolation. . . . We never saw a human being on the whole route . . . hardly a tree or shrub anywhere. Even the olive tree and the cactus, those fast friends of a worthless soil, had almost deserted the country.

"No landscape exists that is more tiresome to the eye than that which bounds the approaches to Jerusalem," he added. "Jerusalem is mournful, dreary, and lifeless. Palestine sits in sackcloth and ashes."[1]

I doubt very much if Twain knew that penning those words was a fulfillment of Bible prophecy, but it was indeed.

The prophecy is found in Deuteronomy 29:

The generation to come of your children that shall rise up after you, and the stranger that shall come from a far land, shall say, when they see the plagues of that land, and the sicknesses which the LORD hath laid upon it; and that the whole land thereof is brimstone, and salt, and burning, that it is not sown, nor beareth, nor any grass groweth therein, like the overthrow of Sodom, and Gomorrah, Admah, and Zeboim, which the Lord overthrew in his anger, and in his wrath: Even all nations shall say, Wherefore hath the Lord done thus unto this land? what meaneth the heat of this great anger? Then men shall say, Because they have forsaken the covenant of the Lord GOD of their fathers, which he made with them when he brought them forth out of the land of Egypt: For they went and served other gods, and worshipped them, gods whom they knew not, and whom he had not given unto them: and the anger of the LORD was kindled against this land, to bring upon it all the curses that are written in this book: and the LORD rooted them out of their land in anger, and in wrath, and in great indignation, and cast them into another land, as it is this day. The secret things belong unto the LORD our God: but those things which are revealed belong unto us and to our children for ever, that we may do all the words of this law. (vv. 22–29)

In 1866, Mark Twain saw what had become of the Holy Land—Israel and Judah—eighteen hundred years after His chosen people were, for the most part, cast into exile for the last time because of disobedience and rebellion, just as predicted in Deuteronomy 29. But Deuteronomy also foresaw that a stranger would come from a far land and record what he saw—sharing it with all the nations. Mark Twain did just that.

As for me, I've been going to the Holy Land frequently, first as a correspondent like Twain, and more recently taking large groups of Americans so they can see what has transpired within the nation-state of Israel since it was reborn in 1948—in a day, just as the Bible prophesied: "Who hath heard such a thing? who hath seen such things? Shall the earth be made to bring forth in one day? or shall a nation be born at once? for as soon as Zion travailed, she brought forth her children" (Isa. 66:8).

Israel is no longer that barren wasteland depicted by Twain in 1866. Indeed, it has become almost a cliché to say the reborn nation has made the deserts bloom again, just as prophesied in Isaiah 35:1: "The wilderness and the solitary place shall be glad for them; and the desert shall rejoice, and blossom as the rose."

Likewise, that land that had trouble growing even weeds in Twain's time is now fulfilling another prophecy from Isaiah: "He shall cause them that come of Jacob to take root: Israel shall blossom and bud, and fill the face of the world with fruit" (27:6).

It's true. Israel is exporting fruit, vegetables, and flowers to the entire world today.

These are all great miracles surrounding Israel, but what's the greatest miracle the world has ever witnessed?

It's happening today before our very eyes—if only the world would see.

We can't see what God did for the children of Israel during the Exodus. We can watch movies about it. We can read about it. We can listen to sermons about it. But we can't see it. But in the Torah we see God identifying Himself over and over again as the one who brought the children of Israel out of the land of Egypt. So mighty was the miracle at the Red Sea that this new identity actually became one of the oft-used names of God. Check out the following verses (italics have been added for emphasis):

> And they shall know that I am *the LORD their God, that brought them forth out of the land of Egypt,* that I may dwell among them: I am the Lord their God. (Ex. 29:46)

> For I am *the Lord that bringeth you up out of the land of Egypt,* to be your God: ye shall therefore be holy, for I am holy. (Lev. 11:45)

I am *the LORD thy God, which brought thee out of the land of Egypt*, from the house of bondage. (Deuteronomy 5:6)

I am *the LORD your God, which brought you out of the land of Egypt*, to be your God: I am the LORD your God. (Num. 15:41)

(See also Lev. 19:36; 22:32–33; 25:38; 26:13.)

It's remarkable how many times God reminded the children of Israel of this miracle. Search it out for yourself sometime. You can read about it in Judges, the books of Samuel, the Psalms, and so on.

Then, all of a sudden, we see an amazing prophecy in Jeremiah 16 that is currently—right now—being fulfilled before our eyes in *this generation*: "Therefore, behold, the days come, saith the LORD, that it shall no more be said, The LORD liveth, that brought up the children of Israel out of the land of Egypt; But, The LORD liveth, that brought up the children of Israel from the land of the north, and from all the lands whither he had driven them: and I will bring them again into their land that I gave unto their fathers" (vv. 14–15). In other words, we see here that the regathering of Israel in the twentieth and twenty-first centuries was a miracle that was to *overshadow the Exodus*. It was bigger and more surprising and more supernatural than the plagues of Egypt, the parting of the Red Sea, the forty years in the wilderness, the pillars of fire, and the victorious entry into the promised land after four hundred years in bondage and oppression.

This is a miracle we are still seeing today—the very existence of the nation of Israel, regathered as no other nation in history from the four corners of the earth to their land after nineteen hundred years.

We also see other prophecies being fulfilled regarding this state. We see Israel surrounded by neighboring states who hate it. We see Jerusalem becoming that burdensome stone (see Zech. 12:3)—the focal point of the entire world's concerns. And we see it surviving miraculously against all human odds.

And still His people doubt.

Jews have been waiting for their Messiah for four thousand years. Some have wrongly assumed that the state of Israel itself is their Messiah. But according to polls, a majority of American Jews don't believe God promised them a land of their own and made good on that promise in the Year of Our Lord 1948. Yet, if seeing is believing, no one alive today on this planet is without excuse.

It should be like witnessing the Red Sea parting. Yet, God Himself says what we are seeing today is evidence of a greater miracle.

As an Arab-American worshipper of Yeshua Ha-Messiach, Jesus the Messiah, who has been mercifully grafted into the promise of redemption and salvation through the line of Abraham, Isaac, and Jacob—I'm very thankful for the opportunity to see these things. To me it is striking evidence that we are on the cusp of seeing the restitution of all things. Even though I live in the real world, among a vast many skeptics and scoffers, I'm not embarrassed to say it.

I look at the evidence and see only one nation in world history that ceased to exist for nearly two thousand years and then came back from the dead—from dry bones, just as it was prophesied in Ezekiel 37. Nations have come and gone, but none except Israel came, went, and came back again, fulfilling the predictions of the Hebrew prophets to a tee.

That Israel defied all odds in being born again after more than nineteen centuries and defended itself successfully for decades against enemies that outnumber Israeli Jews more than a hundred to one is a fact. It's a historical reality no one can deny. It's one of the best evidences that the God of the patriarchs is real and that He lives up to His promises.

Honestly, more than anything else, it's the reality that brought me to my knees in repentance so many years ago and brought me to salvation. It is also what keeps me going back to Israel year after year, to walk in the land that is so precious and meaningful to the Creator, a nation from which He will soon preside over the whole world as King of kings.

I'm very thankful about the nearness of the restitution of all things. It's what gives me hope to get through every tough day. But, if I read my Bible correctly, it's going to be a bumpy road before that day arrives. And from my perspective as a newsman, it's been getting bumpier by the minute as people everywhere seem to be moving further from God's instructions about how we are to live our lives.

Do you feel it?

But, as most books about prophecy dwell on what's coming in the short term, the bumps in the road, this book is focused on the finish line.

One of the things I love about what the Bible tells us about the restitution of all things is that it is great news for everyone in the world—and especially the people of the Middle East. We hear a lot in the news about peace plans for the Middle East. There have been many failed attempts to create one. With all of the violence and terror and hatred we see in the world, and so much of it emanating from the Middle East, it often seems hopeless.

But God has a peace plan. He tells us about it through His prophets. So let's explore God's Mideast Peace Plan, which is strikingly different from Oslo, Camp David, United Nations efforts, Madrid, Taba, the Roadmap, Geneva, and Annapolis.

Now, many Bible students often overlook the promises to the other, non-Jewish peoples of the Middle East—the Arabs, the "brothers from another mother," if you will—promises that begin way back in Genesis, in the tents of Abraham, involving his first son, Ishmael:

> And Abraham said unto God, O that Ishmael might live before thee! And God said, Sarah thy wife shall bear thee a son indeed; and thou shalt call his name Isaac: and I will establish my covenant with him for an everlasting covenant, and with his seed after him. And as for Ishmael, I have heard thee: Behold, I have blessed him, and will make him fruitful, and will multiply him exceedingly; twelve princes shall he beget, and I will make him a great nation. (Gen. 17:18–20)

For you are a holy people to the LORD your God; the LORD your God has chosen you to be a people for His own possession.
—DEUTERONOMY 7:6

While Mark Twain wasn't noted to be a strong Christian believer, he did have a deep appreciation for the plight of the Jews, perhaps sparking his interest in visiting the Holy Land. In 1898 he penned an article for *Harper's* magazine titled "Concerning the Jews."* It ended like this:

> If the statistics are right, the Jews constitute but one per cent of the human race. It suggests a nebulous dim puff of star-dust lost in the blaze of the Milky Way. Properly the Jew ought hardly to be heard of; but he is heard of, has always been heard of. He is as prominent on the planet as any other people, and his commercial importance is extravagantly out of proportion to the smallness of his bulk. His contributions to the world's list of great names in literature, science, art, music, finance, medicine, and abstruse learning are also away out of proportion to the weakness of his numbers.
>
> He has made a marvellous fight in this world, in all the ages; and has done it with his hands tied behind him. He could be vain of himself, and be excused for it. The Egyptian, the Babylonian, and the Persian rose, filled the planet with sound and splendor, then faded to dream-stuff and passed away; the Greek and the Roman followed, and made a vast noise, and they are gone; other peoples have sprung up and held their torch high for a time, but it burned out, and they sit in twilight now, or have vanished.
>
> The Jew saw them all, beat them all, and is now what he always was, exhibiting no decadence, no infirmities of age, no weakening of his parts, no slowing of his energies, no dulling of his alert and aggressive mind. All things are mortal but the Jew; all other forces pass, but he remains. What is the secret of his immortality?*

Every believer needs to know the answer to that question: indeed, the Jews are God's chosen people, unto whom "were committed the oracles of God" (Rom. 3:2).

They are the people now being regathered in their homeland after nineteen hundred years, and they are about to say collectively, "Blessed is He that cometh in the name of the Lord."

> That then the Lord thy God will turn thy captivity, and have compassion upon thee, and will return and gather thee from all the nations, whither the Lord thy God hath scattered thee. If any of thine be driven out unto the outmost parts of heaven, from thence will the Lord thy God gather thee, and from thence will he fetch thee: And the Lord thy God will bring thee into the land which thy fathers possessed, and thou shalt possess it; and he will do thee good, and multiply thee above thy fathers. . . . And thou shalt return and obey the voice of the Lord, and do all his commandments which I command thee this day. (Deut. 30:3-5, 8)

* Mark Twain, "Concerning the Jews," Harper's Magazine, March 1898, https://legacy.fordham.edu/halsall/mod/1898twain-jews.asp

Abraham greatly loved his son Ishmael. For Abraham's sake, God made a promise for this first son, born to Hagar. What was that promise? To make him a great nation.

What nation was that? What was the great nation that would come out of Ishmael? For many years, when I read that promise, I was confused and puzzled by that question. No doubt, nations have been founded by the sons of Ishmael that were great in the sense of being *terrible*. But is that what God meant? Or is there more meaning in that term *great*? Is there yet a promise to Abraham yet to be fulfilled?

The promise is repeated in Genesis 21, this time to Hagar the Egyptian, Ishmael's mother. You know the story: Isaac is weaned. Abraham has a feast. But Ishmael mocks his younger brother, Isaac. And Hagar and Ishmael are cast out. Soon, Hagar finds herself in the wilderness, about to perish, with Ishmael.

> And God heard the voice of the lad; and the angel of God called to Hagar out of heaven, and said unto her, What aileth thee, Hagar? fear not; for God hath heard the voice of the lad where he is.
>
> Arise, lift up the lad, and hold him in thine hand; for I will make him a great nation. (vv. 17–18)

You know the rest. But *what* nation did God promise to Ishmael? Read a little farther:

> And God opened her eyes, and she saw a well of water; and she went, and filled the bottle with water, and gave the lad drink. And God was with the lad; and he grew, and dwelt in the wilderness, and became an archer. And he dwelt in the wilderness of Paran: and his mother took him a wife out of the land of Egypt. (vv. 19–21)

I believe there are clues here—and throughout Scripture—that link Ishmael's promise with the restitution of all things.

Where is the wilderness of Paran? It must be pretty close to

Egypt. Some say it's in Sinai. Others say it's in the Judean desert. Islamic legend says it's Mecca, but I think we can discount that. Hagar was an Egyptian. Ishmael's wife was from Egypt. I'm pretty sure Hagar, after being cast out of Abraham's tent, was on her way back to Egypt. There's a definite Egypt connection here.

What do we learn next about Ishmael? First, we know that he reunited with Isaac at the death of Abraham: "Then Abraham gave up the ghost, and died in a good old age, an old man, and full of years; and was gathered to his people. And his sons Isaac and Ishmael buried him [in Hebron] in the cave of Machpelah, in the field of Ephron the son of Zohar the Hittite, which is before Mamre" (Gen. 25:8–9). We also learn that he died where his people lived—the twelve tribes: "And these are the years of the life of Ishmael, an hundred and thirty and seven years: and he gave up the ghost and died; and was gathered unto his people. And they dwelt from Havilah unto Shur, that is before Egypt, as thou goest toward Assyria: and he died in the presence of all his brethren" (Gen. 25:17–18).

Where are Havilah and Shur?

No one is sure about Havilah, but the consensus is that it is a vast region that encompasses much of the Arabian Peninsula, including Assyria. As for Shur, we find in 1 Samuel that it is "east of Egypt" (15:7). This is where Hagar was heading when she fled from Abraham and Sarai—toward Egypt, her homeland (Gen. 16:7).

So it's reasonable to surmise that the twelve tribes of Ishmael, at the time of his death, were spread out from Egypt to Assyria and possibly south through Arabia—all within reasonable traveling distance to Israel.

Keep that in mind as we explore God's Mideast Peace Plan, which, I believe, ties into God's promised blessing on Ishmael. The outline for this plan is found in Isaiah 19: "The burden of Egypt. Behold, the LORD rideth upon a swift cloud, and shall come into Egypt: and the idols of Egypt shall be moved at his presence, and the heart of Egypt shall melt in the midst of it" (v. 1).

This verse tells us something most believers rarely consider. That

Jesus, when He returns, is not just coming to the Mount of Olives. He's got other business elsewhere. I believe the first verse unequivocally tells us Messiah is actually going to visit Egypt, bringing both judgment and salvation.

It's amazing when you read the prophecies about Jesus' return that He actually personally inflicts judgment on other nations. We know, for instance, from Isaiah that He is going to visit Edom and Bozrah and bring judgment on them:

> Who is this that cometh from Edom, with dyed garments from Bozrah? this that is glorious in his apparel, travelling in the greatness of his strength? I that speak in righteousness, mighty to save. Wherefore art thou red in thine apparel, and thy garments like him that treadeth in the winefat? I have trodden the winepress alone; and of the people there was none with me: for I will tread them in mine anger, and trample them in my fury; and their blood shall be sprinkled upon my garments, and I will stain all my raiment. For the day of vengeance is in mine heart, and the year of my redeemed is come. (Isa. 63:1–4)

It may be hard for some Christians to envision Jesus in this role of conquering King. Remember how difficult it was for the Pharisees to envision Him as their Messiah because He first came as a suffering servant. The expectations of that generation was for a conqueror, someone who would free Israel from foreign occupation. The expectations of many Christians in this generation is for Jesus to look and act as He did back then. That's the trouble with man's traditions, but Scripture is clear.

Where are Edom and Bozrah? They are southeast of Israel. Edom, whose capital city was Bozrah, would correlate with the nations of Jordan and at least part of Saudi Arabia today. There's going to be a judgment of the Lord there. And Isaiah tells us the Lord himself— alone—will bring it about.

Likewise, Jesus is going to ride a swift cloud to Egypt upon His return. Here's what will happen:

And I will set the Egyptians against the Egyptians: and they shall fight every one against his brother, and every one against his neighbour; city against city, and kingdom against kingdom. And the spirit of Egypt shall fail in the midst thereof; and I will destroy the counsel thereof: and they shall seek to the idols, and to the charmers, and to them that have familiar spirits, and to the wizards. And the Egyptians will I give over into the hand of a cruel lord; and a fierce king shall rule over them, saith the Lord, the LORD of hosts. (Isa. 19:2–4)

A civil war is coming in Egypt, and the land will succumb to a cruel king. It's not hard to imagine that scenario today. Egypt has already been racked by infighting. There have been several major power changes since Hosni Mubarak ruled the country. Thanks in large part to the machinations of Barack Obama, Mubarak was replaced briefly by Muslim Brotherhood leader Mohammed Morsi. But, coinciding with some of the largest protests and demonstrations in history, he was replaced through a military coup by President Abdel Fattah al-Sisi.

What's the first thing that comes to mind when you think of Egypt? Probably the Pyramids. So what's the second thing that comes to mind? Undoubtedly, the Nile.

The Nile is the longest river in the world. It has been the story of Egypt's civilization throughout time. As its only major water source, the Nile is also the source of life there, as well as the source of prosperity, the lifeline of the economy. It defines Egypt. Egypt was the breadbasket for the Middle East because of the Nile. And what comes next in Isaiah deals specifically with this river. Pay close attention, because remarkably, something is happening in the Nile region right now—today—that seems surely to be a precursor to fulfilled prophecy:

And the waters shall fail from the sea, and the river shall be wasted and dried up. And they shall turn the rivers far away; and the brooks of defence shall be emptied and dried up: the reeds and flags shall wither. The paper reeds by the brooks, by the mouth of the brooks, and every thing sown by the brooks, shall wither, be driven away, and be no more. The fishers also shall mourn, and all they that cast angle into the brooks shall lament, and they that spread nets upon the waters shall languish. Moreover they that work in fine flax, and they that weave networks, shall be confounded. And they shall be broken in the purposes thereof, all that make sluices and ponds for fish. (Isa. 19:5–10)

What is going on here? The Nile, the source of all water in Egypt, dries up? Impossible! Is this simply an act of God that occurs in the future? Possibly, but new developments in the region now have much of Egypt fearing such an eventuality—and they appear to be the result of man's work, perhaps under God's direction and timing.

With all that has been going on in Egypt in the last several years, the biggest single news story, the preoccupation of the Egyptian people—including Mubarak, Morsi, and al-Sisi—is something most Americans have never heard about. It's a large regional dam project upstream that many Egyptians fear could bring their Nile to a trickle, causing environmental devastation. Egyptian leaders have even threatened to use military action to stop it.

The Grand Ethiopia Renaissance Dam, or GERD for short, will divert an unknown amount of water from the Egyptian Nile after it is finished late in 2017, thus stoking fears of national survival. In 2012, Wikileaks obtained a document revealing Egyptian plans to build an airstrip that would allow its air force to bomb the massive project. In 2013, before he was deposed, Morsi said "all options," including military intervention, were on the table if Ethiopia continued to build the dam on the Blue Nile that feeds Egypt's great river.[2]

Since then, the threat to the Nile, which provides more than 90 percent of Egypt's fresh water, has created near hysteria within Egypt. Why? Because according to strategic analyst Ahmed Abdel Halin, "Egypt sees its Nile water share as a matter of national security."[3]

Richard Tutwiler, a specialist in water resource management at the

American University in Cairo, summed up Egypt's problem: "Egypt is totally dependent on the Nile. Without it, there is no Egypt."[4]

A study by Sameh Kantoush, a professor at Japan's Kyoto University who specializes in dams and water resources, warns of the potential for a number of bleak scenarios involving environmental deterioration or even a collapse that would prove catastrophic for Egypt.[5]

Mohamed Nasr El Din, Egypt's minister of water and irrigation, said of the dam: "It would lead to political, economic and social instability. Millions of people would go hungry. There would be water shortages everywhere. It's huge."[6]

Now think about this:

The Nile River is 4,132 miles long. It flows through Tanzania, Burundi, Rwanda, the Congo, Kenya, Uganda, Sudan, Ethiopia, and into Egypt. The Greek historian Herodotus called this river "the gift of the Nile," because civilization in Egypt depended on its resources. Tutwiler was right: without the Nile there would be no Egypt. To the east and west is desert.

The waters of the Nile have served as the means whereby civilizations have gathered along its banks—even to the days before the pharaohs of Egypt. The natural flow of the Nile is from south to north. Thus, the waters that eventually make their way to Egypt must first pass through southeastern Africa before emptying in the Mediterranean Sea.

Historically, in the spring, the snow on the mountains of East Africa melted, sending a torrent of water that overflowed the banks of the Nile and flooded the river valley. The rushing river picked up bits of soil and plant life, called *silt*. As the annual flood receded, a strip of black soil emerged every year along the banks of the Nile. The silt was rich in nutrients, and it provided the Egyptians with two or three crops every year. This made the Nile Valley ideal for farming since ancient times.

But that's not as true today. Egypt already had water problems before construction on the Ethiopian Grand Renaissance Dam ever began. Bear with me, because this history is important when considering the existential threat posed to Egypt.

In 1970 the Egyptians constructed the Aswan Dam in southern Egypt to provide water for irrigation, to generate electricity, and to control the floodwaters of the Nile. The original Aswan Dam was an embankment dam situated across the Nile River in Aswan, first built by the British in 1902. In the 1960s, Gamal Abdel Nasser began building the high dam. It was a key objective of the socialist Egyptian government following the Egyptian Revolution of 1952. Nasser sought to control flooding, provide water for irrigation, and generate hydroelectricity that would industrialize Egypt.

Nasser's dream was to transform the old-fashioned agricultural economy of Egypt into a modern industrial society. It required electricity—thus the power plant at the dam. It would also require moving people into cities and wiping out the old ways of raising crops that depended on the regular overflow of the banks of the Nile. In fact, 120,000 people, mostly Nubians, were forcibly relocated to build the dam and Lake Nasser, the reservoir into which the Nile flows.

As a result, no longer does the Nile overflow its banks the way it did annually before then. The Aswan Dam controls the flow of water, and no longer are the fertile areas along the Nile the source of natural nutrients flowing out of Africa. All that silt has been accumulating in the Aswan Dam since 1970. And it's filling up with silt and already choking the flow of water into Egypt through the Nile. Some 40 million tons of silt were deposited annually on the banks of the Nile during flooding. Those tons of silt now accumulate every year in Lake Nasser and at the dam, diminishing both the capacity of the lake and the flow of water through the dam.

In other words, Egypt already has a big water problem. And the man most responsible for that water crisis was Gamal Abdel Nasser, the longtime president and Israel-hater, the predecessor to Anwar Sadat.

This water problem has already greatly diminished Egypt's fishing industry because the water no longer carries those natural nutrients it picked up in Africa along the way. And as Egyptians have figured out, it could get a lot worse with the building of the dam in Ethiopia.

Back to how all of this might relate to what the Bible says: There's more about this Nile prophecy in Ezekiel 29. And it has a lot of relevance to Egypt's motivations for building the Aswan Dam:

> Son of man, set thy face against Pharaoh king of Egypt, and prophesy against him, and against all Egypt: Speak, and say, Thus saith the Lord GOD; Behold, I am against thee, Pharaoh king of Egypt, the great dragon that lieth in the midst of his rivers, which hath said, My river is mine own, and I have made it for myself. But I will put hooks in thy jaws, and I will cause the fish of thy rivers to stick unto thy scales, and I will bring thee up out of the midst of thy rivers, and all the fish of thy rivers shall stick unto thy scales. And I will leave thee thrown into the wilderness, thee and all the fish of thy rivers: thou shalt fall upon the open fields; thou shalt not be brought together, nor gathered: I have given thee for meat to the beasts of the field and to the fowls of the heaven. (Eze. 29:2–5)

Isn't it interesting that Egypt is going to be judged for its pride, saying, "My river is mine own, and I have made it for myself"? That is what Egypt said when it built its own high dam at Aswan. That is what it is still saying today as it does battle with Ethiopia over this new dam. Keep that in mind.

The chapter continues, "And the land of Egypt shall be desolate and waste; and they shall know that I am the LORD: because he hath said, The river is mine, and I have made it. Behold, therefore I am against thee, and against thy rivers, and I will make the land of Egypt utterly waste and desolate, from the tower of Syene even unto the border of Ethiopia" (vv. 9–10).

Modern-day Ethiopia, where they are building the dam that threatens Egypt, is not necessarily the same as biblical Ethiopia. Most scholars believe it is Sudan, just to the south of Egypt. Nevertheless, it is certainly interesting that Egypt and Ethiopia are linked in this passage. Of course, no matter which land is called Ethiopia historically, God certainly knew which country would be called Ethiopia at the time of this cataclysm.

So what is "Syene"? That is much more clear. Syene is Aswan. It's still called that today. It's used interchangeably with Aswan. It would seem something is going to happen in Aswan that lays Egypt desolate and waste. And it has to do with a water catastrophe for Egypt. By the way, there are towers at Syene today—monuments celebrating the construction of the Aswan Dam. Now look at these prophetic words:

> And the sword shall come upon Egypt, and great pain shall be in Ethiopia, when the slain shall fall in Egypt, and they shall take away her multitude, and her foundations shall be broken down. Ethiopia, and Libya, and Lydia, and all the mingled people, and Chub, and the men of the land that is in league, shall fall with them by the sword. Thus saith the LORD; They also that uphold Egypt shall fall; and the pride of her power shall come down: from the tower of Syene shall they fall in it by the sword, saith the Lord GOD. And they shall be desolate in the midst of the countries that are desolate, and her cities shall be in the midst of the cities that are wasted. And they shall know that I am the LORD, when I have set a fire in Egypt, and when all her helpers shall be destroyed. In that day shall messengers go forth from me in ships to make the careless Ethiopians afraid, and great pain shall come upon them, as in the day of Egypt: for, lo, it cometh. (Eze. 30:4–9)

Now the catastrophe in Egypt is clearly linked with Egypt's African neighbors. A conflict is taking place. And a conflict is most assuredly brewing in that part of the world right now over Egypt's water supplies.

Let's go back to where we left off in Isaiah 19:

> Surely the princes of Zoan are fools, the counsel of the wise coun-
> sellors of Pharaoh is become brutish: how say ye unto Pharaoh,
> I am the son of the wise, the son of ancient kings? Where are
> they? where are thy wise men? and let them tell thee now, and let
> them know what the LORD of hosts hath purposed upon Egypt.
> The princes of Zoan are become fools, the princes of Noph are
> deceived; they have also seduced Egypt, even they that are the
> stay of the tribes thereof. The LORD hath mingled a perverse spirit
> in the midst thereof: and they have caused Egypt to err in every
> work thereof, as a drunken man staggereth in his vomit. Neither
> shall there be any work for Egypt, which the head or tail, branch
> or rush, may do. In that day shall Egypt be like unto women: and
> it shall be afraid and fear because of the shaking of the hand of
> the LORD of hosts, which he shaketh over it. (vv. 11–16)

Here are more details about the extent of this judgment in Egypt,
a land that has been seduced by its wicked leaders into a perverse
spirit that causes error in every way. We learn that the economy will
be utterly devastated—an economy that revolves almost entirely
around the Nile. Imagine just how little work there would be in
Egypt without either the power generated by the Aswan Dam or
no water flowing from the Nile? There would be plenty of fear, I
can imagine.

Interestingly, there's another kind of fear expressed in the next
few verses: a fear of Israel: "And the land of Judah shall be a terror
unto Egypt, every one that maketh mention thereof shall be afraid
in himself, because of the counsel of the LORD of hosts, which he
hath determined against it. In that day shall five cities in the land
of Egypt speak the language of Canaan, and swear to the LORD of
hosts; one shall be called, The city of destruction" (vv. 17–18)

Now, I have to stop right here and tell you about some amazing
activities I have learned about in Egypt that relate directly to these

prophecies. But understand, again, that Jesus is coming to Egypt to save His people there. He won't just come to the Mount of Olives and sort out everything from Jerusalem. He will actually visit other parts of the world, executing judgment and saving His people.

Who are His people in Egypt? There are not many Jews left there. But there are plenty of long-persecuted Christians—Coptic Christians, which simply means Egyptian Christians.

So why are people in Egypt speaking the language of Canaan in these verses? And what *is* the language of Canaan. *Canaan* is simply another name for Israel today. Israel conquered Canaan, the land given to Abraham. Thus, the language of Canaan is Hebrew.

So why are people in Egypt speaking Hebrew?

This might be shocking news, but Egyptians are indeed studying Hebrew in great numbers. According to an article in Egyptian newspaper *Al-Monitor*:

> Egyptians have diverse motivations for learning about Israel and Hebrew. Some wanted to do business with Israel, before this hope was dashed due to the political pall that has been cast over the countries. Others hope to be hired by the intelligence services or to be employed by the media as Israel experts. Others are simply curious or need to fill a university requirement to study a foreign language. . . .

Nine of the 14 state universities in Egypt, including Al-Azhar Islamic University, have Hebrew departments. Close to 20,000 students study Hebrew at these universities at any given point in time, most in colleges of Middle Eastern Studies. Each year, at least 2,000 students graduate with bachelor's degrees that include the study of Hebrew.[7]

While this odd development is taking place—to the amazement of many in Israel—there is a parallel trend among many Coptic Christians and Egyptian evangelicals. They have been reading Isaiah 19 to understand their fate in these perilous times. Some of them,

I'm told, are banding together and learning Hebrew so they can get a better understanding of the Bible, and Isaiah 19 in particular. Some have also taken the Hebrew-language cue from Isaiah 19, given the importance of what the passage says about the future.

And there's another phenomenon taking place with Christians in Egypt: a great revival. And with Isaiah 19 very much in their minds, they are locating other sources of water in Egypt other than the Nile. It turns out there are many oases throughout the country that have been largely abandoned as the population crowded around the Nile. Some of them are moving back. Others are buying up that land. Still others are making provisions to move to those oases at the first indication of problems with the Nile—which, as you have seen, are already apparent.

Let's get back to Isaiah 19:

> In that day shall there be an altar to the LORD in the midst of the land of Egypt, and a pillar at the border thereof to the LORD. And it shall be for a sign and for a witness unto the LORD of hosts in the land of Egypt: for they shall cry unto the LORD because of the oppressors, and he shall send them a saviour, and a great one, and he shall deliver them. And the LORD shall be known to Egypt, and the Egyptians shall know the LORD in that day, and shall do sacrifice and oblation; yea, they shall vow a vow unto the LORD, and perform it. And the LORD shall smite Egypt: he shall smite and heal it: and they shall return even to the LORD, and he shall be intreated of them, and shall heal them. (vv. 19–22)

There are some 10 million Christians in Egypt. They have suffered great persecution during fourteen centuries of Islamic domination. Clearly, God is hearing their cries, just as He heard the cries of His people during their four hundred years of servitude in Egypt.

Isaiah tells us the Lord is going to smite Egypt and heal it. Not only will the land be healed of this catastrophe that will befall Egypt, but there will be a spiritual redemption as well. The final three verses of Isaiah 19 deal with God's Mideast Peace Plan—and it is an astonishing one that clearly speaks of the restitution of all things:

> In that day shall there be a highway out of Egypt to Assyria, and the Assyrian shall come into Egypt, and the Egyptian into Assyria, and the Egyptians shall serve with the Assyrians. In that day shall Israel be the third with Egypt and with Assyria, even a blessing in the midst of the land: Whom the LORD of hosts shall bless, saying, Blessed be Egypt my people, and Assyria the work of my hands, and Israel mine inheritance. (vv. 22–25)

Imagine that! Egypt and Assyria and Israel, all one big, happy family. Egypt is called God's people. Assyria is called the work of God's hands. And Israel is His inheritance. One-third, one-third, and one-third.

This astonishing message seems to be underscored in Isaiah 27: "And it shall come to pass in that day, that the LORD shall beat off from the channel of the river unto the stream of Egypt, and ye shall be gathered one by one, O ye children of Israel. And it shall come to pass in that day, that the great trumpet shall be blown, and they shall come which were ready to perish in the land of Assyria, and the outcasts in the land of Egypt, and shall worship the LORD in the holy mount at Jerusalem" (vv. 12–13).

And to get back to the question of Ishmael's inheritance, there's that link between Egypt and Assyria I alluded to earlier. It's a link made in Genesis in our exploration of the promise to Abraham and Hagar about Ishmael.

Ishmael's twelve sons settled in the lands from Egypt to Assyria. And thus, we see in Isaiah 19, Ishmael is reconciled with Isaac and Jacob.

There's a special end-time blessing here for the two "great nations" that are linked to Ishmael: Egypt and Assyria. When will they actually be "great nations" in every sense of the phrase? When they are supernaturally blessed through their relationship with Israel, that is, during the period marking the restitution of all things.

Wouldn't Father Abraham be happy about that? In fact, won't the entire world be happy?

Arab and Jew together—God's Mideast Peace Plan, the only one that will actually last for a thousand years.

What is the greatest miracle in history? It's taking place before our eyes. It's the return of the Jews from all over the earth to their homeland. It is what will lead to a one-thousand-year reign of peace, justice, and prosperity for all willing to embrace it—Jew and Gentile alike, Jew and Arab alike.

9

IS THE ANTICHRIST ALIVE AND WELL ON PLANET EARTH TODAY?

And I saw one of his heads as it were wounded to death; and his deadly wound was healed: and all the world wondered after the beast.
—REVELATION 13:3

THEY SAY YOU CAN'T TEACH an old dog new tricks. But that's not in the Bible, so I don't accept it as inspired.

I think the Holy Spirit gives us wisdom to see things in the Bible we've never seen before. How many times have you studied a familiar verse and, all of a sudden, saw it in a whole new light, with renewed clarity? Somehow it's like reading a verse for the first time—even though you've read it a thousand times. It happens to all of us. I believe that is the Holy Spirit working in us.

Throughout this book, there have been two themes:

1. Whether today's Christians might be guilty of the same error as the Pharisees: accepting, almost without question, the teaching of men over the clear teaching of Scripture

2. How repeating this error might lead to confusion over our eternal fate and our destiny in the kingdom of God

I certainly have fallen victim, especially in my early years as a believer, to both of these errors. That's what prompted me to write this book.

With that in mind, I will now dive into the prevalent, modern eschatological belief that the Antichrist will be a European, and Gog, a central figure in Ezekiel's prophecies (and mentioned briefly in Revelation), will be a Russian leader who leads a coalition of nations into battle with Israel in the end-times.

I, too, accepted those teachings for a long time.

I have been studying the Scriptures for about forty years, with a special interest in prophecy. It was prophecy that attracted me to search the Scriptures and that intellectually persuaded me that Jesus was indeed the Messiah. And it is prophecy that strengthens my faith every day.

Half of the many books I have collaborated on are about the Bible, and most of those are about prophecy. Half a dozen I wrote with Hal Lindsey, a man I will always love and admire and at whose feet I sat for more than a decade. I also wrote for Jack Van Impe and Greg Laurie, so I am well familiar with the conventional evangelical view that came out of Dallas Theological Seminary in the 1960s.

But that view did not come down from Mount Sinai. And that's why we need to reconsider it, measuring it against what Scripture actually tells us.

Let's begin with this proposition: The Bible is Israel- and Middle

East–centric. I would further suggest that to really understand the Bible, one must use the prism of its Hebrew and Semitic roots.

In Daniel 12:4, after an angel had interpreted Daniel's vision, the angel told the prophet, "Shut up the words, and seal the book, even to the time of the end: many shall run to and fro, and knowledge shall be increased." That would surely include knowledge of the prophecies about the end-times.

So what am I leading up to?

I don't believe a European Antichrist is ever going to rule over a global government and religious system. Nor do I believe Gog is a future Russian leader. Scripture provides a different paradigm entirely.

What I would like you to do today is put aside your preconceived ideas about the end-times. This is especially crucial since, throughout history, Westerners have tended to project their own, Western view of the world on the Bible, and on prophecy in particular. Americans are always trying to find the United States in *somewhere* in Bible prophecy. We want to know what happens to us in the final conflagrations leading to the return of Jesus.

When I read the Bible, I don't see the United States as a key player. But I do see Israel. I also see many other countries in the Middle East that we can identify with certainty, even if they have different names today than they had when the Scriptures were written.

One guiding principle of understanding the Bible is to start with the easy, clear, straightforward verses before jumping to the more difficult ones that require more interpretation. So let's start with the overwhelming amount of biblical information we have on (1) the major participants involved in attacking Israel in the last days and (2) the nations that Jesus will judge and destroy when He returns.

They are all Middle Eastern countries.

In the popular, traditional view, Rome and Russia are among those who participate in the coalition against Israel. Let's look at what the Bible actually says about this end-time coalition—and the very specific and identifiable nations that the Lord will destroy at the Second Coming.

We'll start way back in Numbers 24, where Balaam prophesies before Balak about the future of both his nation and of Israel. Now, who was Balak and who are his people? Balak was the king of the Moabites, and his allies were the Midianites. (See Numbers 22:1–4.) Here's what Balaam told this Moabite king:

> Come therefore, and I will advertise thee what this people [Hebrews] shall do to thy people [the Moabites] in the latter days. . . . Balaam the son of Beor hath said, and the man whose eyes are open hath said: He hath said, which heard the words of God, and knew the knowledge of the most High, which saw the vision of the Almighty, falling into a trance, but having his eyes open: I shall see him, but not now: I shall behold him, but not nigh: there shall come a Star out of Jacob, and a Sceptre shall rise out of Israel, and shall smite the corners of Moab, and destroy all the children of Sheth. And Edom shall be a possession, Seir also shall be a possession for his enemies; and Israel shall do valiantly. (Num. 24:14–18)

This is a very important prophetic passage pointing to the coming of Messiah, the "Star out of Jacob" and the "Sceptre . . . out of Israel." Which nations are identified here? Moab, Edom, and Seir. No Rome. No Russia.

Where are the ancient lands of Moab, Edom, and Seir? They would be in the modern lands we know as Saudi Arabia and Jordan.

Let's move on to Isaiah:

> He will swallow up death in victory; and the Lord GOD will wipe away tears from off all faces; and the rebuke of his people shall he take away from off all the earth: for the LORD hath spoken it. And it shall be said in that day, Lo, this is our God; we have waited for him, and he will save us: this is the LORD; we have waited for him, we will be glad and rejoice in his salvation. For in this mountain shall the hand of the LORD rest, and Moab shall be trodden down under him, even as straw is trodden down for the dunghill. (25:8–10)

There's Moab again—but not Rome or Russia.

In Micah 5 we read this:

But thou, Bethlehem Ephratah, though thou be little among the thousands of Judah, yet out of thee shall he come forth unto me that is to be ruler in Israel; whose goings forth have been from of old, from everlasting. Therefore will he give them up, until the time that she which travaileth hath brought forth: then the remnant of his brethren shall return unto the children of Israel. And he shall stand and feed in the strength of the LORD, in the majesty of the name of the LORD his God; and they shall abide: for now shall he be great unto the ends of the earth. And this man shall be the peace, when the Assyrian shall come into our land: and when he shall tread in our palaces, then shall we raise against him seven shepherds, and eight principal men. And they shall waste the land of Assyria with the sword, and the land of Nimrod in the entrances thereof: thus shall he deliver us from the Assyrian, when he cometh into our land, and when he treadeth within our borders. (Mic. 5:2–6)

Here we see mention of Assyria, and the Antichrist identified as "the Assyrian"—not the Roman. So again, no Rome. No Russia. Where is Assyria? Today we would be talking about the modern lands of Iraq, part of Iran, Syria, and Turkey.

Did you ever wonder why the Antichrist was referred to as "the Assyrian" so explicitly if he is actually going to be a Roman or a European? This is explicitly an end-time passage, even referring to the birthplace of Jesus, the Messiah, and to His divinity.

Another passage in Isaiah reads:

Who is this that cometh from Edom, with dyed garments from Bozrah? this that is glorious in his apparel, travelling in the great-ness of his strength? I that speak in righteousness, mighty to save. Wherefore art thou red in thine apparel, and thy garments like him that treadeth in the winefat? I have trodden the winepress alone; and of the people there was none with me: for I will tread them in mine anger, and trample them in my fury; and their blood shall be sprinkled upon my garments, and I will stain all my raiment. For the day of vengeance is in mine heart, and the year of my redeemed is come. (63:1–4)

Edom is mentioned here, but again, no Rome and no Russia.

In Habakkuk 3 we read:

God came from Teman, and the Holy One from mount Paran. . . . His glory covered the heavens, and the earth was full of his praise. And his brightness was as the light; he had horns coming out of his hand: and there was the hiding of his power. Before him went the pestilence, and burning coals went forth at his feet. He stood, and measured the earth: he beheld, and drove asunder the nations; and the everlasting mountains were scattered, the perpetual hills did bow: his ways are everlasting. I saw the tents of Cushan in affliction: and the curtains of the land of Midian did tremble. (vv. 3–7)

Teman in this passage is Edom; Paran is Saudi Arabia; Cushan is Arabia; and Midian is Arabia. These are the same lands in which the children of Israel wandered for forty years before entering the promised land. Note what is *not* mentioned.

Here's another passage that speaks of those who attack Israel:

I will also gather all nations, and will bring them down into the valley of Jehoshaphat, and will plead with them there for my people and for my heritage Israel, whom they have scattered among the nations, and parted my land. And they have cast lots for my people; and have given a boy for an harlot, and sold a girl for wine, that they might drink. Yea, and what have ye to do with me, O Tyre, and Zidon, and all the coasts of Palestine? will ye render me a recompence? and if ye recompense me, swiftly and speedily will I return your recompence upon your own head. (Joel 3:2–4)

Here we see Lebanon and Gaza. Interestingly, one is the home of Hezbollah; the other, of Hamas.

In Isaiah 34 we read that there will be a "great slaughter" in Idumea and that Bozrah's "land shall be soaked with blood . . . For it is the day of the Lord's vengeance, and the year of recompenses for the controversy of Zion." Idumea is another name for Edom, and Bozrah was Edom's capital. No other nation is mentioned.

Another very long passage that mentions those the Lord will destroy is Ezekiel 25, where we read of the Ammonites and Rabbah, which represent modern-day Jordan, and a whole lot of other nations and people groups, some of which we've seen before. Missing from the list is any mention of Rome or Russia.

All of these verses are end-time scriptures dealing with the return of Christ and the lands He vanquishes at that time. Not one of them is outside the Middle East. The nations specifically mentioned that come against Israel in the last days are clearly Egypt, Saudi Arabia, Syria, Turkey, Libya, Iran, Jordan, Iraq, Gaza, and Lebanon—every single one of them Muslim and every single one of them a participant in the current turmoil in the Middle East.

There are many, many more examples I could cite.

Without dealing with Ezekiel 38–39, which I'll touch on later, where are the attacks from Rome and elsewhere in the world? Why are all these end-time judgments only on nations that surround Israel?

If you think about it, all of our theories about a Roman Antichrist start and end, pretty much, with interpretations of Daniel and Revelation, the cornerstone of all those scriptures being Daniel 9:26. On the surface, it would seem to be referring to a Roman Antichrist: "And after threescore and two weeks shall Messiah be cut off, but not for himself: and *the people of the prince that shall come shall destroy the city and the sanctuary*; and the end thereof shall be with a flood, and unto the end of the war desolations are determined" (emphasis added).

Who destroyed the city and the sanctuary in AD 70? The Romans. So they must be the "people of the prince that shall come," right? That's what I thought too. I didn't think there was any controversy about who destroyed Jerusalem and the temple that year. And if there isn't, then we know that somehow the prince that shall come must be someone from a revived Roman Empire . . . don't we?

But let's look a little deeper. It's actually not quite that clear-cut when you examine the key words in this verse. This scripture is not referring to a nation or an empire but to a people. So who *were* the people who destroyed the "city and the sanctuary"? Was it the Romans?

No. The people who actually destroyed the city and the temple were *not* Romans; they were Arabs—and they were not even directed to that task by their Roman leaders. In fact, those overwhelmingly Middle Eastern people who destroyed the temple, sacked the city, and committed unspeakable, genocidal atrocities were actually *disobeying* Roman orders.

Does that change your opinion about this verse? It did mine.

Roman historian Tacitus, in his *History*, described who made up the "Roman" army that sacked Jerusalem: "Early in this year Titus Caesar . . . found in Judaea three legions, the 5th, the 10th, and the 15th . . . To these he added the 12th from Syria, and some men belonging to the 18th and 3rd, whom he had withdrawn from Alexandria [Egypt]. This force was accompanied . . . by a strong contingent of Arabs, who hated the Jews with the usual hatred of neighbors."[1]

Did you get that? Syrians and Egyptians and Arabs—and these Arabs "hated the Jews."

Jewish historian Flavius Josephus wrote that "the greatest part of the Roman garrison was raised out of Syria; and being thus related to the Syrian part, they were ready to assist it."[2] The Syrians were actually zealous to help the Roman legions in their oppression of the Jews! And further confirming Syrian involvement, Josephus wrote that "Vespasian sent his son Titus . . . into Syria, where he gathered together the Roman forces, with a considerable number of auxiliaries from the kings in that neighborhood."[3] Additionally, "Malchus also, the king of Arabia, sent a thousand horsemen, besides five thousand footmen."[4]

So, clearly, at this time in the history of the Roman Empire, local peoples were used to supplement the local Roman armies, even to the point of being the majority.

Now let's find out what actually happened with the storming of Jerusalem.

"The multitude of the Arabians, with the Syrians, cut up those that came as supplicants, and searched their bellies," Josephus recorded. "Nor does it seem to me that any misery befell the Jews that was more terrible than this, since in one night's time about two thousand of these deserters were thus dissected."[5]

Who was really responsible, then—what people? Were the Romans overseeing the slaughter and the destruction of the temple and the city?

That doesn't appear to be the case at all. Again, the best history book written on the subject, by Josephus, tells us:

> Now a certain person came running to Titus, and told him of this fire . . . whereupon he rose up in great haste, and, as he was, ran to the holy house, in order to have a stop put to the fire; after him followed all his commanders, and after them followed the several legions, in great astonishment; so there was a great clamor and tumult raised, as was natural upon the disorderly motion of so great an army. Then did Caesar, both by calling to the soldiers that were fighting, with a loud voice, and by giving a signal to them with his right hand, order them to quench the fire.[6]

It does not appear from this account that Titus had any desire to see the temple destroyed. After all, it was not really Rome's nature to simply destroy such a prize. According to Josephus, the emperor's son actually tried to stop it. This was history I had overlooked until very recently. Look what happened next:

> Titus supposing . . . that the house itself might yet be saved, he came in haste and endeavored to persuade the soldiers to quench the fire . . . yet were the regards they had for Caesar, and their

dread of him who forbade them, not as hard as their passion and their hatred of the Jews, and a certain vehement inclination to fight them . . . And thus was the holy house burnt down, without Caesar's approbation.[7]

Do these sound like Roman soldiers disobeying orders from Caesar because of their bloodlust for the Jews? I don't think so. This was a mutiny by local soldiers who had a long-simmering hatred of the Jews.

So who were the people who destroyed Jerusalem and its temple in AD 70? If we are to accept Josephus's account and the corroborating account of Tacitus, they were not Romans. The Romans actually tried to halt the destruction, or "quench the fire," as Josephus put it.

What we have missed historically is that Emperor Augustus, founder of the Roman Empire, made a series of sweeping reforms that led to dramatic changes in the ethnic makeup of the Roman armies he had earlier built. After this time, the armies were increasingly composed of anything but Italian or European soldiers. Instead they were composed of "provincials," or citizens who lived in the provinces, the outer fringes of the empire.

So the army that destroyed the temple and the Holy City was overwhelmingly Middle Eastern, not European—the ancestors of the modern-day inhabitants of the Middle East.

To me, this little-known history was the final thread of the Roman Antichrist theory. Now let's look at where that theory originates.

Besides Daniel 9:26, there are three other passages that hint at a Roman Antichrist:

- Daniel 2, the story of Nebuchadnezzar's dream of a great statue

- Daniel 7, which tells of Daniel's vision of four gruesome beasts

- Revelation 17, which describes the city on seven hills

The traditional interpretation of King Nebuchadnezzar's dream is that the four empires depicted by the statue are:

- the Babylonian Empire

- the Medo-Persian Empire

- the Grecian Empire

- the Roman Empire

The Islamic end-time scenario agrees with the first three of these. But it disagrees with the last. Why? Because Rome never actually conquered Babylon. Remember: this was Babylon's king Nebuchadnezzar's dream, and Daniel, in interpreting the dream, did not tell him about four empires that would conquer *Israel*, which indeed Rome did. He described four empires that would conquer Babylon.

Let's look at those four empires and the land masses they actually vanquished.

First there was the Babylonian Empire, ruled from Babylon.

Next there was the Persian Empire: This can certainly be seen as an empire that would replace that of Nebuchadnezzar. On that everyone should agree.

Third came the Greek Empire. This empire, too, qualifies as a fulfillment of Nebuchadnezzar's dream. The Greeks clearly occupied the entire area of the Babylonian Empire, including Babylon itself.

Finally, let's look at the Roman Empire. What's missing from the lands conquered and occupied by Rome? Babylon is missing. We have a problem here. How can Rome qualify as the fourth empire in Nebuchadnezzar's dream when, in fact, Rome never conquered Babylon?

So, if Rome never actually conquered Babylon, which empire did? What was that fourth kingdom?

Have you ever wondered why we never talk about the empire that followed Rome? Clearly it was Islamic. It still holds Babylon within its grasp today, in modern-day Iraq. Islam conquered much

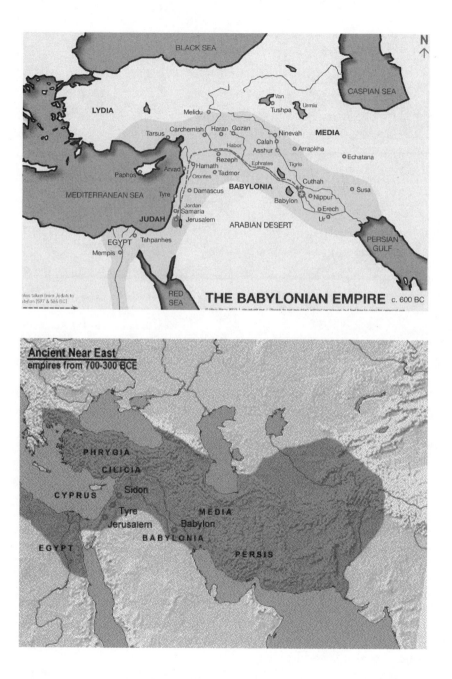

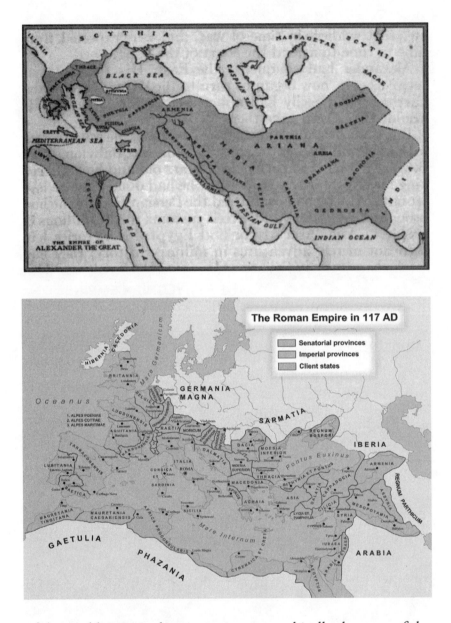

of the world. It was a larger empire geographically than any of the others. It also lasted longer.

In 1917, the Islamic Empire crumbled as Britain defeated the Ottoman Empire in World War I. Then Mustafa Kemal Atatürk secularized Turkey and, for the rest of the world, the Islamic Empire, which had lasted thirteen hundred years, was dead and gone. But it wasn't really dead. It was simply asleep. This oil-rich empire was awakened in 1979 by the Iranian revolution—and it is again one of the most powerful forces in the world today and is on the ascendancy. Unlike the Roman Empire, the Islamic Empire is in revival. Yes, it fell—but it has been revived.

Think about those nations today that surround Israel. They are the armies of the real revived fourth empire. The Romans and Europeans are nowhere in sight.

Here's the important takeaway: study the scriptures and you will find that every single nation that Jesus will fight and conquer at His Second Coming is today an Islamic, Middle Eastern nation.

What about Gog and Magog? Many of us have long assumed that Russia was Magog, especially during the height of the Soviet Union. The evidence is actually pretty thin. There is much more evidence to suggest that Magog is Turkey, which is right now preparing to lead the revived caliphate, just as it did up until World War I.

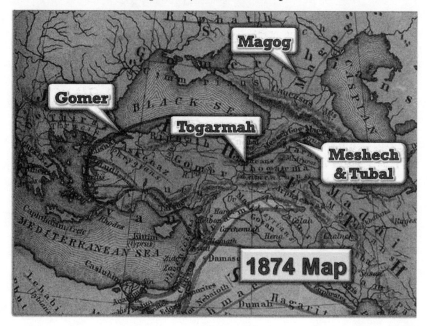

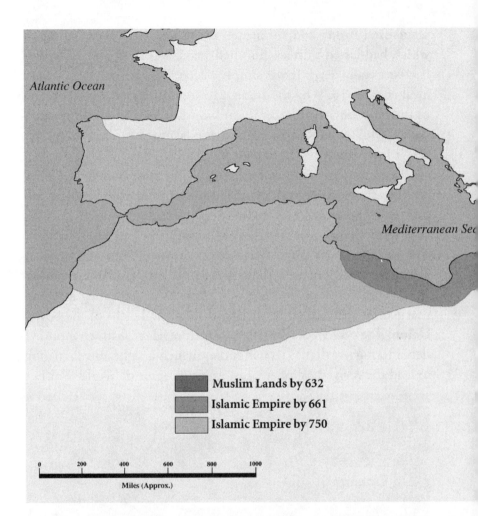

You can look at many ancient maps and see Magog listed as plain as day—not in Russia, not in the Ukraine, but in Turkey. I remember back in the Cold War days when some prophecy teachers were suggesting that Gomer, mentioned in that Magog coalition, was Germany. But in ancient maps, you can see Gomer in Turkey too.

We've been conditioned to believe that the Ezekiel 38–39 invasion is a prelude to the final battle and the return of Jesus. But I'd like to call your attention to a passage in Ezekiel 39 that seems to contradict that idea. That chapter describes the end of a battle waged

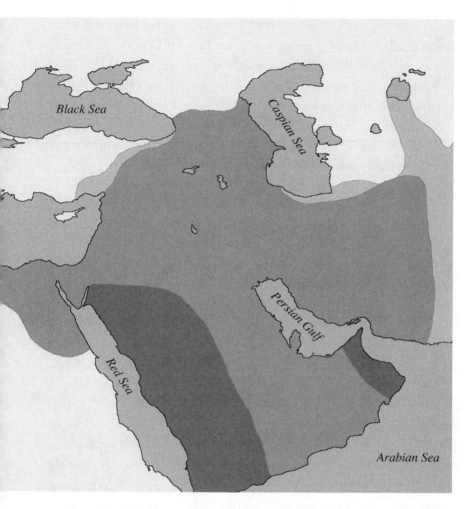

by Gog and Magog—when God defeats this adversary: "So will I make my holy name known in the midst of my people Israel; and I will not let them pollute my holy name any more: and the heathen shall know that I am the LORD, the Holy One in Israel. Behold, it is come, and it is done, saith the Lord GOD; this is the day whereof I have spoken" (vv. 7–8).

If, as proponents of a Russian Gog suggest, the time period we're discussing is a kind of preliminary battle in which Russia is defeated before the ultimate war in which the Antichrist is destroyed, then the worst idolatry and profanity the world has ever known *is yet to come*. The Antichrist is going to declare himself God in the temple. But it says here that after this battle with Gog and Magog, God will no longer allow them, His enemies, to pollute His holy name.

How is it that this battle takes place months or years before the final showdown between Jesus and the Antichrist, yet we're told by God in Ezekiel 39 that He will make His holy name known and that even the heathen will know that He is the Lord?

Do you see my problem here?

If this is your first exposure to the Islamic Antichrist theory, you undoubtedly have many questions. What I have provided here is a brief overview for those who have not yet read Joel Richardson's *New York Times* best seller *The Islamic Antichrist* or his follow-up work, *Mideast Beast*, which I published. If you are interested in pursuing this study in more detail, I recommend those books very highly.

One thing I haven't touched on is the absolutely fascinating way the Islamic end-time scenario lines up in a strange, parallel-universe fashion with Bible prophecy—except that the Muslim apocalyptic vision clearly sees our Jesus as the Antichrist and the Antichrist as the Madhi savior of Islam. This is one of the reasons I see Islam as the perfect antichrist religion. It simply can't be dismissed as an afterthought in any end-time scenario. It stands Bible prophecy on its head. If you expect Russia to lead Islam into battle, you are expecting the tail to wag the dog. Will Russia be involved in some way? No doubt. But even as Vladimir Putin awakens Russia from its imperial slumber, he's hardly Gog.

Islam is the dog, not the tail. And it's a ferocious dog. In fact, it's a ravenous wolf.

If you are expecting some European Antichrist to behead millions of people who won't accept him as God, you are probably going to be very surprised. But who *is* already chopping off people's heads today? Who has been doing it for the last thirteen hundred years?

Ezekiel 31 compares "the Assyrian," another name for this Antichrist figure, to "a cedar." But as Jonathan Cahn points out in

The Harbinger, and in the best-selling documentary *The Isaiah 9:10 Judgment*, the original Hebrew word there is not *cedar*, but *erez*.[8] It's a big tree nevertheless. And here it is associated with the Antichrist. It is also associated with Lebanon, so it could very well be a cedar, the tree for which Lebanon is most famous. It's on the national flag.

Let's take a closer look at Ezekiel 31:

> And it came to pass in the eleventh year, in the third month, in the first day of the month, that the word of the LORD came unto me, saying, Son of man, speak unto Pharaoh king of Egypt, and to his multitude; Whom art thou like in thy greatness? Behold, the Assyrian was a cedar in Lebanon with fair branches, and with a shadowing shroud, and of an high stature; and his top was among the thick boughs. The waters made him great, the deep set him up on high with her rivers running round about his plants, and sent her little rivers unto all the trees of the field. Therefore his height was exalted above all the trees of the field, and his boughs were multiplied, and his branches became long because of the multitude of waters, when he shot forth. All the fowls of heaven made their nests in his boughs, and under his branches did all the beasts of the field bring forth their young, and under his shadow dwelt all great nations. Thus was he fair in his greatness, in the length of his branches: for his root was by great waters. The cedars in the garden of God could not hide him: the fir trees were not like his boughs, and the chestnut trees were not like his branches; nor any tree in the garden of God was like unto him in his beauty. I have made him fair by the multitude of his branches: so that all the trees of Eden, that were in the garden of God, envied him. Therefore thus saith the Lord GOD; Because thou hast lifted up thyself in height, and he hath shot up his top among the thick boughs, and his heart is lifted up in his height; I have therefore delivered him into the hand of the mighty one of the heathen; he shall surely deal with him: I have driven him out for his wickedness. And strangers, the terrible of the nations, have

cut him off, and have left him: upon the mountains and in all the valleys his branches are fallen, and his boughs are broken by all the rivers of the land; and all the people of the earth are gone down from his shadow, and have left him. Upon his ruin shall all the fowls of the heaven remain, and all the beasts of the field shall be upon his branches: To the end that none of all the trees by the waters exalt themselves for their height, neither shoot up their top among the thick boughs, neither their trees stand up in their height, all that drink water: for they are all delivered unto death, to the nether parts of the earth, in the midst of the children of men, with them that go down to the pit. Thus saith the Lord GOD; In the day when he went down to the grave I caused a mourning: I covered the deep for him, and I restrained the floods thereof, and the great waters were stayed: and I caused Lebanon to mourn for him, and all the trees of the field fainted for him. I made the nations to shake at the sound of his fall, when I cast him down to hell with them that descend into the pit: and all the trees of Eden, the choice and best of Lebanon, all that drink water, shall be comforted in the nether parts of the earth. They also went down into hell with him unto them that be slain with the sword; and they that were his arm, that dwelt under his shadow in the midst of the heathen. To whom art thou thus like in glory and in greatness among the trees of Eden? yet shalt thou be brought down with the trees of Eden unto the nether parts of the earth: thou shalt lie in the midst of the uncircumcised with them that be slain by the sword. This is Pharaoh and all his multitude, saith the Lord GOD. (vv. 1–18)

So here we see God likening Pharoah, who is also a type of the Antichrist, to "the Assyrian," which is one of the names of the Antichrist. We find it in Isaiah 10:5: "O Assyrian, the rod of mine anger, and the staff in their hand is mine indignation."

Now we know it is a historical fact that the Assyrians, and the Assyrian king, were used to bring judgment on Israel in the past.

"And it was at Jerusalem the feast of the dedication, and it was winter. And Jesus walked in the temple in Solomon's porch."
– JOHN 10:22–23

Is Hanukkah relevant to Christians?

Today we think of it as one of the "Jewish holidays," and indeed it is. But you won't find any reference to Hanukkah in the Old Testament. You will, however, find Jesus observing it in the New Testament (see John 10:22–23.)

If it was worth Jesus' time, maybe it's worth ours.

So what is Hanukkah all about?

About 175 years before the birth of Jesus, the Greek-Syrian empire ruled over the land of Israel.

The Syrian ruler, Antiochus IV, was a tyrant—a madman, an Antichrist archetype. He sought to suppress all the Jewish laws. Thousands of Jews were killed.

All Jewish worship was forbidden. The scrolls were confiscated and burned. Honoring the Sabbath, circumcision, and the dietary laws were prohibited under penalty of death. Antiochus conspired to depose and later assassinate the righteous high priest, Yochanan. Antiochus' henchmen ordered ninety-year-old Rabbi Eliezer to eat pork as an example to his followers. He refused and was put to death.

In a plot to undermine the strength of the Jewish family and morality, Antiochus decreed that any Jewish maiden who was to be married had to first spend the night with the local governor or commander.

The Syrians, under the command of Holofernes, laid siege to the town of Bethulia. While the town elders discussed a plan to surrender when their food supply ran out, a young and beautiful widow, Yehudit, the daughter of Yochanan the high priest, told the people to maintain faith in their God. She told them she had a plan they would have to accept on faith.

Yehudit took a large basket of cheese, bread, and wine to Holofernes.

She told the commander that, in exchange for mercy on her people, she would tell him how to capture the town. She explained that her people's faith in God remained strong, making the fight against them that much more difficult. However, she said, soon the supply of kosher food would be gone. When that occurred, the people would begin to eat the flesh of unclean animals thus provoking God's anger and causing the town to fall.

She agreed to stay with Holofernes, returning to Bethulia each day to find out how food supplies were holding out. She gained the trust of the commander who was eager to spend time with the beautiful widow as well as to win the siege.

After a few days, Yehudit told Holofernes that Bethulia was now out of food. He had only to wait a few more days for the Jews to begin eating the non-kosher animals. Holofernes invited her to come alone to his tent that night to celebrate. She agreed, inviting him to eat her salty goat-cheese. As he ate, he grew thirsty and Yehudit gave him the wine she had brought with her. While Yehudit pretended to eat and drink, Holofernes became drunk. Soon, he was in a deep sleep. Yehudit took Holofernes' sword and cut off his head. She and her maidservant put his head in a cloth and returned to Bethulia.

Now was the time to attack the Syrians, she said. In disarray at finding their leader dead, the Syrians were overcome and the Jews won the battle.

Defeats like this made Antiochus even more determined to exterminate the Jews, if necessary, to achieve victory.

Hannah and her seven sons were brought before him because they refused to stop studying the Torah, keeping dietary laws, and honoring the Sabbath. Antiochus demanded that they bow down to an idol before him. The eldest son stepped forward and said: "What do you wish from us? We are ready to die rather than transgress the laws of our fathers."

Antiochus ordered him tortured. His tongue, hands, and feet were cut off and he was placed in a cauldron of boiling water. Antiochus turned to the next son and demanded that he worship the idol. The brother refused and was similarly tortured. Antiochus continued down the line and each brother held fast to his faith and gave up his life until only Hannah and her youngest son remained.

Antiochus called the child forward and begged him not to be a martyr for such a small thing as bowing before a statue. The king went so far as to promise him wealth beyond his dreams if he would obey.

Hannah told her youngest child: "My son, I carried you for nine months, nourished you for two years, and have provided you with everything until now. Look upon the heaven and the earth. God is the Creator of it all. Do not fear this tormentor, but be worthy of being with your brothers."

The boy refused to obey the king's commandment and was put to death. As her child lay dying, she cradled his body and asked God that she should be considered worthy to her children in the world to come. She fell to the floor and died.

There were thousands of others who likewise sacrificed their lives as Antiochus' men went from town to town and from village to village to force the inhabitants to worship pagan gods.

One day, the henchmen of Antiochus arrived in the village of Modin where Mattityahu, the old priest, lived. The Syrian officer built an altar in the marketplace of the village and demanded that Mattityahu offer sacrifices to the pagan gods. Mattityahu replied: "I, my sons and my brothers are determined to remain loyal to the covenant which our God made with our ancestors!"

When an accommodating Jew approached the altar to offer a sacrifice, Mattityahu grabbed his sword and killed him, and his sons and friends took on the Syrians, killing many and chasing the rest away. Then they destroyed the altar.

Mattityahu and his sons and friends fled to the hills of Judea. Many Jews joined them. They formed guerrilla armies and attacked the enemy.

Before his death, Mattityahu called his sons together and urged them to continue to fight. In waging warfare, he said, their leader should be Yehuda the Strong. Yehuda was called "Maccabee."

Antiochus sent his army to wipe out Yehuda and his followers, the Maccabees. Though greater in number and arms, the Syrians were defeated by the Maccabees. Antiochus sent out another, bigger army. It, too, was defeated. Finally, he raised an army of forty thousand men to sweep into Judea for a final invasion.

When Yehuda heard of the coming invasion, he exclaimed: "Let us fight unto death in defense of our souls and our Temple!"

God gave the Maccabees their miraculous victory.

When the Maccabees returned to Jerusalem to liberate it, they entered the temple to clear it of the idols placed there by the Syrians. A new altar was built. The golden menorah had been stolen by the Syrians, so the Maccabees made one of cheaper metal. But when they went to light it, they found only a small amount of pure olive oil bearing the seal of the High Priest Yochanan. It was sufficient to light only for one day.

By yet another miracle of God, though, it continued to burn for eight days, until the new oil was made available.

That's how the temple was rededicated and cleansed.

It is this final miracle that Jews commemorate annually with the lighting of candles and the Hanukkah celebration to this day.

Is it not a great day for all freedom-lovers and God-fearers to celebrate, especially those who worship the God of Israel?

And if Yeshua and His disciples took note of this festival, shouldn't His followers today consider it, too, especially since it offers us a prototype foreshadowing of the Antichrist and his abomination of desolation?

But it appears an Assyrian again will play a role in the judgment of Israel: "Wherefore it shall come to pass, that when the Lord hath performed his whole work upon mount Zion and on Jerusalem, I will punish the fruit of the stout heart of the king of Assyria, and the glory of his high looks" (Isa. 10:12).

Has the "whole work upon mount Zion and on Jerusalem" yet been performed? No. So this is a future event. This is a reference to the restitution of all things—the kingdom.

Isaiah 14 is also clearly a prophetic passage about events not yet fulfilled. What do we find there? "I will break the Assyrian in my land, and upon my mountains tread him under foot: then shall his yoke depart from off them, and his burden depart from off their shoulders" (v. 25).

Later, in Isaiah 30:31, we read: "For through the voice of the LORD shall the Assyrian be beaten down, which smote with a rod."

Isaiah 52, a prophetic passage that we know is not yet fulfilled, mentions this Assyrian again:

> For thus saith the Lord GOD, My people went down aforetime into Egypt to sojourn there; and the Assyrian oppressed them without cause. Now therefore, what have I here, saith the LORD, that my people is taken away for nought? they that rule over them make them to howl, saith the LORD; and my name continually every day is blasphemed. Therefore my people shall know my name: therefore they shall know in that day that I am he that doth speak: behold, it is I. How beautiful upon the mountains are the feet of him that bringeth good tidings, that publisheth peace; that bringeth good tidings of good, that publisheth salvation; that saith unto Zion, Thy God reigneth! Thy watchmen shall lift up the voice; with the voice together shall they sing: for they shall see eye to eye, when the LORD shall bring again Zion. Break forth into joy, sing together, ye waste places of Jerusalem: for the LORD hath comforted his people, he hath redeemed Jerusalem. The LORD hath made bare his holy arm in the eyes of all the nations;

and all the ends of the earth shall see the salvation of our God. Depart ye, depart ye, go ye out from thence, touch no unclean thing; go ye out of the midst of her; be ye clean, that bear the vessels of the LORD. For ye shall not go out with haste, nor go by flight: for the LORD will go before you; and the God of Israel will be your reward. Behold, my servant shall deal prudently, he shall be exalted and extolled, and be very high. As many were astonied at thee; his visage was so marred more than any man, and his form more than the sons of men: So shall he sprinkle many nations; the kings shall shut their mouths at him: for that which had not been told them shall they see; and that which they had not heard shall they consider. (vv. 4–15)

This is about Israel recognizing her King and Savior and Messiah for the first time. And once again, we see God defeating the Assyrian.

Micah 5 contains a very familiar verse that identifies the city in which the Messiah will be born. But it is also an end-time passage about this "Assyrian."

Now gather thyself in troops, O daughter of troops: he hath laid siege against us: they shall smite the judge of Israel with a rod upon the cheek. But thou, Bethlehem Ephratah, though thou be little among the thousands of Judah, yet out of thee shall he come forth unto me that is to be ruler in Israel; whose goings forth have been from of old, from everlasting. Therefore will he give them up, until the time that she which travaileth hath brought forth: then the remnant of his brethren shall return unto the children of Israel. And he shall stand and feed in the strength of the LORD, in the majesty of the name of the LORD his God; and they shall abide: for now shall he be great unto the ends of the earth. And this man shall be the peace, when the Assyrian shall come into our land: and when he shall tread in our palaces, then shall we raise against him seven shepherds, and eight principal men. And they shall waste the land of Assyria with the sword, and the land of Nimrod in the entrances thereof: thus shall he deliver us from the Assyrian, when he cometh into our land, and when he treadeth within our borders. (vv. 1–6)

In Ezekiel 31, this Antichrist figure is likened to a cedar. You might say it is his national tree. What's the national tree of Israel?

The fig tree, of course.

In Jonathan Cahn's famous teaching about Isaiah 9:10, he talks about sycamores. But what is the sycamore?

Ficus sycomorus is called the sycamore fig. It is a fig species that has been cultivated since ancient times.

So the fig tree is a sycamore. They are one and the same.

So, think about this: When the leaders of ancient Israel said in Isaiah 9:10 that the sycamores, their national tree, had been cut down, what did they intend to do? Did they intend to ask God why? No. Did they intend to repent? No. Did they intend to reflect on how they had drifted from the ways of the Lord and invited judgment by the Assyrians? No. Not only did they plan to build bigger and stronger in their own strength; not only did they not take God's warning about impending judgment; not only did they not repent . . .

They decided to plant cedars—the national tree of the Assyrian, or Antichrist.

Is it any wonder Israel was judged?

Islam's conquests spread farther than any of the other kingdoms in Daniel's dream. And they lasted nearly thirteen centuries—until World War I. The caliphate was destroyed by Atatürk in the early twentieth century. But it's coming back with a vengeance. It's so obvious we can't see it.

And if this theory is correct, we're a lot closer to the end-times than most people think. Europe is collapsing. Islam is on the rise. The Middle East is in flames. What started out as an "Arab Spring" could turn into a nuclear winter.

Russia is not about to invade Israel. That scenario is nowhere in sight. That's a relic of Cold War thinking. Neither is China amassing a 200 million–man army to march on Jerusalem—but the Arab world is.

Nowhere in the Bible's end-time picture is Israel explicitly attacked by any nation outside the greater Middle East. And nowhere in the Bible does the returning conquering King, Jesus, explicitly fight with any nation except Israel's neighbors—all of whom are Muslims.

Indeed, if there is going to be a global judgment of nations as sheep and goats in the Day of the Lord, as we read about in Matthew 25:32, where do we get the idea that the Antichrist is actually going to preside over the entire world without opposition? The Bible explicitly says the Antichrist will have opposition from nations. Let's hope the United States is one of them—and is thus judged favorably.

10

HOW SHOULD WE PREPARE OURSELVES FOR THE KINGDOM OF GOD?

Wherefore we receiving a kingdom which cannot be moved, let us have grace, whereby we may serve God acceptably with reverence and godly fear.
—HEBREWS 12:28

SO WHAT IS "THE RESTITUTION OF ALL THINGS," that Peter mentioned in Acts 3:21?

It is when Jesus comes again, to bring justice, peace, and prosperity to the world as He rules as the King of kings from Israel. This reign, said Peter, is the fulfillment of that "which God hath spoken by the mouth of all his holy prophets since the world began."

Peter continued:

For Moses truly said unto the fathers, A prophet shall the Lord your God raise up unto you of your brethren, like unto me; him shall ye hear in all things whatsoever he shall say unto you. And it shall come to pass, that every soul, which will not hear that prophet, shall be destroyed from among the people. Yea, and all the prophets from Samuel and those that follow after, as many as have spoken, have likewise foretold of these days. Ye are the children of the prophets, and of the covenant which God made with our fathers, saying unto Abraham, And in thy seed shall all the kindreds of the earth be blessed. Unto you first God, having raised up his Son Jesus, sent him to bless you, in turning away every one of you from his iniquities. (vv. 22–26)

In other words, this millennial kingdom to come is the world's destiny—the great hope for those who find salvation through the atonement of their sins in the sacrifice of Jesus, the Messiah of Israel and the Son of God.

How much thought do believers give to this time, this destiny, in their prayers, their Bible studies, their teachings, their sermons, and their witness to others?

From my experience, very little.

We hear a lot about heaven as our destiny. But was man made for heaven or earth?

You can find many opinions on this subject. But such opinions and human traditions, as we have seen both in Jesus' day and in the so-called church age, have often been dead wrong. The real question should be, what does Scripture tell us?

While there are many mysteries yet to be answered, one thing is abundantly clear through the totality of Scripture: there will be a thousand-year reign over the earth by Jesus, the Messiah and King.

Genesis 1:26 tells us that God said, "Let us make man in our image, after our likeness: and let them have dominion over the fish of the sea, and over the fowl of the air, and over the cattle, and over all the earth, and over every creeping thing that creepeth upon the earth." Man was made for earth in God's perfect vision. He was to live in an earthly paradise.

But man fell. And that has shaped the story ever since.

So what would the "restitution of all things" mean? How would all things be restored?

Logically, it would mean that earth itself would be restored.

One of the dominant themes in the Gospels is the kingdom of God. Over and over, Jesus, like the prophets before Him, spoke of God's reign on the earth. In this chapter, we'll explore what we know about that kingdom from Scripture and how we should be preparing ourselves for it.

We often hear Christians say, "God is doing a new thing." Does God do new things? Of course He does. He's God. But God's nature is unchanging. Because He's perfect, He neither errs nor needs correction. So, we've got to be careful when we say, "God is doing a new thing." What does that mean?

In Isaiah 43, God tells us He does new things. In fact, He suggests that these new things will overshadow the earlier things. It's a message to Israel, who were then in captivity. He promises them a better life—if Israel will return to Him and His commandments: "Remember ye not the former things, neither consider the things of old," He says. "Behold, I will do a new thing; now it shall spring forth; shall ye not know it? I will even make a way in the wilderness, and rivers in the desert" (vv. 18–19).

Just like Israel of old, the people of God today are waiting on God to do a new thing. And He is. I believe that new thing is His bringing an awareness to His people, Messianic Jews and Christians alike, that they need to return to Him and His eternal commandments.

So do Christians live under different rules than those God set forth in the past? Is that what God was suggesting in Isaiah? Not at all. In fact, His plea to His people then was not to forget His eternal commandments, but to return to them.

It's God who does new things to establish and reestablish His relationship with His people. His abilities and His creative spirit are always in motion. But His commandments are the same yesterday, today, and forever. Paul wrote:

Brethren, I count not myself to have apprehended: but this one thing I do, forgetting those things which are behind, and *reaching forth unto those things which are before*, I press toward the mark for the prize of the high calling of God in Christ Jesus. Let us therefore, as many as be perfect, be thus minded: and if in any thing ye be otherwise minded, God shall reveal even this unto you. Nevertheless, whereto we have already attained, *let us walk by the same rule*, let us mind the same thing. (Phil. 3:13–16, emphasis added)

Thus, God does new things, great things, in response the obedience of His people. Are we being obedient today? Or are we just waiting around for God to do new things?

The rebirth of a profoundly obedient Messianic Jewish faith exploding around the world represents a return to the bold, life-changing, turn-the-world-right-side-up, apostolic experience of the first century. They were all Jews who spread the good news of Jesus and the "new thing" He had done. Today, coupled with that expression is a spiritual movement within the non-Jewish church whereby believers are forsaking the traditions of men and returning to God's commandments.

I believe this is actually the beginning of a fulfillment of prophecy:

For, behold, the day cometh, that shall burn as an oven; and all the proud, yea, and all that do wickedly, shall be stubble: and the day that cometh shall burn them up, saith the LORD of hosts, that it shall leave them neither root nor branch. But unto you that fear my name shall the Sun of righteousness arise with healing in his wings; and ye shall go forth, and grow up as calves of the stall. And ye shall tread down the wicked; for they shall be ashes under the soles of your feet in the day that I shall do this, saith the LORD of hosts. Remember ye the law of Moses my servant, which I commanded unto him in Horeb for all Israel, with the statutes and judgments. Behold, I will send you Elijah the prophet before the coming of the great and dreadful day of the LORD: and he shall turn the heart of the fathers to the children, and the heart of the children to their fathers, lest I come and smite the earth with a curse. (Mal. 4)

What does this passage tell us?

There is going to be a judgment, about which countless other prophecy teachers have spoken. The Day of the Lord will be like a terrible swift sword—just but painful for many who have turned their backs to the one true God of Israel.

But for those who fear His name, there will be healing—if we "remember the law of Moses . . . with the statutes and judgments." This is a commandment for those who fear and love God. Yet, what are believers forgetting today, just as Israel forgot so many times in the past? The law of Moses . . . with the statutes and judgments.

What comes next is even more interesting: God is going to send us Elijah the prophet *before* "that great and dreadful Day of the Lord." And what will he do? "He shall turn the heart of the fathers to the children, and the heart of the children to their fathers." That sounds a lot like what I see happening in the world today: a reawakening to the eternal nature of God's commandments among His people.

Jesus Himself spoke of this shortly after the Transfiguration, where He met both Moses and Elijah, speaking to them before three of His disciples, John, Peter, and James (Matt. 17; Mark 9). After witnessing this event, and seeing Elijah for themselves, the disciples asked Jesus why the scribes taught that Elijah must come again, before His return. Jesus answered that, though Elijah had *already* come in their day (referring to John the Baptist; see Matt. 3:3), he must come again to "restore all things" (Matt. 17:11)

What needs to be restored before Jesus comes again? The remembrance of what the Bible says from cover to cover, including what John the Baptist taught, what John the apostle preached, and what Jesus Himself had to say—about the commandments:

If ye love me, keep my commandments. (John 14:15)

He that hath my commandments, and keepeth them, he it is that loveth me: and he that loveth me shall be loved of my Father, and I will love him, and will manifest myself to him. (John 14:21)

If ye keep my commandments, ye shall abide in my love; even as I have kept my Father's commandments, and abide in his love. (John 15:10)

And the dragon was wroth with the woman, and went to make war with the remnant of her seed, which keep the commandments of God, and have the testimony of Jesus Christ. (Rev. 12:17)

Here is the patience of the saints: here are they that keep the commandments of God, and the faith of Jesus. (Rev. 14:12)

Blessed are they that do his commandments, that they may have right to the tree of life, and may enter in through the gates into the city. (Rev. 22:14)

Isaiah, too, spoke of this time of restoration:

Comfort ye, comfort ye my people, saith your God. Speak ye comfortably to Jerusalem, and cry unto her, that her warfare is accomplished, that her iniquity is pardoned: for she hath received of the Lord's hand double for all her sins. The voice of him that crieth in the wilderness, Prepare ye the way of the Lord, make straight in the desert a highway for our God. Every valley shall be exalted, and every mountain and hill shall be made low: and the crooked shall be made straight, and the rough places plain: And the glory of the Lord shall be revealed, and all flesh shall see it together: for the mouth of the Lord hath spoken it. (Isa. 40:1–5)

The Lord, speaking through Isaiah, ended the chapter with: "They that wait upon the LORD shall renew their strength; they shall mount up with wings as eagles; they shall run, and not be weary; and they shall walk, and not faint" (v. 31). Are we honestly waiting on the Lord for this time? Could it be that it is at hand? Are we ready to have our strength renewed? What will it take other than simple obedience and a return to the first-century ways of keeping God's commandments and faith in Jesus?

Is this a new thing that is happening right now? Are we seeing the early evidence of more and more believers—Jews and non-Jews alike—returning to the God of Israel and obedience to His commandments? Is this what Jesus was talking about when He said, "The righteous will shine forth as the sun in the kingdom of their Father" (Matt. 13:43)?

With non-Jewish believers already rediscovering their connection with Israel through Messiah, the trend will explode in the kingdom. The following verse is striking in this regard: "O LORD, my strength, and my fortress, and my refuge in the day of affliction, the Gentiles shall come unto thee from the ends of the earth, and shall say, Surely our fathers have inherited lies, vanity, and things wherein there is no profit" (Jer. 16:19).

This is a prophecy that non-Jews, new to the covenant and the Torah, will come to the Lord realizing they've been duped. Could it be these gentile believers had been following church traditions and the teachings of "church fathers" rather than what the Bible teaches? Truly there is no profit in them. The rewards for following Jesus and observing God's commandments, on the other hand, are great.

In Matthew 19, Peter wondered about his and the other disciples' fate: "Behold, we have forsaken all, and followed thee," he told Jesus. "What shall we have therefore?"

Jesus answered him, "Verily I say unto you, that ye which have followed me, in the regeneration when the Son of man shall sit in the throne of his glory [in the coming kingdom on earth], ye also shall sit upon twelve thrones, judging the twelve tribes of Israel.

And every one that hath forsaken houses, or brethren, or sisters, or father, or mother, or wife, or children, or lands, for my name's sake, shall receive an hundredfold, and shall inherit everlasting life. But many that are first shall be last; and the last shall be first" (vv. 27–30).

The disciples? Sitting on thrones? Is this allegory? Or is it a real promise?

In His coming kingdom, we are promised, we will be just like the resurrected Jesus: "Beloved, now are we the sons of God, and it doth not yet appear what we shall be: but we know that, when he shall appear, we shall be like him; for we shall see him as he is" (1 John 3:2).

Where will He appear? Is this a vision of heaven? No, this is a vision of a future earth, because, as Psalm 115:16 tells us, "the earth hath he given to the children of men."

What will this coming kingdom look like?

First, according to Revelation 20, the thousand-year reign will be a time of perfect peace, justice. and prosperity. Why? Because Jesus will be in charge. What's more, Satan, the great tempter and accuser, will be bound in chains in a bottomless pit (vv. 1–3).

But the most detailed scriptures about this period come in the front of the book—from the Hebrew Scriptures too often neglected by today's Christians.

Isaiah 56 provides one of the best glimpses into our future:

Thus saith the LORD, Keep ye judgment, and do justice: for my salvation is near to come, and my righteousness to be revealed. Blessed is the man that doeth this, and the son of man that layeth hold on it; that keepeth the sabbath from polluting it, and keepeth his hand from doing any evil. Neither let the son of the stranger, that hath joined himself to the LORD, speak, saying, The LORD hath utterly separated me from his people: neither let the eunuch say, Behold, I am a dry tree. For thus saith the LORD unto the eunuchs that keep my sabbaths, and choose the things that please me, and take hold of my covenant; Even unto them will I give in mine house and within my walls a place and a name better than of sons and of daughters: I will give them an everlasting name, that shall not be cut off. Also the sons of the stranger, that join themselves to the Lord, to serve him, and to love the name of the LORD, to be his servants, every one that keepeth the sabbath from polluting it, and taketh hold of my covenant; Even them will I bring to my holy mountain, and make them joyful in my house of prayer: their burnt offerings and their sacrifices shall be accepted upon mine altar; for mine house shall be called an house of prayer for all people. The Lord GOD, which gathereth the outcasts of Israel saith, Yet will I gather others to him, beside those that are gathered unto him.

A few observations:

- In the kingdom, we will be observing the Sabbath. And that begs the question raised in chapter 5: Why aren't we observing it now? It was observed *before* Jesus' time on earth. It was observed *during* His time on earth. It was observed for more than a hundred years *after* His time on earth. And it will be observed during Jesus' one-thousand-year reign as King of kings. If you are not observing the Sabbath, now might be a good time to start learning *how*. You will find that it's not a burden. In fact, it's an immeasurable blessing.

- At last there will be true unity between those of Jewish bloodlines and us "strangers" who have joined ourselves to the house of Israel to take hold of God's covenant. We all—Jew and Gentile alike—will get to worship joyfully in the temple in Jerusalem.

I'll bet you never heard *that* in Sunday school.

But the Hebrew Scriptures also contain dire warnings for those who do not follow God's commandments—perhaps because they have been misled into believing they have been dispensed with and "nailed to the cross":

They that sanctify themselves, and purify themselves in the gardens behind one tree in the midst, eating swine's flesh, and the abomination, and the mouse, shall be consumed together, saith the LORD. For I know their works and their thoughts: it shall come, that I will gather all nations and tongues; and they shall come, and see my glory. And I will set a sign among them, and I will send those that escape of them unto the nations, to Tarshish, Pul, and Lud, that draw the bow, to Tubal, and Javan, to the isles afar off, that have not heard my fame, neither have seen my glory; and they shall declare my glory among the Gentiles. And they shall bring all your brethren for an offering unto the LORD out of all nations upon horses, and in chariots, and in litters, and upon mules, and upon swift beasts, to my holy mountain Jerusalem, saith the LORD, as the children of Israel bring an offering in a clean vessel into the house of the LORD. And I will also take of them for priests and for Levites, saith the LORD. For as the new heavens and the new earth, which I will make, shall remain before me, saith the LORD, so shall your seed and your name remain. And it shall come to pass, that from one new moon to another, and from one sabbath to another, shall all flesh come to worship before me, saith the LORD. And they shall go forth, and look upon the carcases of the men that have transgressed against me: for their worm shall not die, neither shall their fire be quenched; and they shall be an abhorring unto all flesh. (Isa. 66:17–24)

Here, the Lord comes in judgment to set up His kingdom. And when He does, He evidently takes His commandments seriously—including the dietary commandments set forth by Moses. "Clean" and "unclean" are biblical terms you may want to familiarize yourself with.

- The whole world will see the glory of God.

- The ingathering of the Jews to Israel will continue, aided by all nations. They will come to Jerusalem as priests.

- Again, not only will "all flesh" be observing the Sabbath, but also the other feasts (see Leviticus 23). Too many believers see them only as foreshadowings of the coming Messiah. You may want to consider looking into those observances and actually performing some "dress rehearsals" now—before the main act. Just a friendly suggestion.

Here's another great passage about God's coming kingdom:

Therefore my people shall know my name: therefore they shall know in that day that I am he that doth speak: behold, it is I. How beautiful upon the mountains are the feet of him that bringeth good tidings, that publisheth peace; that bringeth good tidings of good, that publisheth salvation; that saith unto Zion, Thy God reigneth! Thy watchmen shall lift up the voice; with the voice together shall they sing: for they shall see eye to eye, when the LORD shall bring again Zion. Break forth into joy, sing together, ye waste places of Jerusalem: for the LORD hath comforted his people, he hath redeemed Jerusalem. The LORD hath made bare his holy arm in the eyes of all the nations; and all the ends of the earth shall see the salvation of our God. Depart ye, depart ye, go ye out from thence, touch no unclean thing; go ye out of the midst of her; be ye clean, that bear the vessels of the LORD. For ye shall not go out with haste, nor go by flight: for the LORD will go before you; and the God of Israel will be your reward. Behold, my servant shall deal prudently, he shall be exalted and extolled, and be very high. As many were astonied at thee; his visage was so marred more than any man, and his form more than the sons of men: So shall he sprinkle many nations; the kings shall shut their mouths at him: for that which had not been told them shall they see; and that which they had not heard shall they consider. (Isa. 52:6–15)

Do you think God still doesn't love Jerusalem? Think again. This will be a time of great blessing for God's servant.

Jesus, whose appearance was once so defaced by mankind, will now astonish mankind, shutting the mouths of kings, and those who had not been told about Him before will consider Him anew.

Speaking of Jesus' suffering on the cross and His scars that He will carry into the millennial kingdom, one of the most astonishing prophecies in the entire Bible is found in Zechariah 12:10: "And I will pour upon the house of David, and upon the inhabitants of Jerusalem, the spirit of grace and of supplications: and they shall look upon me *whom they have pierced*, and they shall mourn for him, as one mourneth for his only son, and shall be in bitterness for him, as one that is in bitterness for his firstborn" (emphasis added).

Can you imagine that scene as the nation of Israel realizes who its Messiah truly is? That is truly when every knee shall bow and every voice utter, "*Baruch haba beshem Adonai*," or, "Blessed is He who comes in the name of the Lord." Jesus will not have heard those words since the day He entered Jerusalem to die on Calvary for the sins of His beloved Israel and the whole world.

This verse from Zechariah reminds me of one less known, in Isaiah 49. There, as Israel fears that the Lord has forgotten her, He assures her that He can *never* forget her. "Behold," He tells her, "I have graven thee upon the palms of my hands; thy walls are continually before me" (v. 16).

In the coming kingdom, the King of kings will sit on the throne of David, we see in Isaiah 16:5: "And in mercy shall the throne be established: and he shall sit upon it in truth in the tabernacle of David, judging, and seeking judgment, and hasting righteousness." And Isaiah tells us:

> And it shall come to pass in the last days, that the mountain of the LORD's house shall be established in the top of the mountains, and shall be exalted above the hills; and all nations shall flow unto it. And many people shall go and say, Come ye, and let us go up to the mountain of the LORD, to the house of the God of Jacob; and he will teach us of his ways, and we will walk in his

paths: for out of Zion shall go forth the law, and the word of the LORD from Jerusalem. And he shall judge among the nations, and shall rebuke many people: and they shall beat their swords into plowshares, and their spears into pruninghooks: nation shall not lift up sword against nation, neither shall they learn war any more. (Isa. 2:24)

What do we learn from this passage?

- People from all nations will come to Jerusalem to learn of His ways.

- The law will go forth out of Jerusalem.

- There won't be weapons anymore—because there won't be war anymore.

"Of the increase of his government and peace there shall be no end, upon the throne of David, and upon his kingdom, to order it, and to establish it with judgment and with justice from henceforth even for ever. The zeal of the LORD of hosts will perform this" (Isa. 9:7).

By the way, do you remember this passage?

And [Jesus] came to Nazareth, where he had been brought up: and, as his custom was, he went into the synagogue on the sabbath day, and stood up for to read. And there was delivered unto him the book of the prophet Esaias. And when he had opened the book, he found the place where it was written, The Spirit of the Lord is upon me, because he hath anointed me to preach the gospel to the poor; he hath sent me to heal the brokenhearted, to preach deliverance to the captives, and recovering of sight to the blind, to set at liberty them that are bruised, to preach the acceptable year of the Lord. And he closed the book, and he gave it again to the minister, and sat down. And the eyes of all them that were in the synagogue were fastened on him. And he began to say unto them, This day is this scripture fulfilled in your ears. (Luke 4:16–21)

If ye love me, keep my commandments. —JOHN 14:15

You've no doubt heard the term *Judaizing*. Perhaps you have heard your pastor explain what it means. You may even have explored the controversy of Judaizing in the first century. But do you understand it?

It's most often associated with Galatians 2:14, where Paul wrote: "But when I saw that they walked not uprightly according to the truth of the gospel, I said unto Peter before them all, If thou, being a Jew, livest after the manner of Gentiles, and not as do the Jews, why compellest thou the Gentiles to live as do the Jews?"

This is one of those *hard* verses in the Bible. And there are many. But understanding them comes with knowing something about the Hebraic roots of our faith.

What has prevented so many Christians from discovering the truth about the totality of Scripture is a misinterpretation of this passage in Galatians and what the neo-Pharisaical tradition of the "church" over nineteen centuries has taught to preserve the false notion that Jesus came to start a new religion—one that did away with the law. Jesus did not speak against the law but against additions to the law, the oral traditions of the rabbis. Jesus' primary indictment against the Pharisees throughout the Gospels was that they added to the law.

But, it may surprise critics to learn I agree entirely with what Paul was saying here: No man is justified by the works of the law. We are saved by grace through Jesus' sacrifice on the cross. That said, the law is not dead—not for Jews or for Gentile believers who come to salvation through grace. Both Jew and Gentile can be saved only by grace. However, we are still accountable to the eternal laws of God.

Again, as John wrote in his gospel and his letters over and over again, obedience to God's commandments is the way we demonstrate our love of God (see John 14:15). It's how we show that we know Him, and that we know the truth and are not liars (see 1 John 2:3). It's how we avoid committing sin after we are saved (see 1 John 3:4).

Two issues I have sought to make plain through this book: we are all accountable for our sins and we can be saved only through repentance and the atoning sacrifice of Jesus.

James explained in Acts 15 concerning the very controversy Paul was addressing in Galatians, there was never a question about the validity of the law and the Gentiles' need to keep it. The question was, how could the disciples evangelize a people who first needed to be circumcised and knowledgeable of the law—before they could even fellowship with them? James proffered a solution: he suggested that new, Gentile believers be given a short list of commandments to follow: abstaining from pollutions of idols, from fornication, and from things strangled, and from blood, with the understanding that they would learn the rest of the law in the synagogues every Sabbath. So, it wasn't a question of *if* all believers would be accountable for their transgressions of the law (sins); it was a question of *when*.

There was still some confusion even among the apostles in the beginning of Acts, as addressed in chapter 2, concerning pharisaical oral traditions that prohibited direct contact with Gentiles, whom they saw as "unclean." The great sin of the Pharisees—adding to the law—was still afflicting some of the apostles, including Peter, in the early part of Acts. That's the basis for this accusation of "Judaizing" by Paul in Galatians. It apparently took a concerted effort by the apostles to break the yoke of the Pharisees even after all the criticism Jesus directed toward them in the Gospels.

It's not a question of grace versus the law. It's not a question of being saved through obedience to the law. All the apostles made that clear. Paul wrote "For as many as are of the works of the law are under the curse: for it is written, Cursed is every one that continueth not in all things which are written in the book of the law to do them" (Gal. 3:10).

Are we *of* the works of the law? No. We indisputably and unarguably are *of* the saving spirit of faith and grace. But does that mean we are no longer accountable to the laws of God? No. Knowledge of the law, accountability to the law, and obedience to the law are how we demonstrate we *know* God, *love God, and* avoid sin after we are saved.

What was all that about?

It was Jesus' way of announcing, for those who had ears and discernment, that He was the Messiah. It was also a hint that He would *not* at that time, restore all things. He would have to come again to do that.

Here is the passage Jesus was reading from. Notice where He closed the book: "The Spirit of the Lord God is upon me; because the Lord hath anointed me to preach good tidings unto the meek; he hath sent me to bind up the brokenhearted, to proclaim liberty to the captives, and the opening of the prison to them that are bound; To proclaim the acceptable year of the Lord . . ." (Isa. 61:1–2).

That's where Jesus closed the book. But what follows those words?

> . . . and the day of vengeance of our God; to comfort all that mourn; to appoint unto them that mourn in Zion, to give unto them beauty for ashes, the oil of joy for mourning, the garment of praise for the spirit of heaviness; that they might be called trees of righteousness, the planting of the Lord, that he might be glorified. And they shall build the old wastes, they shall raise up the former desolations, and they shall repair the waste cities, the desolations of many generations. And strangers shall stand and feed your flocks, and the sons of the alien shall be your plowmen and your vinedressers. But ye shall be named the Priests of the Lord: men shall call you the Ministers of our God: ye shall eat the riches of the Gentiles, and in their glory shall ye boast yourselves. For your shame ye shall have double; and for confusion they shall rejoice in their portion: therefore in their land they shall possess the double: everlasting joy shall be unto them. For I the Lord love judgment, I hate robbery for burnt offering; and I will direct their work in truth, and I will make an everlasting covenant with them. And their seed shall be known among the Gentiles, and their offspring among the people: all that see them shall acknowledge them, that they are the seed which the Lord

hath blessed. I will greatly rejoice in the LORD, my soul shall be joyful in my God; for he hath clothed me with the garments of salvation, he hath covered me with the robe of righteousness, as a bridegroom decketh himself with ornaments, and as a bride adorneth herself with her jewels. For as the earth bringeth forth her bud, and as the garden causeth the things that are sown in it to spring forth; so the Lord GOD will cause righteousness and praise to spring forth before all the nations.

Isn't that amazing? Jesus didn't read any further than verse 2 because the time of restoration was not yet at hand. It was not yet a time of vengeance. It was a time to hear the good news and to "proclaim the acceptable year of the Lord." Only upon His Second Coming would judgment and justice follow.

Here's a vivid kingdom picture from Isaiah 60:

Arise, shine; for thy light is come, and the glory of the LORD is risen upon thee. For, behold, the darkness shall cover the earth, and gross darkness the people: but the LORD shall arise upon thee, and his glory shall be seen upon thee. And the Gentiles shall come to thy light, and kings to the brightness of thy rising. Lift up thine eyes round about, and see: all they gather themselves together, they come to thee: thy sons shall come from far, and thy daughters shall be nursed at thy side. Then thou shalt see, and flow together, and thine heart shall fear, and be enlarged; because the abundance of the sea shall be converted unto thee, the forces of the Gentiles shall come unto thee. The multitude of camels shall cover thee, the dromedaries of Midian and Ephah; all they from Sheba shall come: they shall bring gold and incense; and they shall shew forth the praises of the LORD. All the flocks of Kedar shall be gathered together unto thee, the rams of Nebaioth shall minister unto thee: they shall come up with acceptance on mine altar, and I will glorify the house of my glory. Who are these that fly as a cloud, and as the doves to their windows? Surely the isles shall wait for me, and the ships of Tarshish first, to bring thy sons from far, their silver and their gold with them, unto the name of the LORD thy God, and to the Holy One of Israel, because he hath glorified thee. And the sons of strangers shall build up thy walls, and their kings shall minister unto thee: for in my wrath I smote thee, but in my favour have I had mercy on thee. Therefore thy gates shall be open continually; they shall not be shut day nor night; that men may bring unto thee the forces of the Gentiles, and that their kings may be brought. For the nation and kingdom that will not serve thee shall perish; yea, those nations shall be utterly wasted. The glory of Lebanon shall come unto thee, the fir tree, the pine tree, and the box together, to beautify the place of my sanctuary; and I will make the place of my feet glorious. The sons also of them that afflicted thee shall come bending unto thee; and all they that despised thee shall bow themselves down at the soles of thy feet; and they shall call thee; The city of the LORD, the Zion of the Holy One of Israel. Whereas thou has been forsaken and hated, so that no man went through thee, I will make thee an eternal excellency, a joy of many generations. Thou shalt also suck the milk of the Gentiles, and shalt suck the breast of kings: and thou shalt know that I the LORD am thy Saviour and thy Redeemer, the mighty One of Jacob. For brass I will bring gold, and for iron I will bring silver, and for wood brass, and for stones iron: I will also make thy officers peace, and thine exactors righteousness. Violence shall no more be heard in thy land, wasting nor destruction within thy borders; but thou shalt call thy walls Salvation, and thy gates Praise. The sun shall be no more thy light by day; neither for brightness shall the moon give light unto thee: but the LORD shall be unto thee an everlasting light, and thy God thy glory. Thy sun shall no more go down; neither shall thy moon withdraw itself: for the LORD shall be thine everlasting light, and the days of thy mourning shall be ended. Thy people also shall be all righteous: they shall inherit the land for ever, the branch of my planting, the work of my hands, that I may be glorified. A little one shall become a thousand, and a small one a strong nation: I the Lord will hasten it in his time.

This prophetic passage speaks of a time of great prosperity for Israel. Nations that don't serve Israel will perish and be laid waste. There will be no more violence in the land, no more destruction. Israel will no more need the light of the sun or the moon because of God's presence. And all Israel will be righteous.

Revelation 22 offers a similar picture:

And he shewed me a pure river of water of life, clear as crystal, proceeding out of the throne of God and of the Lamb. In the midst of the street of it, and on either side of the river, was there the tree of life, which bare twelve manner of fruits, and yielded her fruit every month: and the leaves of the tree were for the healing of the nations. And there shall be no more curse: but the throne of God and of the Lamb shall be in it; and his servants shall serve him: And they shall see his face; and his name shall be in their foreheads. And there shall be no night there; and they need no candle, neither light of the sun; for the Lord God giveth them light: and they shall reign for ever and ever. (vv. 1–5)

Notice how Israel- and Jerusalem-centric this imagery is. Jesus doesn't come to be the president of the United States. He doesn't come to be the secretary-general of the United Nations. He doesn't come to rule the European Union or sit in the Vatican.

He comes to rule and reign in Jerusalem as the King of the Jews. But He will also rule over the entire world from there.

Why is God so Israeli-centric? The answer is provided many times in Scripture, but nowhere as clearly as in Jeremiah 3:14: "Turn, O backsliding children, saith the Lord; *for I am married unto you: and I will take you one of a city, and two of a family, and I will bring you to Zion*" (emphasis added). That's how God thinks of Israel—as a bride who has played the harlot. Henceforth, though, Isaiah tells us, Israel will be known as "the holy people, the redeemed of the LORD: and thou shalt be called, Sought out, a city not forsaken" (Isa. 62:12).

But what's going to be happening on the ground? What's life going to be like in this millennial kingdom? Much of it, we know, is offered from the perspective of Israel, the apple of God's eye. In Ezekiel 28, we learn that Israel will build houses, plant vineyards, and "dwell with confidence" (v. 26). That may not sound like much to the untrained ear. But it should sound like a big deal in Israel, where no one dwells in confidence. Life in Israel today is full of risks from terrorism—a threat that much of the rest of the world is beginning to experience as well. But there's something else that caught my attention here—the idea of building houses.

Do you know that Israel has been under pressure from the United States, Europe, and most of the Arab and Muslim world *not* to build houses, apartments, and new communities? It's a fact. The United Nations and the world powers are attempting to shut down the building of homes even in and around Jerusalem, the nation's capital. Israel can't even build homes for its burgeoning population without facing boycott threats, sanctions, and criticism from the rest of the world. One thing for sure, in the millennial kingdom, no one will tell Israel not to build.

Ezekiel 36 tells us that after God cleanses Israel of all its iniquities, the most desolate land will be tilled and "become like the garden of Eden" (vv. 33–35). Given that much of Israel is desert, blooming like the garden of Eden would be a miracle indeed. And, ultimately, the restitution of all things means the whole world will be closer to being one big garden of Eden than it has been since Adam and Eve were expelled.

In chapter 8 we discussed the shocking prophecy of Egypt's Nile drying up, which, ultimately leads to the return of the Lord—to Egypt, to save His people. Zechariah 14 prophesies that when His feet touch down on the Mount of Olives, there will be a tremendous earthquake. When that happens, we're told, "living waters shall go out from Jerusalem; half of them toward the former sea, and half of them toward the hinder sea: in summer and in winter shall it be" (v. 8). These are healing waters, and the rest of the story is found in Ezekiel 47, a truly amazing millennial miracle:

> Then said he unto me, These waters issue out toward the east country, and go down into the desert, and go into the sea: which being brought forth into the sea, the waters shall be healed. And it shall come to pass, that every thing that liveth, which moveth, whithersoever the rivers shall come, shall live: and there shall be a very great multitude of fish, because these waters shall come thither: for they shall be healed; and every thing shall live whither the river cometh. And it shall come to pass, that the fishers shall stand upon it from Engedi even unto Eneglaim; they shall be a place to spread forth nets; their fish shall be according to their kinds, as the fish of the great sea, exceeding many. (vv. 8–10)

Which sea do these waters flow into? The Dead Sea. If you have ever visited Israel, you have no doubt experienced this unusual body of "water," immensely more saline than any other. It is also the lowest place on earth—1,388 feet below sea level and reaching about 1,200 feet deep. It's 50 miles long and 15 miles wide.

The Dead Sea is 34 percent saline—nine times more so than the ocean. Yet, what this passage tells us is that this very dead sea is going to come alive during the millennial kingdom. How do we know these verses in Ezekiel are about the Dead Sea? They can scarcely be about any other, given that En Gedi is named as beachfront property. En Gedi is an Israeli town today, a mere stone's throw from the now-retreating banks of the Dead Sea. We also know the location because of a parallel prophecy in Joel 3:18: "And it shall come to pass in that day, that the mountains shall drop down new wine, and the hills shall flow with milk, and all the rivers of Judah shall flow with waters, and a fountain shall come forth out of the house of the LORD, and shall water the valley of Shittim." The valley of Shittim is well-known today as one near the Dead Sea.

What do we know about the other nations of the world during this period? Zechariah provides some insight. According to this prophetic book, not only will Israel be the center of the world geographically, as it always has been, but it will truly be the spiritual and political epicenter too: "And it shall come to pass, that every one that is left of all the nations which came against Jerusalem shall even go up from year to year to worship the King, the LORD of hosts, and to keep the feast of tabernacles" (Zech. 14:16).

The "feast of tabernacles"? From Leviticus 23. Isn't that just for the Jews? Didn't Jesus fulfill that through His first coming? Apparently not. In the millennial kingdom it's mandatory, and not just for the Jews but for the other nations too.

Isaiah 11 provides a beautiful picture of the kingdom. This is what it will be like in God's perfect world:

> The wolf also shall dwell with the lamb, and the leopard shall lie down with the kid; and the calf and the young lion and the fatling together; and a little child shall lead them. And the cow and the bear shall feed; their young ones shall lie down together: and the lion shall eat straw like the ox. And the sucking child shall play on the hole of the asp, and the weaned child shall put his hand on the cockatrice' den. They shall not hurt nor destroy in all my holy mountain: *for the earth shall be full of the knowledge of the LORD, as the waters cover the sea.* (vv. 6–9, emphasis added)

Here's a parallel passage:

> But be ye glad and rejoice for ever in that which I create: for, behold, I create Jerusalem a rejoicing, and her people a joy. And I will rejoice in Jerusalem, and joy in my people: and the voice of weeping shall be no more heard in her, nor the voice of crying. There shall be no more thence an infant of days, nor an old man that hath not filled his days: for the child shall die an hundred years old; but the sinner being an hundred years old shall be

accursed. And they shall build houses, and inhabit them; and they shall plant vineyards, and eat the fruit of them. They shall not build, and another inhabit; they shall not plant, and another eat: for as the days of a tree are the days of my people, and mine elect shall long enjoy the work of their hands. They shall not labour in vain, nor bring forth for trouble; for they are the seed of the blessed of the LORD, and their offspring with them. And it shall come to pass, that before they call, I will answer; and while they are yet speaking, I will hear. The wolf and the lamb shall feed together, and the lion shall eat straw like the bullock: and dust shall be the serpent's meat. They shall not hurt nor destroy in all my holy mountain, saith the LORD. (Isa. 65:18–24)

What about the blight of anti-Semitism in the world? Will there be any vestige of it in the kingdom? Not according to Zechariah: "Yea, many people and strong nations shall come to seek the LORD of hosts in Jerusalem, and to pray before the LORD. Thus saith the LORD of hosts; In those days it shall come to pass, that ten men shall take hold out of all languages of the nations, even shall take hold of the skirt of him that is a Jew, saying, We will go with you: for we have heard that God is with you" (Zech. 8:22–23).

What will those of us not living in Israel be doing? In Revelation 1, John tells us that Jesus Christ, the "faithful witness, and the first begotten of the dead, and the prince of the kings of the earth" has "made us kings and priests unto God and his Father" (vv. 5–6). That's encouraging. He added in chapter 5 that we will reign with Him (v. 10). James 2:5 affirms that: "Hearken, my beloved brethren, Hath not God chosen the poor of this world rich in faith, and heirs of the kingdom which he hath promised to them that love him?"

The nations of the world shouldn't feel left out, because Revelation 11:15 tells us that "the kingdoms of this world are become the kingdoms of our Lord, and of his Christ, and he shall reign for ever and ever."

This kingdom should scarcely be a secret to believers today. The angel Gabriel announced it to Mary when he told her, "Behold, thou shalt conceive in thy womb, and bring forth a son, and shalt call his name Jesus. He shall be great, and shall be called the Son of the Highest: and the Lord God shall give unto him the throne of his father David: And he shall reign over the house of Jacob for ever; and of his kingdom there shall be no end" (Luke 1:31–33).

Mary, probably a teenager at the time, got it! When she visited her cousin Elizabeth, who would become the mother of John the Baptist, she gave a remarkable prophecy of her own, embedded in words of praise:

> My soul doth magnify the Lord, and my spirit hath rejoiced in God my Saviour. For he hath regarded the low estate of his handmaiden: for, behold, from henceforth all generations shall call me blessed. For he that is mighty hath done to me great things; and holy is his name. And his mercy is on them that fear him from generation to generation. He hath shewed strength with his arm; he hath scattered the proud in the imagination of their hearts. He hath put down the mighty from their seats, and exalted them of low degree. He hath filled the hungry with good things; and the rich he hath sent empty away. He hath helped his servant Israel, in remembrance of his mercy; as he spake to our fathers, to Abraham, and to his seed for ever. (Luke 1:46–55)

That's the kingdom some of us alive today on earth may experience—soon. Are you ready? Do you understand it and welcome it the way Mary did? Are you expectant and hopeful about it? Do you really long for peace, justice, and prosperity—on God's terms?

I don't know about you, but I'm ready for His coming.

I've noticed that it's more difficult for the younger generation to relate to such instantly world-changing events. They're still getting to know this world of ours the way it is—or the way they think it is. To young people, their world is just beginning. They're developing plans for the future, looking for fulfillment through relationships and opportunities through education and careers. Many of them are reluctant to talk about prophecy or even to learn about it. You can understand why they might not be looking forward to an upside-down world suddenly turning right side up. They likely don't even see the world in quite such a desperate state as we do. After all, it's the only world they have known. Some of them may even subconsciously feel that these end-time events that they cannot control might rob them of their own dreams and aspirations.

But that is not God's intent. He wants to give them—and us—a brand-new world free of hate, free of war, free of injustice, free of deception and lies, free of corruption, free of violence, free of robbery.

We were not meant to love this world the way it is.

It's easy to feel despair and anxiety living in times like these. It reminds me of an apocryphal story about a man named Morris, an old Jewish man who goes to the Western Wall in Jerusalem to pray twice every day.

A reporter learns about Morris and decides to interview him about his motivation. She goes to the wall and watches him pray for forty-five minutes. When he turns to leave, using a cane and moving very slowly, she approaches him.

"Pardon me, sir," she says. "I'm Rebecca Smith from CNN. What's your name?"

"Morris Feinberg," he replies.

"Sir, how long have you been coming to the Western Wall and praying?" she asks.

"For about sixty years."

"Sixty years!" she repeats, shocked. "That's amazing! What do you pray for?"

"I pray for peace between the Christians, Jews, and the Muslims," he answers. "I pray for all the wars and all the hatred to stop. I pray for all our children to grow up safely as responsible adults and to love their fellow man. I pray that politicians tell us the truth and put the interests of the people ahead of their own interests."

"How do you feel after doing this for sixty years?" the reporter asks at last.

Morris answers: "Like I'm talking to a wall!"

Let me close with one of my favorite passages from Isaiah. The prophet was clearly feeling as though all of his work had come to nothing—as if *he'd* been talking to a wall. He was living in a time not unlike ours. Right was wrong. Up was down. Evil was good. And he felt despair. So he cried out to the Lord. Here's the story:

> Then I said, I have laboured in vain, I have spent my strength for nought, and in vain: yet surely my judgment is with the LORD, and my work with my God. And now, saith the LORD that formed me from the womb to be his servant, to bring Jacob again to him, Though Israel be not gathered, yet shall I be glorious in the eyes of the LORD, and my God shall be my strength. And he said, It is a light thing that thou shouldest be my servant to raise up the tribes of Jacob, and to restore the preserved of Israel: I will also give thee for a light to the Gentiles, that thou mayest be my salvation unto the end of the earth. Thus saith the LORD, the Redeemer of Israel, and his Holy One, to him whom man despiseth, to him whom the nation abhorreth, to a servant of rulers, Kings shall see and arise, princes also shall worship, because of the LORD that is faithful, and the Holy One of Israel, and he shall choose thee. Thus saith the LORD, In an acceptable time have I heard thee, and in a day of salvation have I helped thee: and I will preserve thee, and give thee for a covenant of the people, to establish the earth, to cause to inherit the desolate heritages; That thou mayest say to the prisoners, Go forth; to them that are in darkness, Shew yourselves. They shall feed in the ways, and their pastures shall be in all high places. They shall not hunger nor thirst; neither shall the heat nor sun smite them: for he that hath mercy on them shall lead them, even by the springs of water shall he guide them. And I will make all my mountains a way, and my highways shall be exalted. (Isa. 49:4–11)

You're not talking to a wall. The Creator of the universe is listening. He's got plans for you that are better than any you could possibly devise for yourself—much better than those a corrupt and fallen world could offer you. And those plans will become a reality for you—*if* you are faithful and obedient to Him until He comes, in a moment, in the twinkling of an eye, to bring "the restitution of all things" . . .

To bring us back to the Garden.

Shalom.

APPENDIX

A COMPREHENSIVE LIST OF SEVENTH-DAY SABBATH SCRIPTURES

WHAT THE BIBLE HAS TO say about the seventh-day Sabbath:

GENESIS 2:1–3 "Thus the heavens and the earth were finished, and all the host of them. And on the seventh day God ended his work which he had made; and he rested on the seventh day from all his work which he had made. And God blessed the seventh day, and sanctified it: because that in it he had rested from all his work which God created and made."

EXODUS 16:23 "And he said unto them, This is that which the Lord hath said, To morrow is the rest of the holy sabbath unto the Lord: bake that which ye will bake to day, and seethe that ye will seethe; and that which remaineth over lay up for you to be kept until the morning."

EXODUS 16:25–26 "And Moses said, Eat that to day; for to day is a sabbath unto the Lord: to day ye shall not find it in the field. Six days ye shall gather it; but on the seventh day, which is the sabbath, in it there shall be none."

EXODUS 20:8 "Remember the sabbath day, to keep it holy."

EXODUS 31:13–18 "Speak thou also unto the children of Israel, saying, Verily my sabbaths ye shall keep: for it is a sign between me and you throughout your generations; that ye may know that I am the LORD that doth sanctify you. Ye shall keep the sabbath therefore; for it is holy unto you: every one that defileth it shall surely be put to death: for whosoever doeth any work therein, that soul shall be cut off from among his people. Six days may work be done; but in the seventh is the sabbath of rest, holy to the LORD: whosoever doeth any work in the sabbath day, he shall surely be put to death. Wherefore the children of Israel shall keep the sabbath, to observe the sabbath throughout their generations, for a perpetual covenant. It is a sign between me and the children of Israel for ever: for in six days the LORD made heaven and earth, and on the seventh day he rested, and was refreshed. And he gave unto Moses, when he had made an end of communing with him upon mount Sinai, two tables of testimony, tables of stone, written with the finger of God."

EXODUS 34:21 "Six days thou shalt work, but on the seventh day thou shalt rest: in earing time and in harvest thou shalt rest."

EXODUS 35:2–3 "Six days shall work be done, but on the seventh day there shall be to you an holy day, a sabbath of rest to the LORD: whosoever doeth work therein shall be put to death. Ye shall kindle no fire throughout your habitations upon the sabbath day."

LEVITICUS 19:30 "Ye shall keep my sabbaths, and reverence my sanctuary: I am the LORD."

LEVITICUS 23:1–4 "And the LORD spake unto Moses, saying, Speak unto the children of Israel, and say unto them, Concerning the feasts of the LORD, which ye shall proclaim to be holy convocations, even these are my feasts. Six days shall work be done:

but the seventh day is the sabbath of rest, an holy convocation; ye shall do no work therein: it is the sabbath of the LORD in all your dwellings. These are the feasts of the LORD, even holy convocations, which ye shall proclaim in their seasons."

NUMBERS 15:32–36 "And while the children of Israel were in the wilderness, they found a man that gathered sticks upon the sabbath day. And they that found him gathering sticks brought him unto Moses and Aaron, and unto all the congregation. And they put him in ward, because it was not declared what should be done to him. And the LORD said unto Moses, The man shall be surely put to death: all the congregation shall stone him with stones without the camp. And all the congregation brought him without the camp, and stoned him with stones, and he died; as the LORD commanded Moses."

NUMBERS 28:25 "And on the seventh day ye shall have an holy convocation; ye shall do no servile work."

DEUTERONOMY 5:12–15 "Keep the sabbath day to sanctify it, as the LORD thy God hath commanded thee. Six days thou shalt labour, and do all thy work: But the seventh day is the sabbath of the LORD thy God: in it thou shalt not do any work, thou, nor thy son, nor thy daughter, nor thy manservant, nor thy maidservant, nor thine ox, nor thine ass, nor any of thy cattle, nor thy stranger that is within thy gates; that thy manservant and thy maidservant may rest as well as thou. And remember that thou wast a servant in the land of Egypt, and that the LORD thy God brought thee out thence through a mighty hand and by a stretched out arm: therefore the LORD thy God commanded thee to keep the sabbath day."

2 CHRONICLES 2:4 "Behold, I build an house to the name of the LORD my God, to dedicate it to him, and to burn before him sweet incense, and for the continual shewbread, and for the

burnt offerings morning and evening, on the sabbaths, and on the new moons, and on the solemn feasts of the LORD our God. This is an ordinance for ever to Israel."

NEHEMIAH 13:15-22 "In those days saw I in Judah some treading wine presses on the sabbath, and bringing in sheaves, and lading asses; as also wine, grapes, and figs, and all manner of burdens, which they brought into Jerusalem on the sabbath day: and I testified against them in the day wherein they sold victuals. There dwelt men of Tyre also therein, which brought fish, and all manner of ware, and sold on the sabbath unto the children of Judah, and in Jerusalem. Then I contended with the nobles of Judah, and said unto them, What evil thing is this that ye do, and profane the sabbath day? Did not your fathers thus, and did not our God bring all this evil upon us, and upon this city? yet ye bring more wrath upon Israel by profaning the sabbath. And it came to pass, that when the gates of Jerusalem began to be dark before the sabbath, I commanded that the gates should be shut, and charged that they should not be opened till after the sabbath: and some of my servants set I at the gates, that there should no burden be brought in on the sabbath day. So the merchants and sellers of all kind of ware lodged without Jerusalem once or twice. Then I testified against them, and said unto them, Why lodge ye about the wall? if ye do so again, I will lay hands on you. From that time forth came they no more on the sabbath. And I commanded the Levites that they should cleanse themselves, and that they should come and keep the gates, to sanctify the sabbath day. Remember me, O my God, concerning this also, and spare me according to the greatness of thy mercy."

ISAIAH 56:2-8 "Blessed is the man that doeth this, and the son of man that layeth hold on it; that keepeth the sabbath from polluting it, and keepeth his hand from doing any evil. Neither let the son of the stranger, that hath joined himself to the LORD, speak, saying, The LORD hath utterly separated me from his people: neither let the eunuch say, Behold, I am a dry tree. For thus saith the LORD unto the eunuchs that keep my sabbaths, and choose the things that please me, and take hold of my covenant; Even unto them will I give in mine house and within my walls a place and a name better than of sons and of daughters: I will give them an everlasting name, that shall not be cut off. Also the sons of the stranger, that join themselves to the LORD, to serve him, and to love the name of the LORD, to be his servants, every one that keepeth the sabbath from polluting it, and taketh hold of my covenant; Even them will I bring to my holy mountain, and make them joyful in my house of prayer: their burnt offerings and their sacrifices shall be accepted upon mine altar; for mine house shall be called an house of prayer for all people. The Lord GOD, which gathereth the outcasts of Israel saith, Yet will I gather others to him, beside those that are gathered unto him."

ISAIAH 58:13–14 "If thou turn away thy foot from the sabbath, from doing thy pleasure on my holy day; and call the sabbath a delight, the holy of the LORD, honourable; and shalt honour him, not doing thine own ways, nor finding thine own pleasure, nor speaking thine own words: Then shalt thou delight thyself in the LORD; and I will cause thee to ride upon the high places of the earth, and feed thee with the heritage of Jacob thy father: for the mouth of the LORD hath spoken it."

ISAIAH 66:23 "And it shall come to pass, that from one new moon to another, and from one sabbath to another, shall all flesh come to worship before me, saith the LORD."

JEREMIAH 17:21–27 "Thus saith the LORD; Take heed to yourselves, and bear no burden on the sabbath day, nor bring it in by the gates of Jerusalem; Neither carry forth a burden out of your houses on the sabbath day, neither do ye any work, but hallow ye the sabbath day, as I commanded your fathers. But they obeyed not, neither inclined their ear, but made their neck stiff, that they might not hear, nor receive instruction. And it shall come to pass, if ye diligently hearken unto me, saith the LORD, to bring in no burden through the gates of this city on the sabbath day, but hallow the sabbath day, to do no work therein; Then shall there enter into the gates of this city kings and princes sitting upon the throne of David, riding in chariots and on horses, they, and their princes, the men of Judah, and the inhabitants of Jerusalem: and this city shall remain for ever. And they shall come from the cities of Judah, and from the places about Jerusalem, and from the land of Benjamin, and from the plain, and from the mountains, and from the south, bringing burnt offerings, and sacrifices, and meat offerings, and incense, and bringing sacrifices of praise, unto the house of the LORD. But if ye will not hearken unto me to hallow the sabbath day, and not to bear a burden, even entering in at the gates of Jerusalem on the sabbath day; then will I kindle a fire in the gates thereof, and it shall devour the palaces of Jerusalem, and it shall not be quenched."

LAMENTATIONS 2:6 "And he hath violently taken away his tabernacle, as if it were of a garden: he hath destroyed his places of the assembly: the LORD hath caused the solemn feasts and sabbaths to be forgotten in Zion, and hath despised in the indignation of his anger the king and the priest."

EZEKIEL 20:12-24 "Moreover also I gave them my sabbaths, to be a sign between me and them, that they might know that I am the LORD that sanctify them. But the house of Israel rebelled against me in the wilderness: they walked not in my statutes, and they despised my judgments, which if a man do, he shall even live in them; and my sabbaths they greatly polluted: then I said, I would pour out my fury upon them in the wilderness, to consume them. But I wrought for my name's sake, that it should not be polluted before the heathen, in whose sight I brought them out. Yet also I lifted up my hand unto them in the wilderness, that I would not bring them into the land which I had given them, flowing with milk and honey, which is the glory of all lands; Because they despised my judgments, and walked not in my statutes, but polluted my sabbaths: for their heart went after their idols. Nevertheless mine eye spared them from destroying them, neither did I make an end of them in the wilderness. But I said unto their children in the wilderness, Walk ye not in the statutes of your fathers, neither observe their judgments, nor defile yourselves with their idols: I am the LORD your God; walk in my statutes, and keep my judgments, and do them; And hallow my sabbaths; and they shall be a sign between me and you, that ye may know that I am the LORD your God. Notwithstanding the children rebelled against me: they walked not in my statutes, neither kept my judgments to do them, which if a man do, he shall even live in them; they polluted my sabbaths: then I said, I would pour out my fury upon them, to accomplish my anger against them in the wilderness. Nevertheless I withdrew mine hand, and wrought for my name's sake, that it should not be polluted in the sight of the heathen, in whose sight I brought them forth. I lifted up mine hand unto them also in the wilderness, that I would scatter them among the heathen, and disperse them through the countries; Because they had not executed my judgments, but had despised my statutes, and had polluted my sabbaths, and their eyes were after their fathers' idols."

EZEKIEL 22:8 "Thou hast despised mine holy things, and hast profaned my sabbaths."

EZEKIEL 22:26 "Her priests have violated my law, and have profaned mine holy things: they have put no difference between the holy and profane, neither have they shewed difference between the unclean and the clean, and have hid their eyes from my sabbaths, and I am profaned among them."

EZEKIEL 23:38 "Moreover this they have done unto me: they have defiled my sanctuary in the same day, and have profaned my sabbaths."

EZEKIEL 44:24 "And in controversy they shall stand in judgment; and they shall judge it according to my judgments: and they shall keep my laws and my statutes in all mine assemblies; and they shall hallow my sabbaths."

EZEKIEL 45:17 "And it shall be the prince's part to give burnt offerings, and meat offerings, and drink offerings, in the feasts, and in the new moons, and in the sabbaths, in all solemnities of the house of Israel: he shall prepare the sin offering, and the meat offering, and the burnt offering, and the peace offerings, to make reconciliation for the house of Israel."

EZEKIEL 46:1–4 "Thus saith the Lord GOD; The gate of the inner court that looketh toward the east shall be shut the six working days; but on the sabbath it shall be opened, and in the day of the new moon it shall be opened. And the prince shall enter by the way of the porch of that gate without, and shall stand by the post of the gate, and the priests shall prepare his burnt offering and his peace offerings, and he shall worship at the threshold of the gate: then he shall go forth; but the gate shall not be shut until the evening. Likewise the people of the land shall worship at the door of this gate before the LORD in the sabbaths and in the new moons. And the burnt offering that the prince shall offer unto the LORD in the sabbath day shall be six lambs without blemish, and a ram without blemish."

EZEKIEL 46:12 "Now when the prince shall prepare a voluntary burnt offering or peace offerings voluntarily unto the LORD, one shall then open him the gate that looketh toward the east, and he shall prepare his burnt offering and his peace offerings, as he did on the sabbath day: then he shall go forth; and after his going forth one shall shut the gate."

HOSEA 2:11 "I will also cause all her mirth to cease, her feast days, her new moons, and her sabbaths, and all her solemn feasts."

MATTHEW 12:1–14 "At that time Jesus went on the sabbath day through the corn; and his disciples were an hungred, and began to pluck the ears of corn and to eat. But when the Pharisees saw it, they said unto him, Behold, thy disciples do that which is not lawful to do upon the sabbath day. But he said unto them, Have ye not read what David did, when he was an hungred, and they that were with him; how he entered into the house of God, and did eat the shewbread, which was not lawful for him to eat, neither for them which were with him, but only for the priests? Or have ye not read in the law, how that on the sabbath days the priests in the temple profane the sabbath, and are blameless? But I say unto you, that in this place is one greater than the temple. But if ye had known what this meaneth, I will have mercy, and not sacrifice, ye would not have condemned the guiltless. For the Son of man is Lord even of the sabbath day.

"And when he was departed thence, he went into their synagogue: And, behold, there was a man which had his hand withered. And they asked him, saying, Is it lawful to heal on the sabbath days? that they might accuse him. And he said unto them, What man shall there be among you, that shall have one sheep, and if it fall into a pit on the sabbath day, will he not lay hold on it, and lift it out? How much then is a man better than a sheep? Wherefore it is lawful to do well on the sabbath days. Then saith he to the man, Stretch forth thine hand. And he stretched it forth; and it was restored whole, like as the other. Then the Pharisees went out, and held a council against him, how they might destroy him."

MATTHEW 24:20–22 "But pray ye that your flight be not in the winter, neither on the sabbath day: for then shall be great tribulation, such as was not since the beginning of the world to this time, no, nor ever shall be. And except those days should be shortened, there should no flesh be saved: but for the elect's sake those days shall be shortened."

MATTHEW 28:1 "In the end of the sabbath, as it began to dawn toward the first day of the week, came Mary Magdalene and the other Mary to see the sepulchre."

MARK 1:21 "And they went into Capernaum; and straightway on the sabbath day he entered into the synagogue, and taught."

MARK 2:23–28 "And it came to pass, that he went through the corn fields on the sabbath day; and his disciples began, as they went, to pluck the ears of corn. And the Pharisees said unto him, Behold, why do they on the sabbath day that which is not lawful? And he said unto them, Have ye never read what David did, when he had need, and was an hungred, he, and they that were with him? How he went into the house of God in the days of Abiathar the high priest, and did eat the shewbread, which is not lawful to eat but for the priests, and gave also to them which were with him? And he said unto them, The sabbath was made for man, and not man for the sabbath: Therefore the Son of man is Lord also of the sabbath."

MARK 3:1–6 "And he entered again into the synagogue; and there was a man there which had a withered hand. And they watched him, whether he would heal him on the sabbath day; that they might accuse him. And he saith unto the man which had the withered hand, Stand forth. And he saith unto them, Is it lawful to do good on the sabbath days, or to do evil? to save life, or to kill? But they held their peace. And when he had looked round about on them with anger, being grieved for the hardness of their hearts, he saith unto the man, Stretch forth thine hand. And he stretched it out: and his hand was restored whole as the other. And the Pharisees went forth, and straightway took counsel with the Herodians against him, how they might destroy him."

MARK 6:2 "And when the sabbath day was come, he began to teach in the synagogue: and many hearing him were astonished, saying, From whence hath this man these things? and what wisdom is this which is given unto him, that even such mighty works are wrought by his hands?"

MARK 15:42 "And now when the even was come, because it was the preparation, that is, the day before the sabbath . . ."

MARK 16:1 "And when the sabbath was past, Mary Magdalene, and Mary the mother of James, and Salome, had bought sweet spices, that they might come and anoint him."

LUKE 4:16 "And he came to Nazareth, where he had been brought up: and, as his custom was, he went into the synagogue on the sabbath day, and stood up for to read."

LUKE 4:31 "And [he] came down to Capernaum, a city of Galilee, and taught them on the sabbath days."

LUKE 6:1–5 "And it came to pass on the second sabbath after the first, that he went through the corn fields; and his disciples plucked the ears of corn, and did eat, rubbing them in their hands. And certain of the Pharisees said unto them, Why do ye that which is not lawful to do on the sabbath days? And Jesus answering them said, Have ye not read so much as this, what David did, when himself was an hungred, and they which were with him; How he went into the house of God, and did take and eat the shewbread, and gave also to them that were with him; which it is not lawful to eat but for the priests alone? And he said unto them, that the Son of man is Lord also of the sabbath."

LUKE 6:6–11 "And it came to pass also on another sabbath, that he entered into the synagogue and taught: and there was a man whose right hand was withered. And the scribes and Pharisees watched him, whether he would heal on the sabbath day; that they might find an accusation against him. But he knew their thoughts, and said to the man which had the withered hand, Rise up, and stand forth in the midst. And he arose and stood forth. Then said Jesus unto them, I will ask you one thing; is it lawful on the sabbath days to do good, or to do evil? to save life, or to destroy it? And looking round about upon them all, he said unto the man, Stretch forth thy hand. And he did so: and his hand was restored whole as the other. And they were filled with madness; and communed one with another what they might do to Jesus."

LUKE 13:14–17 "And the ruler of the synagogue answered with indignation, because that Jesus had healed on the sabbath day, and said unto the people, There are six days in which men ought to work: in them therefore come and be healed, and not on the sabbath day. The Lord then answered him, and said, Thou hypocrite, doth not each one of you on the sabbath loose his ox or his ass from the stall, and lead him away to watering? And ought not this woman, being a daughter of Abraham, whom Satan hath bound, lo, these eighteen years, be loosed from this bond on the sabbath day? And when he had said these things, all his adversaries were ashamed: and all the people rejoiced for all the glorious things that were done by him."

LUKE 14:1–6 "And it came to pass, as he went into the house of one of the chief Pharisees to eat bread on the sabbath day, that they watched him. And, behold, there was a certain man before him which had the dropsy. And Jesus answering spake unto the lawyers and Pharisees, saying, Is it lawful to heal on the sabbath day? And they held their peace. And he took him, and healed him, and let him go; and answered them, saying, Which of you shall have an ass or an ox fallen into a pit, and will not straightway pull him out on the sabbath day? And they could not answer him again to these things."

LUKE 23:54–56 "And that day was the preparation, and the sabbath drew on. And the women also, which came with him from Galilee, followed after, and beheld the sepulchre, and how his body was laid. And they returned, and prepared spices and ointments; and rested the sabbath day according to the commandment."

JOHN 5:16–17 "And therefore did the Jews persecute Jesus, and sought to slay him, because he had done these things on the sabbath day. But Jesus answered them, My Father worketh hitherto, and I work."

JOHN 7:22–24 "Moses therefore gave unto you circumcision; (not because it is of Moses, but of the fathers;) and ye on the sabbath day circumcise a man. If a man on the sabbath day receive circumcision, that the law of Moses should not be broken; are ye angry at me, because I have made a man every whit whole on the sabbath day? Judge not according to the appearance, but judge righteous judgment."

JOHN 9:14–16 "And it was the sabbath day when Jesus made the clay, and opened his eyes. Then again the Pharisees also asked him how he had received his sight. He said unto them, He put clay upon mine eyes, and I washed, and do see. Therefore said some of the Pharisees, This man is not of God, because he keepeth not the sabbath day. Others said, How can a man that is a sinner do such miracles? And there was a division among them."

JOHN 19:31 "The Jews therefore, because it was the preparation, that the bodies should not remain upon the cross on the sabbath day, (for that sabbath day was an high day,) besought Pilate that their legs might be broken, and that they might be taken away."

ACTS 1:12 "Then returned they unto Jerusalem from the mount called Olivet, which is from Jerusalem a sabbath day's journey."

ACTS 13:14 "But when they departed from Perga, they came to Antioch in Pisidia, and went into the synagogue on the sabbath day, and sat down."

ACTS 13:27 "For they that dwell at Jerusalem, and their rulers, because they knew him not, nor yet the voices of the prophets which are read every sabbath day, they have fulfilled them in condemning him."

ACTS 13:42–44 "And when the Jews were gone out of the synagogue, the Gentiles besought that these words might be preached to them the next sabbath. Now when the congregation was broken up, many of the Jews and religious proselytes followed Paul and Barnabas: who, speaking to them, persuaded them to continue in the grace of God. And the next sabbath day came almost the whole city together to hear the word of God."

ACTS 15:19–21 "Wherefore my sentence is, that we trouble not them, which from among the Gentiles are turned to God: But that we write unto them, that they abstain from pollutions of idols, and from fornication, and from things strangled, and from blood. For Moses of old time hath in every city them that preach him, being read in the synagogues every sabbath day."

ACTS 17:2 "And Paul, as his manner was, went in unto them, and three sabbath days reasoned with them out of the scriptures."

ACTS 18:4 "And he reasoned in the synagogue every sabbath, and persuaded the Jews and the Greeks."

COLOSSIANS 2:16–22 "Let no man therefore judge you in meat, or in drink, or in respect of an holyday, or of the new moon, or of the sabbath days: which are a shadow of things to come; but the body is of Christ. Let no man beguile you of your reward in a voluntary humility and worshipping of angels, intruding into those things which he hath not seen, vainly puffed up by his fleshly mind, and not holding the Head, from which all the body by joints and bands having nourishment ministered, and knit together, increaseth with the increase of God. Wherefore if ye be dead with Christ from the rudiments of the world, why, as though living in the world, are ye subject to ordinances, (Touch not; taste not; handle not;) which all are to perish with the using;) after the commandments and doctrines of men?"

HEBREWS 4:1–12 "Let us therefore fear, lest, a promise being left us of entering into his rest, any of you should seem to come short of it. For unto us was the gospel preached, as well as unto them: but the word preached did not profit them, not being mixed with faith in them that heard it. For we which have believed do enter into rest, as he said, As I have sworn in my wrath, if they shall enter into my rest: although the works were finished from the foundation of the world. For he spake in a certain place of the seventh day on this wise, and God did rest the seventh day from all his works. And in this place again, If they shall enter into my rest. Seeing therefore it remaineth that some must enter therein, and they to whom it was first preached entered not in because of unbelief: Again, he limiteth a certain day, saying in David, To day, after so long a time; as it is said, To day if ye will hear his voice, harden not your hearts. For if Jesus had given them rest, then would he not afterward have spoken of another day. There remaineth therefore a rest to the people of God. For he that is entered into his rest, he also hath ceased from his own works, as God did from his. Let us labour therefore to enter into that rest, lest any man fall after the same example of unbelief. For the word of God is quick, and powerful, and sharper than any twoedged sword, piercing even to the dividing asunder of soul and spirit, and of the joints and marrow, and is a discerner of the thoughts and intents of the heart."

NOTES

CHAPTER 1: DID JESUS COME TO START A NEW RELIGION?
1. AllAboutGod.com, "Religious Pluralism," All About Religion, accessed June 14, 2016, http://www.allaboutreligion.org/religious-pluralism.htm.
2. See, for example, Matthew 22:18; 23:13–15, 23, et al.

CHAPTER 2: WHAT DID THE FIRST-CENTURY FAITH LOOK LIKE?
1. Steven Ertelt, "58,586,256 Abortions in America Since Roe v. Wade in 1973," LifeNews.com, January 14, 2016, http://www.lifenews.com/2016/01/14/58586256-abortions-in-america-since-roe-v-wade-in-1973/.

CHAPTER 3: WHAT DOES IT MEAN TO BE A "CHRISTIAN" TODAY?
1. For more on cheap grace, see Dietrich Bonhoeffer, *The Cost of Discipleship* (SCM, 1959; New York: Touchstone, 1995).

CHAPTER 5: WHY DON'T WE OBSERVE THE SABBATH ANYMORE?
1. Samuele Bacchiocchi, *From Sabbath to Sunday: A Historical Investigation of the Rise of Sunday Observance in Early Christianity*, 18th ed. (Rome: Pontifical Gregorian University Press, 1977; 1980), 153. Citations are to the 1980 edition.
2. Harcel Simon, *Verus Israel: A Study of the Relations Between Christians and Jews in the Roman Empire AD 135–425*, trans. H. McKeating (n.p.: Littman Library of Jewish Civilization, 1996), 235.
3. Stephen M. Wylen, *The Jews in the Time of Jesus: An Introduction* (Mahwah, NJ: Paulist Press, 1995),190–92.
4. Tacitus, *The Annals* (ca, 117) (New York: Palatine Press, 2015), 15.44
5. Simon, *Verus Israel.*
6. S. R. E. Humbert, Adversus Graecorum Calumnias, in J. P. Mina, *Patrologia Graeca*, p. 143.
7. Bacchiocchi, *From Sabbath to Sunday.*
8. Ibid.
9. Ibid.
10. Ibid.

CHAPTER 6: HOW EARLY DID REPLACEMENT THEOLOGY BEGIN?

1. See, for example, *Encyclopædia Britannica Online*, s.v. "Origen," http://www.britannica.com/biography/Origen; and *Wikipedia*, s.v. "Origen," https://en.wikipedia.org/wiki/Origen, both accessed June 22, 2016.
2. C. A. Patrides, "The Salvation of Satan," *Journal of the History of Ideas* 28, no. 4 (October–December 1967), 467–78.
3. Edward Gibbon, *History of the Decline and Fall of the Roman Empire*.
4. Ibid.
5. Augustine, *Confessions*, 12.14.17.
6. John Chrysostom, *Against the Jews*, Homily 1:5.
7. Martin Luther, "On the Jews and Their Lies," Luther's Works, Volume 47, translated by Martin H. Bertram, Philadelphia: Fortress Press, 1971.
8. John Calvin, "A Response to Questions and Objections of a Certain Jew," from Gerhard Falk, *The Jew in Christian Theology: Martin Luther's Anti-Jewish Vom Schem Hamphoras, Previously Unpublished in English, and Other Milestones in Church Doctrine Concerning Judaism* (Jefferson, NC, and London: McFarland, 2013).
9. D. Thomas Lancaster, *Restoration: Returning the Torah of God to the Disciples of Jesus* (Littleton, CO: First Fruits of Zion, 2015), 25, emphasis added.
10. *Encyclopedia Judaica*, CD-ROM ed., v. 1.0, s.v. "Fiscus Judaicus,"
11. Ecclesiastical History by Theodoret. Book 1 Chapter 9.

CHAPTER 8: WHAT IS THE GREATEST MIRACLE IN HISTORY?

1. Mark Twain, *The Innocents Abroad*, originally published in 1869, chap. 45.
2. Noel, "Stratfor Sources Reveal Egypt, Sudan Contingency Plans to Secure Nile Water Resources," Wikileaks Press, August 31, 2012, http://wikileaks-press.info/stratfor-sources-reveal-egypt-sudan-contingency-plans-to-secure-nile-water-resources/.
3. Cam McGrath, "Egypt Gets Muscular over Nile Dam," Inter Press Service, March 21, 2014, http://www.ipsnews.net/2014/03/egypt-prepares-force-nile-flow/.
4. Malcolm Dash, "Egypt, Ethiopia and the Nile," *Jerusalem Post*, March 14, 2016, http://www.jpost.com/Opinion/Egypt-Ethiopia-and-the-Nile-447910.
5. Walaa Hussein, "Will Renaissance Dam flood Egypt's Mediterranean coast?" *Al-Monitor*, January 2016, http://www.al-monitor.com/pulse/originals/2016/01/ethiopia-egypt-renaissance-dam-flooding-sea-environment.html#.
6. Bradley Hope, "Ethiopia's giant dam muddies the waters downstream in Egypt," *National*, April 23, 2012, http://www.thenational.ae/news/world/middle-east/ethiopias-giant-dam-muddies-the-waters-downstream-in-egypt.
7. Jacky Hugy, "Egyptians Show High Interest in Israeli Literature, Culture," *Al-Monitor*, April 16, 2013, http://www.al-monitor.com/pulse/originals/2013/04/egyptians-interest-in-israeli-culture.html#.

CHAPTER 9: IS THE ANTICHRIST ALIVE AND WELL ON PLANET EARTH TODAY?

1. Tacitus, *The History*, new ed., bk. 5.1, ed. Moses Hadas, trans. Alfred Church and William Brodribb (New York: Modern Library, 2003).
2. Flavius Josephus, *The Wars of the Jews, or History of the Destruction of Jerusalem*, bk. 2, chap. 13.
3. Flavius Josephus, *The Complete Works of Josephus: The Wars of the Jews, or the History of the Destruction of Jerusalem*, bk. 3, chap. 1, par. 3.
4. Ibid., chap. 4, par. 2.
5. Flavius Josephus, *The Wars of the Jews: History of the Destruction of Jerusalem*, trans. William Whiston, bk. 5, chap. 13, par. 4.
6. Ibid., bk. 6, chap. 4.
7. Ibid.
8. Jonathan Cahn, *The Harbinger: The Ancient Mystery that Holds the Secret of America's Future* (Lake Mary, FL: FrontLine, 2012), 89–90.

INDEX

SCRIPTURE INDEX